ASPECTS OF ROTHERHAM
2

ASPECTS OF ROTHERHAM

Discovering Local History – 2

Edited by
Melvyn Jones

Wharncliffe Publishing Limited

First Published in 1996 by
Wharncliffe Publishing Limited

Copyright © Wharncliffe Publishing Limited 1996

For up-to-date information on other titles produced under the
Wharncliffe imprint, please telephone or write to:

Wharncliffe Publishing Limited
FREEPOST
     47 Church Street
     Barnsley
     South Yorkshire S70 2BR
     Telephone (24 hours): 01226 - 734555

ISBN: 1-871647-32-0

Cover illustration: Rotherham Parish Church and Chapel on the Bridge,
from a hand-coloured engraving, *c.*1830.

A CIP catalogue record of this book is available from the
British Library.

Printed in Great Britain by Redwood Books, Trowbridge,
Wiltshire

CONTENTS

INTRODUCTION

by Melvyn Jones

The *Aspects* Series has proved that there is much high quality local history research activity in South Yorkshire and that there is a large readership for the fruits of that research. Part of the attraction of the series is its unique blend of family, community, economic, social and landscape history which has encouraged original research from new and experienced writers alike. Although aimed at the general reader, each volume published so far has included studies of considerable historical importance. The present volume is no exception.

Hot on the heels of the runaway success of *Aspects of Rotherham 1*, this second collection of essays on aspects of the history of the Metropolitan District is, arguably, more varied than the first volume with family history, historical biography and landscape history being particularly well represented.

Following his meticulously documented study of Thomas Rotherham's College in *Aspects of Rotherham 1*, Stephen Cooper continues his research into Tudor Rotherham by providing, through a detailed study of wills, a fascinating insight into the preoccupation of our Tudor forbears with their preparations for death and the disposal of their earthly goods. His carefully researched study reveals their beliefs, attitudes and perceptions, some of them peculiar to their age, others surprisingly like our own.

Family history and historical biography are particularly well represented in this second volume. John Goodchild's study of Lionell Copley, a Doncaster (Wadworth) man, who operated furnaces and forges in the Rotherham area in the seventeenth and early eighteenth centuries, sheds welcome light on a particularly interesting and complex character, and early capitalist. Towards the other end of the occupational scale, Joan Jones's study of Thomas Salkeld, the painter on the Wentworth estate in the first half of the nineteenth century, not only reveals the working life of an individual who must have had unique access into the most intimate recesses of a large aristocratic estate, but also the domestic comforts enjoyed by a highly trusted estate employee of long-standing. Tony Munford's study of the engineer, Sir Donald Bailey, and Ray Hearne's essay on the work of the writer, Mike Haywood, acquaint us with the qualities and energies of

two of Rotherham's most famous twentieth century sons. Alex
Fleming's study of the Paynes of Newhill in the parish of Wath in the
eighteenth and nineteenth centuries shows the outlook and pre-occu-
pations of an important local Quaker family, a particularly important
aspect of the study being the way in which the family papers reveal
the reactions of members of the family to national and international
events.

Landscape history is also well represented. Melvyn Jones's reconstruction of the boundaries and landscape features of the deer
park at Kimberworth shows that there is much of interest to learn
about this very important medieval land use that was once widely
distributed in South Yorkshire. Tony Dodsworth's study of Rawmarsh
Common reveals much that was not previously widely known, not
least the extensive rabbit warrens that once existed there. Likewise,
Brian Elliott's investigations into dovecotes in Rotherham's countryside have led to a number of surprising discoveries. Alice Rodgers's
painstakingly documented study of the revealing of the remains of
Roche Abbey between the middle of the nineteenth century and the
1930s, shows the way in which the work of the landscaper Capability
Brown was painstakingly removed to reveal the Abbey's ground plan.
We take public libraries for granted. Freda Casson's study of early
lending libraries in Rotherham carefully charts the ways in which the
reading public was catered for in the days before the local authority
provided such a service and then outlines the setting up of the local
authority service. The study documents the enterprise of a number of
individuals and agencies in establishing mechanisms for the
borrowing of books and the reading of newspapers and journals; it
also emphasises the voracious appetite for reading among the towns-
people, both as a leisure pursuit and as a means of extending their
knowledge and understanding.

Industrial history, as is only right and proper in a town like
Rotherham, has not been neglected. Tony Munford's investigation
into the derivation of the name 'Oil Mill Fold' has revealed something
of the little known industry of oil seed crushing in the town, while
John Goodchild's study of ruddle mining and milling at Micklebring
and Braithwell respectively, sheds more light on another little known
episode in the mining and manufacturing industry of the area.
Finally, Trevor Lodge's carefully researched and well illustrated
history of Templeborough Steelworks is a fitting tribute to one of the
town's major industrial undertakings.

Rotherham's role as a market town is often overlooked. Tom
Beastall's study of its important role as a market centre for the rich

agricultural areas to the east is underlined by the proposal for a railway from the town to Bawtry at the beginning of the 1880s. The study reveals what a rich vein of information railway proposals are, this one also emphasising the potential for the expansion of stone quarries at Whiston, Wickersley and Roche, suburban development in the villages along the line and for recreational outings to the 'Roche Abbey valley' and the 'picturesque village of Maltby'.

As with the first volume, this book could not have been produced without the help and support of a number of key individuals. I would like to thank Timothy Hewitt and Alan Twiddle of Wharncliffe Publishing for their continued confidence in and support for the *Aspects* Series. Brian Elliott, as originator of the Series, has been a great source of encouragement. I also acknowledge the help of Hazel Undy in word processing, Neil Donovan for technical help with discs, and Bob Warburton for drawing a number of key maps. Staff in Rotherham Central Library's Archives and Local Studies Section have been, as usual, patient and helpful, and their assistance to contributors is gratefully acknowledged. Finally, my heartfelt thanks must go to the contributors for once again meeting deadlines, making my job as editor relatively painless and, most important, for providing for all our potential readers another first-class volume of rigorously researched, lucidly written and superbly illustrated studies of local history at its best.

Anyone wishing to be considered as a contributor to *Aspects of Rotherham 3* (which, subject to commercial viability, will be published in the Autumn of 1998) should, in the first instance, contact Melvyn Jones, Editor: *Aspects of Rotherham*, c/o Wharncliffe Publishing Ltd, 47 Church Street, Barnsley, S70 2AS, enclosing a brief description of the proposed contribution.

1. 'In the Name of God Amen': Tudor Will-Makers of Rotherham

by Stephen Cooper

WILLS ARE AN IMPORTANT SOURCE of social history, and many more survive from the Tudor period than from preceding centuries. Fortunately, these include a good number made by men (and women) who inhabited the parish of Rotherham.[1] These wills are about both God and Mammon, about the spiritual and the material. They include wills made by priests associated with Thomas Rotherham and his College of Jesus, which have much to tell us about religious beliefs, but they also include wills made by men concerned with landed property and trade. When we read these wills, we see charity and parsimony at work. We learn of people and places held dear, but also of treasured heirlooms. Wills provide us with a fascinating insight into the material world, as well as the psychology, of those who came before us.

Religious beliefs and burial arrangements

Most, though not all, wills made in the early Tudor period began with the words *In the Name of God Amen*, or its Latin version, *In Dei Nomine Amen*. This opening is significant – men and women apparently put their immortal souls first. One such individual was John Bokyng, master of the grammar school in the College of Jesus, founded by Thomas Rotherham in 1482.[2] When he made a will (1483), he bequeathed his soul to Almighty God, the Blessed Mary and all the Saints[3], as did the widow Margaret Tayliour (1484)[4] and William Greybarn, first Provost of Rotherham College (1501).[5] This formula was typical, expressing the orthodox Catholic view that God, Mary and the Saints all had a part to play in salvation.

Few people expressed this view as fully as the priest Thomas Swift, originally from Tinsley and sometime rector of Wickersley (1535):[6]

> *. . . I bequeath my soul to him which created and redeemed the same, Christ Jesus, beseeching humbly Almighty God, Son, and the Holy Ghost, three Persons and one God, to have mercy of me sinful creature, praying also His Godhead to have pity of me, and of his infinite mercy to put His most excellent passion between my soul and His righteous judgement; and if I for my manifold sins and trespasses have not made*

true confession, due contrition and satisfaction as I ought to have done,
I therefore ask grace and forgiveness, meekly beseeching the most
glorious Virgin, our Lady Saint Mary, all Angels, Archangels, Apostles,
Evangelists, Martyrs, Confessors, and Virgins, with all the celestial citi-
zens and glorious company of heaven, to be my advocates, to pray for
me unto God for remission of my sin, that my soul may be saved and
come to the bliss that never shall have end . . .

Does this priest 'protest too much'? It has been suggested that there
was a 'preoccupation with orthodoxy' in the early Tudor period, which
arose from the fact that the existence of heresy was all too real[7]; and
it is curious that even Archbishop Thomas Rotherham himself took
the trouble to protest his unswerving adherence to all the tenets of
Roman Catholicism, when one might have thought that this could be
taken for granted. His will, made in 1498 closes with the following
remarkable declaration:

. . . I hesitate in no article of the faith, nor have ever hesitated. And if
by chance, which God avert, by the infirmity of disease or from some
cause I shall pronounce otherwise in my last moments, I deny it now,
henceforth and forever renouncing and detesting now and always what-
ever shall be repugnant to the bride of Christ, his holy church, because
I wish to die, I desire to die a true Christian, and I pray and again I
pray, that I may so die.[8]

After the Reformation, new religious beliefs could be openly
expressed;[9] and we find that the wills of Robert Swift the mercer,
whose fine wall-brass may still be seen in Rotherham church (1560)[10]
and John Rudyerde, gentleman (1601)[11] bequeath their souls simply
to God Almighty, or to God and Christ, while the former hopes that
he will be saved 'through Jesus Christ . . .' The Virgin, Saints and
'whole company of Heaven' are left out, in accordance with the
dictates of Protestant theology.[12] A full statement of the new creed can
be found in a model will recommended for use by practising lawyers
by a Rotherham writer, William West, in his collection of forms and
precedents, entitled *Symbolaeographie*, and published in 1590:

I do . . . most joyfully commit my soul into the hands of Almighty God
my creator, whom I most humbly beseech to accept the same, and to
forgive me all my sins through his mercy, and by, and for the passion,
death, and merits of our Lord and only saviour Jesus Christ, who of
his infinite mercie and love hath redeemed me from the bondage of hell,

death, and everlasting damnation, that made full satisfaction to his heavenly father for all my sins.[13]

The new sentiments also appear in monumental inscriptions, for example on Thomas Woodhouse's tomb (1606):

In Adam's fall, sin made us thrall
to death and dreadful pain,
But Christ and Cross hath payd our loss,
and got us life again.[14]

Before the Reformation, the belief in the power of prayer to relieve souls languishing in purgatory was very strong – as can be seen by looking at the will of Henry Carnebull, Thomas Rotherham's Archdeacon. Henry made his will when he began to suffer from an illness at Rotherham College on 12 July, 1512.[15] He had already given considerable thought to the welfare of his soul, having paid a large sum for permission to found two chantries in 1505;[16] and Thomas Rotherham had decreed that Henry be remembered in all prayers offered in the College.[17] But now, on his sickbed, Henry declared that he wanted to be buried in Rotherham, if he died there. A marble stone was to be placed over his grave, with an inscription inviting visitors to pray for him. There was to be a dirge and masses, followed by an obit a week later, with doles for the clergy and the poor. He went on to endow his two chantries, and said that his executors should dispose of his moveable goods 'as they shall seem (i.e. think) best for the health of my soul'. Two days later, still 'lying full sick in the College of Rotherham', he made a codicil to his will, adding various gifts, including 26s 8d to the four orders of friars at York. Sad to say, Henry did not recover. He died, and was duly buried at Rotherham on 10 August, 1512.

Carnebull was not alone in wanting to reduce his time in purgatory. For the same reason Thomas Rotherham directed that 1,000 masses be celebrated as quickly as possible after his death![18] Many bequests, legacies and residuary gifts were made with purgatory in mind. William Rawson, provost of Rotherham College in 1495, left ten shillings a year for two years for an anniversary mass.[19] He bequeathed four gowns to his executors, with directions that they be sold and the proceeds applied for the salvation of his soul; and the residue of his goods was to be applied for the same purpose. A few years later, provost Greybarn provided a quarterly obit for three years and left the residue of his goods to fund minor scholarships for poor scholars, at the grammar school and the University of Oxford. John Lillie, who was Vicar of Rotherham in 1513 and whose will is shown in Figure 1 asked, if his 'poor substance' would allow it, for a dirge and a solemn mass on the day of his burial, at the 'month's mind' and 'year's mind', and he also gave the priest Robert Morton seven marks to sing and say masses for a year.[20] Seven marks was about the going rate: Lilly's contemporary Thomas Gree had left that amount a few years earlier (1505).[21] Thomas Reresby also asked (1522) that a priest should say and sing for his soul in the parish church for a year, and (though he was only a layman) specified the prayers to be used: 'which priest I will shall say weekly *Placebo, Dirige with Commendation* and *Mass* four times in the week'.[22] Soon after (1525) Thomas Swift left £37 6s 8d to pay for a chantry for his soul for eight years. The money was to be kept safe by the provost and fellows of Rotherham College; and the priest of the chantry was to be John Addy, master of the writing school. Addy was to say *Placebo, Dirige* and *Commendations* three times a week, and Masses at specified intervals.

Some testators had very precise wishes as to the place of burial. John Bokyng specified

> in the south chancel of Rotherham church near and next to the pew in which the wife of Richard Lilly the bailiff of Rotherham and my own wife sit.[23]

These seating arrangements tell us that the bailiff was an important person; and we find confirmation of this in the later will of William Whitmore, who was the Earl of Shrewsbury's bailiff in 1553 and in 1556.[24] When he married Cecily Parker on 16 August, 1558, the parish clerk described him as Mr William Whitmore, the 'Mr' being a mark of distinction;[25] and when Whitmore made his will in 1568 he described himself as 'gentleman'.

The new Jesus Chapel was a favourite place for burial, chosen by provosts Greybarn and Rawson and by Henry Carnebull, who specified that he be 'laid low under foot afore the altar there'. Carnebull further directed that his tombstone be of marble, even writing the inscription for it, while naturally leaving the date of death blank! Vicar Lillie wanted to be buried within our Lady's choir 'nigh to my father, Richard Lilly'. Robert Hertley of Rotherham (1521), whose bequests of 'mills' and a 'cutler wheel' suggest his occupation, wanted to lie 'in the church of All Hallows of Rotherham, fast by my wife'.[26] The priest William Sarbirne (1502) wanted to lie in the choir,[27] Thomas Reresby in the south aisle, Thomas Swift 'before the door of

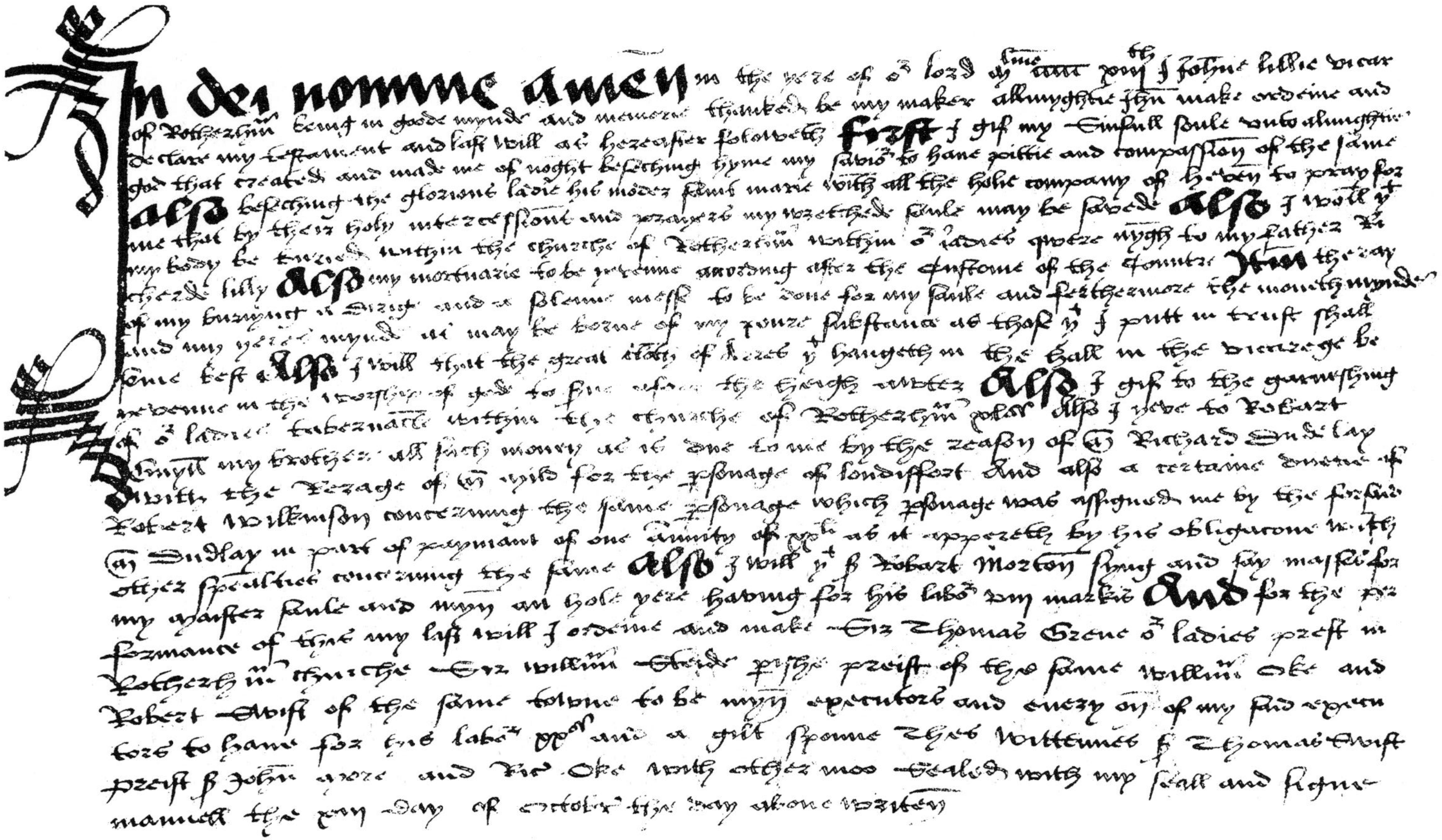

Figure 1. The will of John Lilly, 1513. *Borthwick Institute of Historical Research*

our Lady's choir', Robert Swift the mercer in the 'rood choir'. Others
were not so particular. Widow Tayliour (1484) was amongst those who
simply stated that she wanted to buried in the church, as did Thomas
Bone of Doncaster (1506)[28] and Richard Edmondes the innkeeper
(1608),[29] while John Rudyerde (1601) mentioned the church, or
churchyard.

We would expect the funerals of the provosts of Rotherham College
to be grand affairs; and so they were;[30] but the provosts were not the
only testators who left detailed directions as to how their funerals were
to be conducted. Robert Hertley seems to have been fond of candles.
He described very precisely how his executors could maximise the
number which could be kept burning:

> *I give my best candlestick, that I had of Roger Hardy, to hang before*
> *the Rood in the Rood choir; and Laurence Ashton to have 8d to hang*
> *it on a pole. I will that there be made for every flower of the candlestick*
> *a taper of wood, that there may be nine cierges of wax set upon, and*
> *three pounds of wax to be in a cierge; and my cierge that standeth before*
> *Saint Margaret shall be taken down and broken, and three pounds to*
> *be taken to make nine little cierges to the said candlestick.*

These instructions suggest that Robert Hertley had an eye for detail
– which he perhaps found useful in his business as a cutler.

William Swift of Rotherham, second son of Robert Swift the
mercer, directed (1568) that on the day of his burial there should be
'a substantial honest dinner for all my worshipful and honest friends';
and he provided black gowns with hoods of fine cloth for his sister,
nephews, brother in law, friend, and their wives. His wife and children
must be 'clothed in black after the ancient custom of this realm'.[31]
Richard Edmundes left vicar Thomas Jopson ten shillings 'to make a
sermon at my burial'.

Bequests and legacies

Rotherham church frequently received bequests and legacies. John
Bokyng and Margaret Tayliour each left their 'best animal' in payment
of mortuaries – a kind of ecclesiastical death duty, while Vicar Lillie
doubtless intended the same thing when he said that his mortuary
should be paid 'according after the custom of the county'. John
Bokyng also gave 3s 4d for the fabric and 2s to the high altar 'for tithes
forgot'. Margaret Tayliour left 12d to the high altar and 3s 4d for the
fabric of the church and her burial. Provost Greybarn left 6s 8d for
the church bells, while provost Rawson left five yards of linen for an

altar cloth. Robert Holden (1505) left 13s 4d for the repair of the chancel and the glazing of a window.[32] Vicar Lillie left 40s 'to the garnishing of our Lady's tabernacle', and he also bequeathed a tapestry:

> *I will that the great cloth of Arras that hangeth in the hall in the vicarage be given in the worship of God to serve afore the high altar.*

Thomas Swift left 20s 'for the church works and needs'. In addition to the candles already mentioned, Robert Hertley left 3s 4d 'to the repairing of our lady's vestment' – presumably worn by the priest when peforming certain ceremonies at Our Lady's altar – and he also left 'to our Lady's altar a vestment that I bought of Roger Padley, with a superaltar and a sacring bell'. The church was even remembered by some whose first allegiance lay elsewhere: Dame Elizabeth Fitzwilliam of Aldwark[33] made gifts (1503) to the Friars of Tickhill, York Minster, the high altars at Ecclesfield and Rawmarsh, Roche Abbey, Monk Bretton Priory, both orders of Friars at Doncaster[34] and other churches; but she also left 6s 8d to the high altar at Rotherham 'for tithes forgot'.[35] We shall see that her relative Thomas Clarel had also left gifts to Rotherham church, when he made his will in 1493.[36]

Testators also remembered the chapel on Rotherham bridge. In a legacy which has become famous, since it enables historians to date the building, John Bokyng left 3s 4d 'to the fabric of the Chapel to be built on Rotherham bridge'. In a less famous legacy made the following year (1484), Margaret Tayliour also left 3s 4d, referring to the chapel as 'the chapel of the Blessed Mary'. In the following year Arnold Reresby esquire left 6s 8d 'to the making or glazing of a window in the chapel of the Blessed Mary upon Rotherham bridge'.[37]

Prior to the dissolution of the monasteries, testators made gifts to Rufford Abbey, which owned the manor of Rotherham, collected the tithes, and appointed its vicar. In 1490 Thomas Webster left 20d[38] and in 1525 Thomas Swyft left a great silver salt-cellar (to the Abbey) and 'a girdle with harness silver gilt' (to the abbot). There were also gifts to Rotherham College and its pupils. The most generous benefactors were the founder Thomas Rotherham and his archdeacon Henry Carnebull;[39] but there were also gifts by Bokyng, of land worth 8s a year, by provost Greybarn, and by provost Rawson, who left several books to the College library.

Gifts to the poor were a common feature of Tudor wills, which is not surprising when we consider that plague and dearth were common and the role of the State was limited. William West's

Symbolaeographie contained model clauses relating to the relief of
poverty. Among the many gifts for the benefit of his soul, Henry
Carnebull included one of a penny 'to every poor man, woman and
child' asking alms at his funeral. Provosts Greybarn and Rawson each
left money for the poor. Thomas Reresby left land to the 'commonalty' of Rotherham but he also left 'all my corns or grains to the poor'.
'Mr' Thomas Lilly, who may have been a merchant, possibly a mercer,
also left land to the 'Commonalty of Rotherham' and he gave no less
than £6 13s 4d 'to be distributed to and among the poor people in
Rotherham'.[40] He also gave 'to twenty of the poorest men and women
in Rotherham to every of them a gown cloth price 4s'. William Swift
issued what might seem to some a very rash invitation: he asked that
every poor man and woman should attend the 'substantial honest
dinner' to be held after his funeral: they were each to have something
to eat and a penny in silver. One doubts the wisdom of such a provision because many years later, in 1810, Thomas Tuke
of Wath-upon-Dearne left a penny to every poor child who should
attend his funeral; and it is said that 700 came.[41]

The late sixteenth century saw the foundation of the Feoffees of the
Common Lands of Rotherham, a corporation which still exists. They
were given their Charter by Queen Elizabeth in 1589, undertaking a
variety of duties now carried out by local and central government. The
first of these was 'the relief of the poor people'; and it is interesting to
note that some of the original Feoffees made personal provision for
the poor, when they made their wills. One of these Feoffees was
Thomas Woodhouse, a prosperous yeoman. When he died in 1606, he
owned one house in the Crofts, several in 'Westgate Green' and
another in Westgate itself. He also owned land in Rotherham,
Brinsworth, Tinsley and Greasbrough. He left substantial legacies to
relatives and friends, including his sister Alice Caland. He made two
gifts to the poor of Rotherham: the first of £33 6s 8d, the second of
two pieces of land (or closes) in Greasbrough.[42] Shortly after
Woodhouse died, his sister made further provision for the poor of
Kimberworth, Masborough and Gilberthorp-hill.[43]

One of Thomas Woodhouse's colleagues was Nicholas Mounteney.
He is recorded in the court rolls of the manor of Ecclesfield for 1591
as 'Nicholas Mountney of Rotherham mercer son of John Mountney
then lately of Creswick deceased'. The same records describe him as
'gentleman' in 1592. He was greave to the Feoffees in 1600 and may
have been a churchwarden in 1605, when his name appears in the
marriage and burial registers for the parish of Rotherham.[44] He died
in 1615, leaving £3 6s 8d to the poor of Rotherham town and fifteen

shillings to the poor of Ecclesfield town and parish. He also left all his old clothes to his 'needful friends and customers for malt'.[45]

Testators sometimes remembered local roads and bridges which stood in need of repair. Perhaps this reflected Rotherham's position as a market town, whose communications with surrounding communities were important – though West's *Symbolaeographie* contained a suggested forms of words, which may mean that gifts of this nature were in any event commonplace. Provost Greybarn left 3s 4d for the repair of Rotherham bridge. Henry Carnebull directed that £6 13s 4d 'be delivered to the factors of Rawmarsh causey which is now sore decayed'. Robert Hertley left 3s 4d 'to the paving in the lane going to Greasborough . . . to be wared[46] from John Haryngton's stable northward'. Thomas Swift left money for the repair of the 'gate' (meaning road) at Tinsley.[47] The bailiff William Whitmore left 20s 'to the mending of the highways about the town of Rotherham'.[48] Most strikingly, Thomas Webster left a series of such legacies in 1490:

> *to the making of a bridge called Rotherbridge, 20s. Also to the making of a road called Welgate, in Rotherham, 3s 4d . . . Also I leave to the making of a road called Ardsley lane, 20d.*

Material possessions

The source of most wealth in Tudor times was land; and landed property was frequently mentioned in wills. When the Feoffee Nicholas Mounteney died in 1615 he left property in Micklehill Field, Cross of the Ash Field, Canklow Field and Elsemorefield, which suggests that Rotherham had four open arable fields, though other documents refer to three.[49] When the bailiff William Whitmore made his will (1568) he disposed of land in Nottinghamshire, and left his wife Cecily his 'farm and lease of Eastwood . . . in full recompense of her jointure and dowry'. He left his son all his timber 'lying at Eastwood hewn and ready to build', mentioned a farm at Masborough, and left sums of money to five named servants.[50]

But, apart from land, there were other items of property which men valued, and wanted to hand on to posterity. Sometimes it was books, sometimes clothing, sometimes a bed or bed linen, or a tapestry, sometimes items of personal adornment or household silver.

Provost Rawson left four books to the library at Rotherham College. He also bequeathed vestments to several of his friends: a coverlet with figures and geese; a red cloak; a short gown and hood; a blue gown and hood, and another of musterdevilles. The four gowns left to his executors were described in detail: the first was blue and had fur in the hood, the second was violet and had a hood lined with red silk, the third was green with a hood similar to the second's and the fourth was russet, with a plain hood.[51] Thomas Swift left provost Nevile 'my best gown crimson furred with martrons with my best surplice, a bag of black velvet with ring of silver and gilt, a girdle harnessed with silver and gilt having a flower on the buckle, and another in the pendent.' Rawson and Swift were both members of the clergy; but the laity could be equally smart: Thomas Lilly made bequests of his sword, his best jacket of damask, his gown of worsted, his 'best' gown, and even his night gown. And the memorial brass of Robert Swift in Rotherham church shows him with a long loose gown trimmed with fur.[52]

As to beds, provost Rawson bequeathed 'the tester, blankets and sheets' in his lower room. Thomas Swift left to John Addy (master of the writing school at Rotherham College and the man who was to be his chantry priest) 'a featherbed that he lieth on, with bolster, tester and sciller, with a gown'. Nicholas Mounteney made various bequests of beds and bedding, describing the latter very precisely: 'two pillows viz my second best'; 'my second green rug'; 'one bolster my best save two'. He even said where exactly they might be found:

> one seeled bedstead standing in the parlour next the hall . . . one feather bed and one coverlet usually lying on the same bed.

Richard Edmondes was an innkeeper. His wife supplied a gallon of ale and some bread to the workmen when the Hood Cross was set up in 1595. 14d was left unpaid, and the debt was only settled by the town greaves two years later.[53] Edmondes described himself as 'innholder' when he made his will in 1608. He left his maidservant Frances Maison:

> the furniture of the bed whereon I lie usually viz the featherbed mattress bolster pillow pillowcase a blanket sheets and two coverlets

This gift was made in consideration of her 'long and diligent service', doubtless in Edmondes' inn.

The wealthier members of society owned jewellery. William Swift was such a man. His will (1568) contains gifts of a chain of fine gold, two rings of gold engraved with his arms and cognizance, one ring of fine gold engraved with the five wounds of our Lord, two gold brooches, which he had been 'accustomed to wear' upon his hats. He

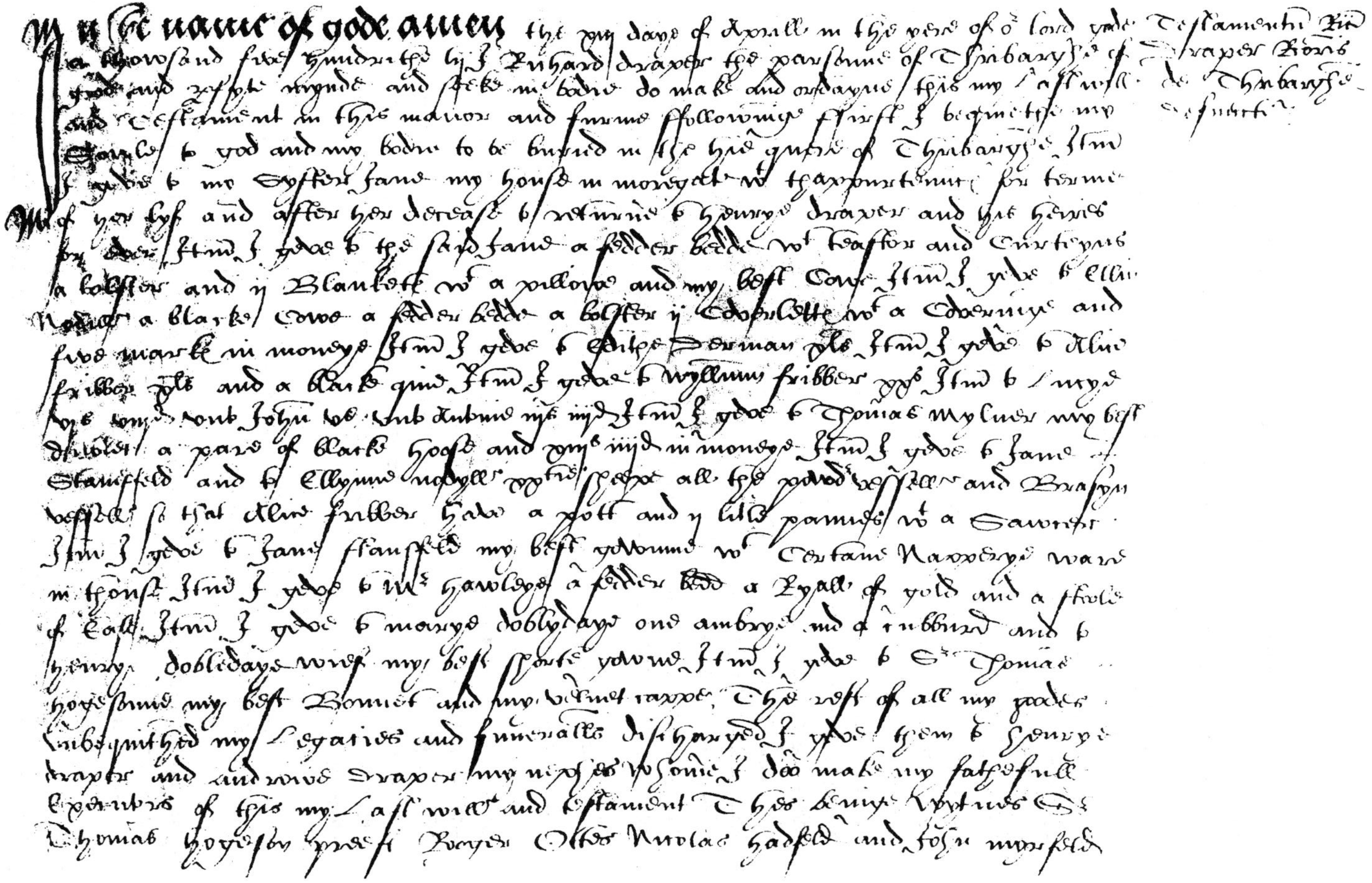

Figure 2. The will of Richard Drapper, 1552. *Borthwick Institute of Historical Research*

must have cut a most impressive figure. Swift also left each of his godsons one or two 'old angels', an angel being a gold coin worth 6s 8d; but these coins were probably not for spending. The angel coin sometimes served as a talisman. In particular, angels were used by the Tudor monarchs when they touched for the King's Evil. They were given to the sufferer afterwards, to be worn around the neck.[54] A few years before, Thomas Lilly had bequeathed angels to his mother-in-law and his sister, while Richard Drapper, who once taught grammar at Rotherham school, and whose will of 1552 is shown in Figure 2, left 'a ryal of gold'.[55] Nicholas Mounteney's will contained various legacies of 'current money', or cash, but also seven 'pieces of gold', two of them earmarked for the purchase of gold rings.

There were other items in the homes of the better-off, which were passed down from one generation to the next. Thomas Swift left his kinsman Robert Swift 'a macer with a cover of silver and gilt having a roebuck upon it' – the roebuck being a family emblem. In 1560, Robert Swift in turn left his godson a 'gilt goblet with a cover having an R & S on the top', and his daughter 'a standing cup with a cover all gilt'. In 1568 his son William left one basin, a silver ewer, two silver livery pots, two 'nests' of gilt bowls with their covers, one 'nest' of large cups, four cups with covers, one dozen silver trencher plates, two great 'salts', two dozen spoons 'with knobs of the Apostles', and one dozen spoons 'with knobs'.

A woman's touch can be detected in the will of Margaret Tayliour (1484): she left her son William two silver spoons, and her daughter Agnes her best gown. She left Richard Tayliour eight lengths of woollen, and 42 lengths of linen cloth. She also left her servant Katherine a cooking pot, a number of dishes and pans, four pieces of furniture and four linen cloths. A person who did not want to list such items individually might refer to them as 'huslements', as did Thomas Gree the chantry priest in 1505, when he left them to his sisters.

Animals were sometimes mentioned. Margaret Tayliour left her best cow to Margaret Crosse, and when he made his will Robert Hertley gave a special direction: 'I have two mares with foal and when they foal, I give the better to Master Mownforth'. We have also seen that it was common to leave an animal to pay the mortuary fees due to Mother Church.

Psychology

Some wills tell us much about the way men thought. Thomas Clarel was a relative of Dame Elizabeth Fitzwilliam and therefore of the Clarels of Aldwark; but he became a grocer in London. In the fifteenth century, grocers were not what they are today. They exported wool and cloth and imported luxury goods and raw materials from the Mediterranean – spices, fruit, wax, and dyes. The Grocers' Company had been founded in 1345, its first name being the Guild of Pepperers. Around 1447, Thomas Clarel was apprenticed to a leading grocer and wool exporter, Nicholas Wyfold, who became Lord Mayor of London in 1450. Clarel was admitted to the freedom of the Grocers' Company in 1454, and elected to the livery – the minority of senior men entitled to wear the Company's distinctive gown – in 1461. In 1473, he was elected as one of the two wardens of the Company.[56] When he made his will (1493) he described himself as grocer and citizen of London. He wanted to be buried in the Pardon Churchyard at St Paul's, though he lived in the parish of St Giles, Cripplegate.[57]

Clarel had spent his working life in London, but he remembered his roots, for he left one third of his estate for vestments and copes to be given to Rotherham church, Rawmarsh church and 'other churches 10 miles about'. He also left 'a black cloth with a white cross thereon made and a maul to carry it in'. He also left to Rotherham church:

> *my cloth of Arras of the passion of our Lord, to hang before the roodloft there for as long as it will endure, and my stained cloth of the battle between the Lord Scales and the Bastard . . .*

It seems a strange thing, to leave a picture of a tournament to a church; but when we probe behind the surface we can perhaps see why Thomas Clarel made this bequest.

We must first of all understand what this 'battle' was. Lord Scales was Anthony Woodville, brother in law to King Edward IV. The Bastard was a natural son of the Duke of Burgundy, sometimes referred to as the Grand Bastard, or 'my Lord Bastard'. These two knights fought each other at Smithfield in London on Thursday and Friday 11 and 12 June, 1467, to promote relations between England and Burgundy. On the first day, they met on horseback with lance and sword, until the Bastard's horse rammed its head into Scales's saddle and deposited him on the ground. On the second day, they came on foot, hammering each other with battleaxes until the King broke off the combat and made them swear an oath of friendship. The fight attracted much attention – rather like a modern boxing match; but there is perhaps a more particular reason why Thomas Clarel came into possession of his picture of it, for on the day after the tourna-

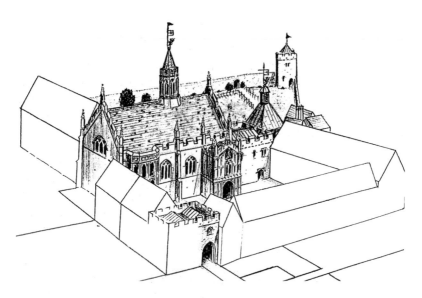

Figure 3. A reconstruction of Grocers' Hall, *c.*1500. *Centre for Metropolitan History*

ment, the King entertained the Bastard in Grocers' Hall (see Figure 3), when a total of £35 2s 9d was spent on the feast, which lasted for two days.[58] In view of the location of the feast, it is reasonable to suppose that Thomas Clarel was there, especially since he now belonged to the elite group of grocers permitted to wear the livery; and perhaps it was through his attendance there that he acquired the picture of the joust, which he clearly valued, and kept for many years.

In giving his stained cloth of the tournament to Rotherham, Thomas Clarel doubtless thought that he was giving something which would adorn the church; but perhaps he also thought that it would remind the locals of what he had become, for in addition he left 'a vestment of white damask with my arms upon it and with the grocers arms upon the same'. Clarel was a local boy who had made good in the City, and wanted people to know it. We should also remember that it was in the late fifteenth century that Rotherham church was rebuilt. It is likely that Clarel made his bequest in the knowledge that others were contributing to the restoration, notably his fellow Yorkshireman, Thomas Rotherham, then also engaged in building the College of Jesus.

Lastly, we return to the will of William Swift (1568). William's father, Robert Swift, had been 'the great advancer of the family'. It is reasonable to suppose that his wealth derived from the fact that he was a mercer – a dealer in luxury cloths such as silk – for the mercers of London were even wealthier than the grocers.[59] William Swift was clearly determined to carry on his father's work. He was entitled to certain rents; and he left precise instructions as to how this income should be dealt with. The money was to be collected annually by his five bailiffs and brought to his house in Rotherham, called the Swan. There, it was to be put into a chest, kept in the study. The chest was made of ashwood and was 'covered and bound with strong iron bands'. It had three locks and three keys. These were kept by his wife, cousin, and nephew. When the bailiffs came, the keyholders were to 'take pains' to meet at the Swan, so that the chest could be opened. These arrangements remind us that there were no banks in the 1560s, at least not in Rotherham; but Swift was evidently a prudent man, determined to see that his money was safe nonetheless. This impression is reinforced when we look at the directions he gives concerning his two daughters. He wants one of them to marry his ward Ralph Byston, and Ralph can marry whichever girl he 'shall like best of'. Swift leaves the girls a substantial part of his estate; but if either of them

> *use themselves wantonly or lightly without giving due obedience to their mother, and following the wise counsel of my friends in their choice of marriage . . .*

she is to get nothing, for

> *it would grieve me to know that any of my goods should be wasted with youthful and dissolute persons.*

Here is the authentic voice of the Tudor parent, worrying about the younger generation and its profligate ways, and determined to see that his family continues to prosper.[60]

If wills can explain how our ancestors thought, they can occasionally even suggest how they spoke. In 1552 the former grammar master at Rotherham school, Richard Drapper, made his will. When he did so he mentioned certain items which were in 'thouse'; and by this he clearly meant 'the house'. Yorkshire pronunciation has not changed much in 500 years.

Glossary

ANGEL: a gold coin worth 6s 8d, minted in 1464. Discontinued in the reign of Charles II
CAUSEY: a single or double line of flagstones laid where a road is worn away
CIERGE: a candle, especially a large candle used in religious ceremonies
CLOTH OF ARRAS: a tapestry
CODICIL: a supplementary document, modifying a will
COGNIZANCE: badge or heraldic device
DAMASK: rich silk fabric woven with elaborate designs and figures
DIRGE: song of mourning sung at a burial
GRAINS: the refuse malt left over after brewing, often fed to cattle and swine
DOWRY: property or money brought by bride to her husband
GATE: road
GREAVE: officer or supervisor
JOINTURE: estate settled on wife for period during which she survives her husband
LIVERY POTS: pots to put refreshment in for the night
MACER: bowl
MARK: 13s 4d
MARTRON: marten
MAUL: a trunk or travelling bag
MERCER: dealer in textiles, especially silks and other costly materials
MUSTERDEVILLES: a kind of mixed grey woollen cloth, much used in the 14th and 15th
    centuries
OBIT: memorial service, usually on the anniversary of someone's death
ROOD: the Cross of Christ
ROODLOFT: gallery on top of the screen between the nave and chancel of a church, which bore
    the rood
RYAL: a gold coin minted in 1464 worth 10s. Otherwise known as a noble
SALT: salt-cellar
SACRING BELL: a small bell rung at the elevation of the host
SCILLER: (or celure) the vertical part at the head of the bed which ascends and sometimes supports
    the canopy
STAINED: ornamented with coloured pictures or designs
SUPERALTAR: slab of stone consecrated for use on unconsecrated altar
TESTATOR: a person who has made a will
TESTER: the canopy over a bed
TO WARE: to spend
WHERE: choir

Notes and References

I have modernised spelling throughout. Before 1971 there were four farthings in a penny, twelve
pennies in a shilling and twenty shillings to the pound; and the abbreviations for pounds, shillings
and pence were £, s and d.
    The handwriting and terminology of Tudor wills is not easy to decipher and understand. The St
Anthony's Press at the BIHR publishes guides to contemporary handwriting e.g. *Sixteenth and
Seventeenth Century Handwriting*. Series 1 compiled by Ann Rycraft, 3rd edn. 1972. As for archaic
words, which are sometimes used in wills, see *The Oxford English Dictionary* and *The English Dialect
Dictionary*, ed. Joseph Wright, Oxford, 1898–1905.

Abbreviations used in references:

Aspects 1: *Aspects of Rotherham, Discovering Local History*, ed. by Melvyn Jones, Wharncliffe
    Publishing Ltd, 1995.
BIHR: Borthwick Institute of Historical Research, University of York, St Anthony's Hall, Peasholme
    Green, York YO1 2PW.
DNB: *Dictionary of National Biography*.
Eastwood: *History of the Parish of Ecclesfield*, Rev J Eastwood, London, 1862.
f: folio.
Guest: *Historic Notices of Rotherham* by John Guest FSA, Robert White, Worksop, 1879.
Hey, Packmen: *Packmen, Carriers and Packhorse Roads* by David Hey, Leicester University Press,
    1980.

Hey, South Yorkshire: *The Making of South Yorkshire* by David Hey, Moorland Publishing, 1979.

HH: *Hallamshire, The History and Topography of the Parish of Sheffield in the County of York* by Joseph Hunter, 3rd edition, 1975, ed. by the Rev. Alfred Gatty.

HSY: *The History and Topography of the Deanery of Doncaster*, by Joseph Hunter, 1828–31, republished by EP Publishing in collaboration with Sheffield City Council, 1974.

Nightingale: *A Medieval Mercantile Community, The Grocers' Company and the Politics and Trade of London 1000–1485* by Pamela Nightingale, Yale University Press, 1995.

Richardson: *The Local Historian's Encyclopaedia* by John Richardson, Historical Publications Ltd, 1974.

Surtees: Publications of the Surtees Society.

Tate: *The Parish Chest* by W. E. Tate, Phillimore, 1983.

TRHS: *Transactions of the Royal Historical Society*.

v: volume.

YASRS: Yorkshire Archaeological Society Record Series.

Youings: *Sixteenth Century England* by Joyce Youings, Penguin, 1984 (The Pelican Social History of Britain).

References

1. Eileen Power pointed out the importance of wills as a historical source many years ago: *Medieval People*, Methuen & Co Ltd, revised edition, 1986, p. 157. More recently, David Hey has pointed out that the practice of making a will spread down the social scale in the Tudor period: *Family History & Local History in England*, Longman, 1987, p. 52.

2. For Thomas Rotherham's College see the author's *Sumptuously Builded of Brick: Thomas Rotherham's College, 1482–1550* in *Aspects 1*.

3. YASRS 33 p. 141; Guest p. 122.

4. BIHR V 23 f. 322r.

5. YASRS 33 p. 167; Guest p. 120.

6. YASRS 33 p. 172; HH p. 364; Guest p. 259; Surtees 79 p. 196; Guest p. 259.

7. *The Stripping of the Altars, Traditional Religion in England 1400–1580*, Eamonn Duffy, Yale University Press, 1992 p. 326.

8. *Aspects 1*; Guest p. 142.

9. However, a number of writers have pointed out that we should beware of accepting religious formulae at face value, since wills were often drawn up by a small number of people, often parish priests, who suggested the words which should be used, just as a solicitor would nowadays: David Hey, op. cit. p. 52, Youings p. 197. I am grateful to my friend Dr C.R.J. Currie of the Institute of Historical Research for reminding me of this point.

10. Guest pp. 519, 259; HH p. 364.

11. Guest p. 259.

12. Youings p. 197.

13. *Symbolaeographie*, 1590, section 406. Various editions of this work are in Rotherham Central Library, Local Studies Section. For William West see: the DNB; *William West, Seneschal of Hallamshire*, Chapter 6 in T. Walter Hall, *Incunabula of Sheffield History*, Sheffield, J. W. Northend Ltd., 1937; *The Writers of Tudor Yorkshire* by A. G. Dickens TRHS 5th Series 13, 1963 pp. 49–76.

14. HSY vol II p. 18.

15. YASRS 33 p. 169; Guest p. 258. Carnebull may have been at school with Thomas Rotherham: HSY vol II p. 6.

16. YASRS 107, p. 133; Kreider p. 82.

17. YASRS 33 p. 144.

18. Guest p. 136.

19. YASRS 33 p. 143; Surtees 1868 IV p. 111.

20. BIHR v 26, f. 141r.

21. BIHR v 25, f. 163v; Guest p. 258.

22. YASRS 33, p. 171; Surtees 79, p. 151; Guest p. 259.

23. We learn from this that Bokyng was not a priest, but a married man, as was his successor Robert Coliour, who died intestate in 1509.

24. Guest pp. 158, 377. He may previously have been a greave: ibid   p. 382.

25. Guest p. 235.

26. Surtees 79 p. 128.

27. Guest p. 258.
28. Surtees 1868, II vol IV, p. 98(n).
29. BIHR v 31A, f. 98v.
30. See Aspects 1, p. 16.
31. Guest p. 519; Surtees 121 (1912) p. 51.
32. YASRS 33, p. 143; Guest p. 124.
33. Aldwark was an outlying dependency of the parish of Ecclesfield, though nearer to Rotherham: HSY vol II p. 51; Eastwood pp. 167, 488. For Elizabeth Fitzwilliam see HSY vol II pp. 53–4 and the pedigree at p. 56.
34. The two orders of Friars at Doncaster were the Carmelites (or White Friars) and the Franciscans or Friars Minor (Grey Friars): see HSY vol I pp. 17–19. The two fell out in the 1530s: see *Aspects* 1 p. 17.
35. Surtees (1868) IB p. 309.
36. Surtees 116 (1908) p. 62.
37. Surtees 1855 *Testamenta Eboracensa* p. 282 (n).
38. Guest p. 37.
39. See *Aspects 1* p. 14.
40. Guest p. 377.
41. *A History of the ancient Parish of Wath-upon-Dearne*, W. Keble Martin, Wath, 1920, p. 79.
42. BIHR v 30A, f. 93r.
43. HSY vol II p. 13 (n2). Hunter calls her Alice Ealand.
44. T. Walter Hall, *South Yorkshire Historical Sketches*, 1931 pp. 24, 25; HH p. 390. Monteney's son Richard became a barrister, was a prominent figure in Rotherham, and owned a house near the Hood Cross: Guest pp. 203–4.
45. BIHR v 33B, f. 387r.
46. See glossary.
47. In that part of England occupied by the Danes, 'gate' often meant road or street.
48. BIHR v 18, f. 28r.
49. BIHR v 33B, f. 486v. For the names of the open fields see Guest pp. 368, 383, 386.
50. BIHR v 18, f. 28r. These servants had been remembered twelve years earlier by Whitmore's son in law Thomas Lilly, who left two shillings 'to every servant in my father Whitmore's house': Guest p. 377.
51. Thomas Rotherham's Statutes specified the gowns to be worn by Fellows and choristers: see *Aspects 1* p. 15.
52. See *Aspects 1* p. 25.
53. Guest pp. 388–9. Guest thought that the Hood Cross was merely 'a stone cross'; but it is more likely to have been a building, used in connection with the market. Most market towns had one. It was usually a vaulted polygonal structure with an open archway on each side: Oxford English Dictionary; Hey, South Yorkshire p. 69. One reason for thinking that Rotherham's Hood Cross was a building, not a simple cross is that the Feoffees incurred considerable expense in repairing it, notably in 1603 and 1640: Guest pp. 389, 395. The bills suggest that it was a covered building, like that erected in Shaftesbury in 1570, 'for all those who sold butter, cheese, eggs, poultry, or the like to stand or sit dry in during the market': *The Agrarian History of England and Wales*, ed. Joan Thirsk, vol IV 1500–1640, Cambridge University Press, 1967 p. 48.
54. The King's Evil was scrofula, the tubercular inflammation of the lymph glands of the neck. For the ceremony of touching, much developed by Henry VII see Tate, p. 157–161.
55. BIHR v 29, f. 107. For Richard Drapper's dubious career, see *Aspects 1* pp. 19–20.
56. Information supplied by Mr Roy Hawkins, Beadle to the Grocers' Company. In the late fifteenth century the livery was changed every three years. As warden, Thomas Clarel was provided with it at the expense of the Company: Nightingale p. 523. For Nicholas Wyfold, see Nightingale pp. 491, 494–6.
57. HSY vol II p. 53.
58. *Warwick the Kingmaker and the Wars of the Roses*, Paul Murray Kendall, Cardinal, 1973, pp. 206–7; *The Paston Letters*, Everyman's Library, Dent, London 1956, pp. 44, 50. The present Grocers' Hall is the fifth and dates from the 1960s, but stands on the site of the hall which Thomas Clarel knew (see Figure 3). The accounts of the feast survive. The average amount spent on election feasts in the 1440s was between £25 and £36 – Nightingale pp. 467, 541.
59. Nightingale pp. 523, 552.
60. He succeeded. His son was made a knight by James I in 1603: HSY vol I pp. 205–6.

Acknowledgements

I thank the Borthwick Institute of Historical Research for permission to reproduce extracts from the wills of Vicar John Lillie and Master Richard Drapper, and Professor David Crouch, Dr Derek Keene and the Centre for Metropolitan History for permission to reproduce the sketch of the medieval Grocers' Hall.

2. Lionell Copley: A Seventeenth Century Capitalist

by John Goodchild, M. Univ.

LIONELL COPLEY APPEARS TO HAVE BEEN the first major capitalist in the West Riding iron industry, a man who came to control ironstone mines, charcoal-productive woodlands, blast furnaces, iron-working forges and a major market in iron. In addition, he was the owner of a substantial country estate, had major interests in coalmining, was a producer of bar iron for nailmaking and had a concern with steel making, as well as taking an active part in local affairs.

What was Copley's background? He was baptised at Wadworth in December 1607 and was the younger of the sons of William Copley of Wadworth Hall (see Figure 1); his father was head of a junior branch of the family of Copley of Sprotbrough. As a young man, Lionell Copley was Muster Master General when the Parliamentary Army was raised in 1642, while his elder brother Christopher was a major and later a lieutenant-colonel in that Army, being the co-victor at the Battle of Sherburn in 1645, having commanded one of three regiments of horse at the Battle of Nantwich in 1644, under Lord Fairfax.[1]

Lionell Copley was to marry a London widow, herself a native of Cheshire, and to have four children. His brother Colonel Copley died in 1653, and the Colonel's only son in 1658, whereupon Lionell Copley succeeded to the family's Wadworth Hall estate and became a landed gentleman.[2] Wadworth Hall had been rebuilt by Colonel Copley in 1644, at a cost of at least £600, and he had planted orchards, hopyards and timber there from 1632. Lionell Copley's own only surviving son, Lionell junior, was educated at Oxford and was successively Governor of Hull and Governor of the Colony of Maryland in North America; by the failure of male heirs in the Copleys of Sprotbrough, the estate there was to come to Lionell's own descendants in 1709.[3]

Both before and after his accession to the Wadworth Hall estate, Lionell Copley's interests were widespread, while he was a man of marked character. As early as 1638 he was sued for a substantial £20 in wages, claimed by employees for leading coal: Copley challenged the right of the West Riding Quarter Sessions to deal with the matter, but the justices affirmed their right under statute to adjudicate, and

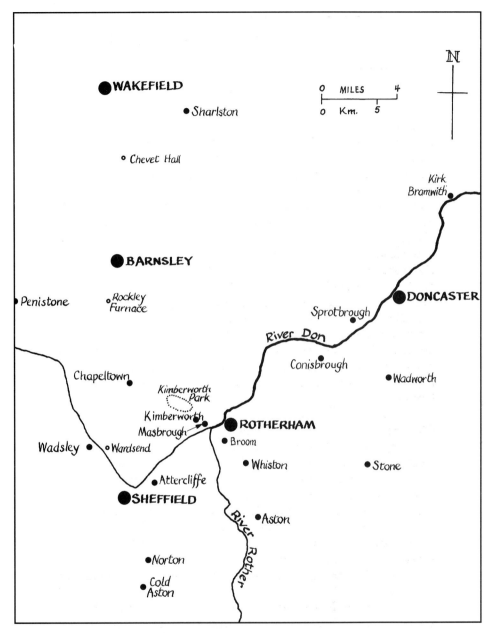

Figure 1.   South Yorkshire and adjacent parts of West Yorkshire showing the location of places mentioned in the text.

they ordered him to pay. Copley then 'uttered very disgraceful and uncivile speeches against Sir William Savile then present in open cort' and the magistrates were about to commit Copley for contempt when Savile interceded for him. The justices were somewhat mollified, and dismissed him 'hoping he will hereafter carrye himself more discretly in Court of Justice and to persons of quality'. [4]

Much later, in 1664, he was indicted at the Assizes for having beaten one Richard Firth and having then put a bridle in his mouth and ridden him about for half an hour, kicking him to make him move. [5] But apart from his ready tongue and his apparently curious sense of humour, Copley was a keen sportsman and was mentioned as an illegal taker of game – of partridges – in 1637, while his own letters of the 1650s also refer to his interest in game. [6] He had more serious interests too, and early in the period of the restored monarchy, and in a period of marked persecution, he became in 1663 a trustee of an endowment for ejected nonconformist ministers, and in the 1640s he was taking an active part in the new ecclesiastical administration of the West Riding: he had powers to oversee the choice by the inhabitants of Penistone of a new minister, although in the event they chose one not to Copley's liking. [7] He was also a Rotherham (charities) Feoffee. [8]

In 1666 a conspiracy to defraud Copley came into court, the instigator of the conspiracy being one Francis Mountney of Rotherham, gentleman. Incidentally, Copley was said later to have joined the Parliamentarians in the Civil War through mistake and fright – probably a calumny upon him; he was said to have supplied Sheffield Castle with armaments.

How did Copley first come into ironmaking? His first known association with the iron industry dates from 1635, when he was in his late twenties and when he was fined for having been responsible for the deposit of 'iron hammers lying in Marshgate' in Doncaster, to the obstruction of the highway: Doncaster was the uppermost limit of natural navigation on the river Don. In 1638 he and two partners obtained powers to erect an ironworks at Conisbrough, and in 1639 he was the senior of four partners, including his own elder brother, who agreed to lease, from the Earl of Arundel and others, land in the parish of Ecclesfield and in Kimberworth, Attercliffe and Sheffield, on which the lessees would erect two forges. [9] In 1648 Captain Adam Eyre's diary records calling upon Colonel Copley at the forge in Sheffield. [10] Before 1640, Lionell Copley was also a quarter partner in the iron forge at Stone in Tickhill. In 1639 he was living at what was described as Browne, presumably the later Broom House in Whiston, a mile from Rotherham.

In 1655, a patent was granted to a Captain Copley for smelting and forging iron with pit coal, and he erected works near Bristol and in Kingswood Forest there. This is probably a mere coincidence of surnames; certainly this Captain Copley, one of several to experiment with coal at this period, failed in his intentions.[11] The charcoal blast furnace reigned supreme in the West Riding, as elsewhere: a reference occurs to a furnace at or near Thurgoland in 1567, and references to furnaces at Kimberworth and at Wadsley in 1587.[12] It seems possible that it was under this 1587 lease that iron forges were also opened at Wadsley, forges which Copley took in 1651 together with 100 or 150 tons of iron a year to come from Foxbrook Furnace, together with the necessary hammers, anvils and tools. At Chapeltown in Ecclesfield parish, a furnace was in existence in 1637, and in 1652 Copley controlled this latter forge too.[13] By the end of 1646, the Copley brothers and their two partners – being a royal Clerk of the Kitchen and a Kent man – were liable to pay the enormous rent of £2,120, but owing to the Wars they claimed that 'the works pays not the rent reserved and the arrears are more worth than the term'.[14] But a year later, in 1647, Attercliffe and Wadsley forges were claimed to be worth £200 a year in clear profit, despite the claimed losses, and as the times settled down, the ironworks were continued successfully. Lionell Copley succeeded his erstwhile partners, and in relation to the Rotherham and Sheffield area works, in 1666, and for a lease period of ten years, Lionell Copley alone became the tenant of Rotherham Forge, Chapel Furnace at Chapeltown, Wardsend Forge near Sheffield and Attercliffe Forge, with the right to mine ironstone at Sheffield and Ecclesfield and to a supply of charcoal wood, Rotherham Forge being converted under the terms of the lease to a slitting mill (see Figure 2).[15]

Now for a time Chapel Furnace and Kimberworth Forge near Rotherham had been in the hands of one Francis Nevile, of Chevet Hall near Wakefield, a country gentleman and sometime MP; he was for some years the agent for the South Yorkshire estates of the Earl of Pembroke & Montgomery later belonging to the Countess of Arundel & Surrey, and like the Countess, but unlike the Copley brothers, Nevile had supported the royalist cause in the Civil Wars, and subsequently was heavily fined (£1000) as a Royalist delinquent. As early as 1632 Nevile had leased both land and timber from the Copleys of Sprotbrough, and in 1652 he was reported as having had a lease of Kimberworth Park and the ironworks near Rotherham, and as being owed substantial sums by his employer (as agent), the Countess of

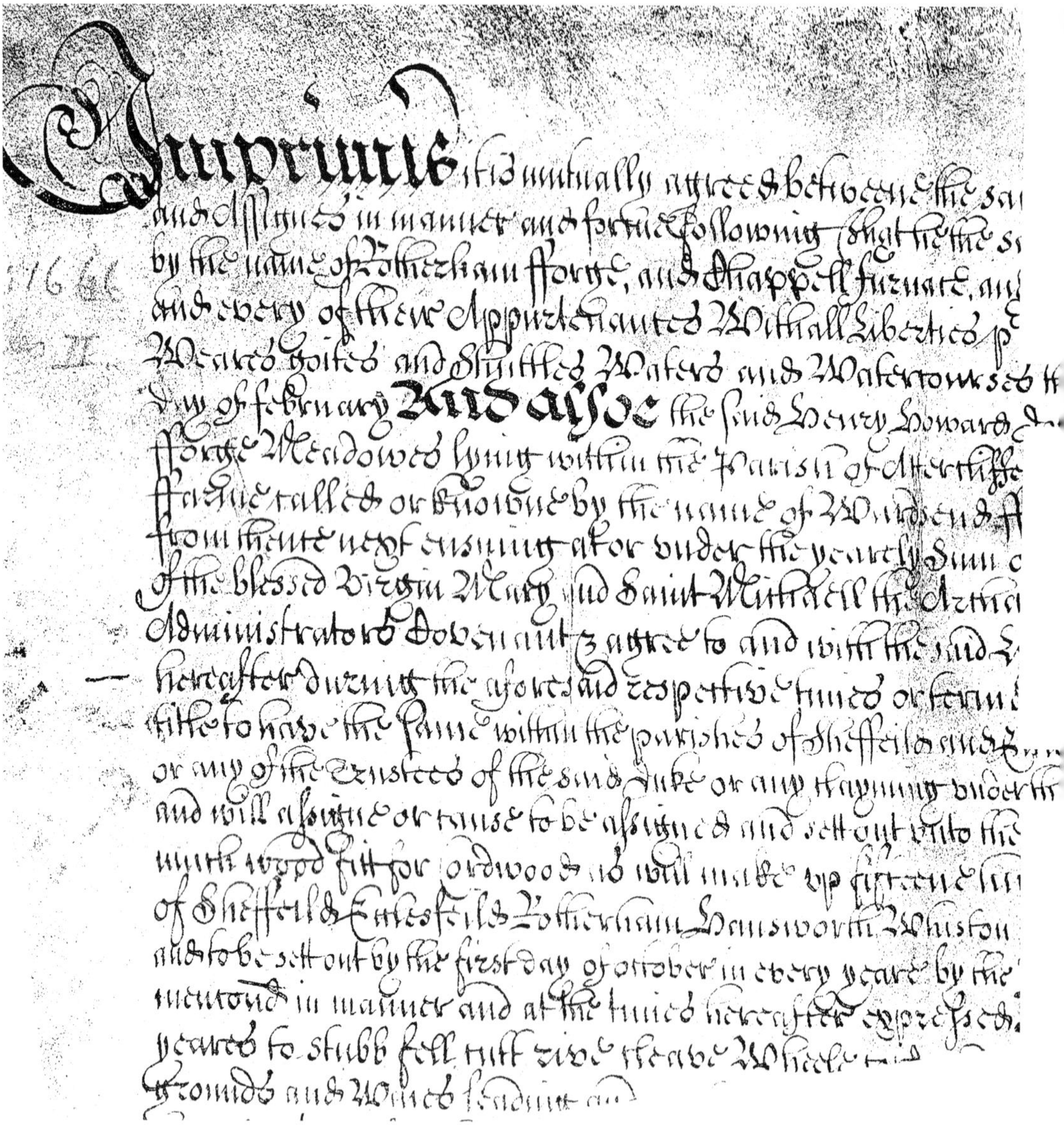
1666
Imprimis it is mutually agreed betweene the sai
and Assignes in manner and forme following that the the s
by the name of Rotherham fforge, and Chappell furnace, an
and every of theire Appurtenances With all Liberties p
Weares goites and Shuttles Waters and Watercourses
day of february And alsoe the said Henry Howard
fforge Meadowes lying within the Parish of Attercliffe
ffarme called or knowne by the name of Wardsend f
from thence next ensuing at or under the yearely Sum
of the blessed Virgin Mary and Saint Michaell the Archa
Administrators Covenant & agree to and with the said
hereafter during the aforesaid respective times or term
title to have the same within the parishes of Sheffield and E
or any of the Trustees of the said Duke or any claymeing under th
and will assigne or cause to be assigned and sett out unto the
much wood fitt for cordwood as will make up fifteene hun
of Sheffield Ecclesfield Rotherham Handsworth Whiston
and to be sett out by the first day of october in every yeare by the
mentioned in manner and at the times hereafter expressed
yeares to stubb fell cutt rive cleave Wheele
grounds and Wayes leading

Figure 2. Beginning of the agreement made in 1666 between Lionell Copley and Henry Howard of Norfolk, second son of the late Henry, Earl of Arundel and Surrey, under which Copley leased Rotherham Forge, Chapel Furnace, Wardsend Forge and Attercliffe Forge. It was also agreed that he could mine ironstone in Sheffield and Ecclesfield parishes and cordwood for charcoal making on the Howard estate in the parishes of Sheffield, Ecclesfield, Rotherham, Handsworth, Whiston and Treeton. *The original is in Rotherham Central Library, Archives and Local Studies Section*

Arundel & Surrey. That good lady, a goddaughter incidentally of Queen Elizabeth, had prudently and with her husband retired to Holland and then Italy during the Wars at home, and as a widow she lived on until 1654. Nevile, whom the Countess addressed in surviving letters as cousin, and from whom she received personal as well as financial advice in the early 1650s, had from 1632 at least had interests in woods (for charcoal), and in 1639 he paid for charcoal timber used in the Kimberworth ironworks, becoming (as a renewal?) tenant there in 1645 at £100 a year, and he was tenant too of Chapel Furnace. It was this small ironworking empire which Nevile handed over, presumably owing to his financial difficulties, to Lionell Copley, who addresses Nevile in letters as 'Good Cozen' – a phrase not necessarily at that period suggesting literal cousinly relationship, but suggesting some family connection.[16]

In 1652 then, Copley (alone) took Chapel Furnace and Kimberworth Forge (both on lease, of course), with their stock of 332 tons of raw iron in bars, paying £612 for the works and £1963 12s 8d for the stock, plus one ton of bar iron which was paid to Nevile at Bradley near Huddersfield (did the Colne Bridge Forge there exist then?), and a yet further £172 2s 6d for cordwood for charcoal making. Nevile was to remain as head tenant, but Lionell Copley was to pay the £100 a year rent and to maintain a stock worth at the least £2000. The owner, the Countess, agreed to the new arrangement and for a supply of timber for charcoaling for so long as her timber reserves 'shall Contynue'. The agreement provided further that if the average price of iron sold at the works rose two shillings above £15 a ton, or above £16 a ton at Hull and York, then the price for a cord of wood should increase from 4s 6d to 5s. A careful and detailed valuation of the stock at both Chapel Furnace and Kimberworth Forge was made, its date being 16 June, 1652, signed by both Copley and his manager, John Kaye. This valuation is apparently unique locally for its period, and lists the whole stock of the two works.[17]

It will be apparent that the sparseness of the surviving documentation makes it impossible to report in detail the growth of Lionell Copley's ironmaking interests and their ancillaries in raw materials supply and in regard to markets, but in the case of Chapel Furnace and Kimberworth Forge a little of what was involved is described in some detail, and one sees something of the huge capital investment involved.

Continuing his business's growth – and possibly also envisaging the desirability of forestalling potential opposition and rivalry – in 1653 Copley further extended his business by taking a lease of three acres of land on which to build a furnace at Rockley, near Worsbrough, at a site provided with the necessary water power to power bellows, and just downwind of the lessor's (Francis Rockley's) house nearby. Copley was to pay a rent based upon output: a mere £5 ground rent, but also five shillings for every ton of iron cast there.[18] Rockley himself was also to be allowed by a slightly later agreement to cast forty tons of iron a year there, using Copley's utensils. Ironworks there had existed earlier, and in 1646 they had been accounted valueless as no profit was made, and Rockley had had trouble with his steward-manager, William Hayford, while Rockley himself was in prison in London. Hayford's descendants were later to become ironmasters on their own account in the West Riding. Lionell Copley probably used timber from the adjacent owner's well-wooded estate – that of Thomas Edmunds of Worsbrough. He owed him £300 in 1645, i.e., before he took the lease to build Rockley Furnace.

Copley added further to his iron empire when in 1669 he entered into an agreement with Gervase Nevile (son of Francis of Chevet) to take over Norton Forge and Furnace, just south of Sheffield. Nevile was to assign his own interest to Copley, and to procure the confirmation of Mrs Bullock, late of Norton, widow, who presumably was the lessor. The papers refer to iron boshes to the furnace, and to Copley acquiring with the works the ironstone 'on ye delph [i.e., ironstone pits] hills neare Cold Aston', in Derbyshire.[19]

During the Commonwealth period, Copley had worked collieries at Kimberworth and at Whiston, paying respectively £100 and £55 rents for what were almost certainly the largest collieries in the Don valley at that time. In 1655 he was concerned with the matter of the rating of his coal mines at Whiston, where he may have been tenant of the Stringers, lords of the manors of Whiston and of Sharlston near Wakefield, at which latter place they extensively exploited their own coal resources.[20]

In 1664 and in 1670 Copley was concerned with the acquisition of the available timber on the Aston estate, and in the 1660s he was a member of a cabal of ironmasters who indulged in price-fixing. In 1665, curiously, he was stated to be an ironmaster but not a founder of iron – suggesting that his concern was in the production of iron rods (partly used in nailmaking), rather than with the making of iron castings: he was said not to be concerned in iron with the 'working of it up'. This may not have been the case earlier, for as well as working iron forges, he had agreed in 1659 to buy 100 to 150 tons of pig iron a year over a seven-year period.[21] Copley was certainly both a large-scale and geographically widespread ironmaster, even if he had written in the early 1650s that 'I am noe Lawyer nor Good Clerk'.[22] How financially successful he was in so widespread an empire is difficult to tell.

Copley's business interests also extended widely into ironstone mining: he aimed to control raw materials as well as iron production and working-up: ironstone getting, charcoal timber supply, iron making, iron rolling and slitting, were all his concerns, along with marketing, while he probably possessed a virtual monopoly in the Rotherham area coal markets also. He had had a house in Rotherham during the 1650s, and lived there, presumably removing to Wadworth Hall subsequent to his nephew's death in 1658, when he became its master. He continued as an ironmaster until his death, making his will on 20 November, 1675 and dying in London only seventeen days later, on 7 December, 1675, and being buried at Wadworth[23] on the 19th of the same month. Only a very few years earlier, he had been assessed in 1672 to the Hearth Tax for 'Brome farme', on five hearths in Whiston, and (described as an esquire) for the seventeen hearths of Wadworth Hall; and it was apparently he who in 1672 was also assessed for the fourteen hearths of the 'Collidge' in Rotherham, for the one hearth of Attercliffe Forge and – most interestingly – for the four hearths in Kimberworth of the 'Steele Furnish' there.[24] His widow lived on until 1696, when she died at the age of 85. The 'iron' empire is said to have been disposed of about 1678, in debt.

Copley was of course from 1658 a country gentleman as well as an ironmaster: he was in the tradition which was to be continued by the Spencers of Cannon Hall near Barnsley and the Cottons of Haigh Hall, after his death. Some undated propositions in the hand of (and signed by) Lionell Copley, in relation to a proposed marriage settlement – but after his accession to the Wadworth Hall estate – list his estates and their annual value to him. Of these, the first three were in part in his own occupation, and all of course were his own property – i.e., the list excludes his leaseholds:

	£	s	d	
Wadworth	123	15	4	
Hensall	126	10	4	
Bramwith	161	12	0	
Broom	130	0	0	
Masbrough	30	0	0	being a house and land
	£571	17	8[25]	

This was a handsome income for a country gentleman. The Nonconformist Register of the Revs Oliver Heywood and Thomas Dickenson refers to Copley's death: 'Mr Lionell Copley of Rotherham died at London bur. in Yorkshire... aged 60, rich'.[26]

References

1. *Yorkshire Diaries*, Surtees Society, Volume 65, 1877, p. 109n; Hunter, J., *South Yorkshire*, Vol.1, 1828, p. 252.
2. Hunter, *South Yorkshire*, Vol.1, p. 251.
3. *Burke's Landed Gentry*, 1925 Edition, p. 394.
4. West Riding Quarter Session Records, *Yorkshire Archaeological Journal*, Vol. 5, p. 372.
5. *Yorkshire Diaries*, p. 109n.
6. The John Goodchild Collection, Wakefield: Misc. Iron MSS Boxes.
7. *Yorkshire Diaries*, p. 109n; West Riding Quarter Session Records, *Yorkshire Archaeological Society Record Series*, Vol. 53, 1915, p. 19n.
8. Guest, J., *Historic Notices of Rotherham*, 1879, p. 399.
9. *Catalogue of the Arundel Castle Manuscripts*, Sheffield City Libraries, 1965, p. 37.
10. *Yorkshire Diaries*, p. 109n.
11. *Calendar of State Papers Domestic*, 1875–86; Smiles, S., *Industrial Biography*, 1863, pp. 57–58; Nef, J.U., *Rise of the British Coal Industry*, Vol 1, 1932, p. 249n.
12. *Catalogue of the Arundel Castle Manuscripts*.
13. John Goodchild Collection.
14. Royalist Composition Papers, *Yorkshire Archaeological Society Record Series.*, Vols 15, 18, 20.
15. Rotherham Archives, 139B.
16. John Goodchild Collection.
17. John Goodchild Collection.
18. Wilkinson, J., *Worsborough: Its Historical Associations and Rural Attractions*, 1872, pp. 75–76.
19. John Goodchild Collection.
20. West Yorkshire Archives, West Riding Quarter Sessions Order Books.
21. Riden, P. (Ed), *George Sitwell's Letterbook 1662–66*, Derbyshire Record Society, Vol. X, 1985, p. 227.
22. John Goodchild Collection.
23. Hunter, *South Yorkshire*, p. 251.
24. Wakefield Library Headquarters, West Riding Hearth Tax Returns, 1672.
25. John Goodchild Collection.
26. Turner, J. H. (ed.), *Northowram Registers*, 1881.

3. Thomas Salkeld (1778–1844): Estate Worker, Wentworth

by Joan Jones

A country estate and its labour force

LARGE COUNTRY ESTATES SUCH AS the Fitzwilliam estate centred on Wentworth Woodhouse were complex organisations in the eighteenth and nineteenth centuries and were substantial employers of labour.[1] Direct employment was greatly increased if they had mining and manufacturing interests as well as agricultural ones. Direct employment in coal mining on the Wentworth estate, for example, increased from 79 in 1795 to 869 in 1845.[2] Additionally, many people, for example agricultural tenants, local craftmen and tradesmen and suppliers in local towns, were indirectly dependent for their livelihoods on country estates.

The size and complexity of the Wentworth estate labour force in the early Victorian period has been recorded in a series of documents compiled for the purpose of distributing the St Thomas' Day charity donation on 21 December each year and the Collop Monday charity in March each year.[3] It is not clear when these two charities began or when they ceased but detailed nineteenth century lists have survived for the period 1811–28 and 1841–56.[4] At the back of the 1841 lists of employees there is a 'Rule of Admissibility' to a claim for the St Thomas' Day donation: 'Any person regularly employed in the Service of Earl Fitzwilliam and employed at that time. Persons employed at that time at a merely occasional job are not entitled.'[5] A quantity of meat and a sum of money were given on St Thomas' Day (Figure 1) and meat only on Collop Monday. The charity appears not to have extended to the indoor staff at the mansion.

The list of Fitzwilliam employees compiled in December 1841 names 1017 persons then employed by the Earl on the Wentworth estate. The largest group of employees were miners, 181 at Elsecar New and Jump Colliery, 168 at Elsecar Old Colliery, 126 at Parkgate Colliery, 55 at Strafford Main Colliery, 54 at Stubbin Colliery, 24 at the ironstone mining grounds at Tankersley and 12 constructing Thorncliffe Drift, a major mine drainage project stretching from Elsecar to Thorncliffe. There were also 54 persons employed at Elsecar Ironworks and 65 employed on building 'Greasbro New

Figure 1. Distributing the St Thomas Day charity. *Eric Leslie*

Coach Road'. Another large group of employees was engaged on expanding or maintaining the fabric of the estate and these included 40 carpenters, 35 masons, eight sawyers, six joiners and four plumbers. The agricultural land 'in hand' employed 61 farm labourers at the home farm, 19 woodmen and five blacksmiths. The pleasure grounds at Wentworth and the parks at Wentworth and Tankersley were also substantial employers: there were 36 gardeners, seven botanical gardeners, nine gatekeepers, six employed at the menagerie, three gamekeepers, three park keepers, eight at Earl Fitzwilliam's stud, two saddlers, a 'boat tenter', a rat catcher and a 'stable bed maker'. The list also included three tailors, three maltsters, two millers, a brewer and a brewer's assistant, a cooper, a butcher and a postman. Additionally, twelve former employees were listed who were resident at the hospital (Barrow almshouses). Last but not least were two painters: Thomas Salkeld, the principal painter and Robert Pepper, the painter's apprentice (Figure 2).

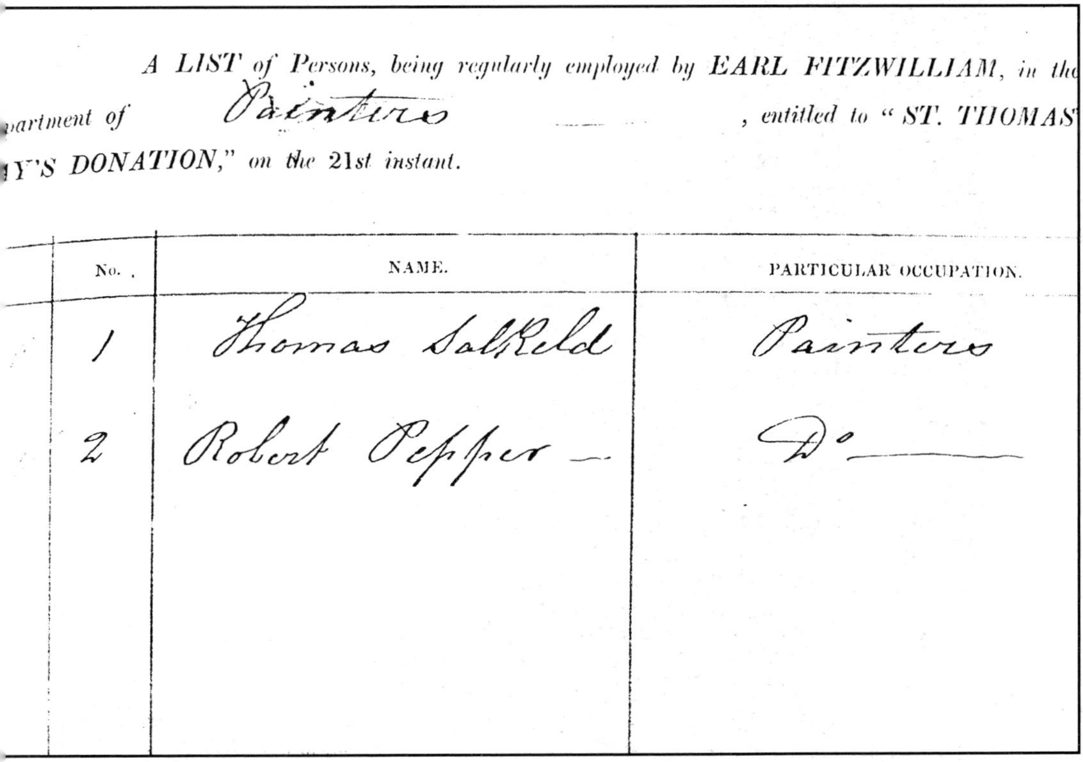

A LIST of Persons, being regularly employed by EARL FITZWILLIAM, in the
partment of Painters *, entitled to "ST. THOMAS*
Y'S DONATION," on the 21st instant.

No.	NAME.	PARTICULAR OCCUPATION.
1	Thomas Salkeld	Painters
2	Robert Pepper	Do

Figure 2. Thomas Salkeld and his grandson Robert Pepper identified in the St Thomas Day lists of 1843. *Wentworth Woodhouse Muniments WWM A-1414*

The Salkeld family

The first known documented reference to a Salkeld at Wentworth is for 1771 when John Salkeld married Mary Mercer. John Salkeld's occupation was given as painter. We know that he was the estate painter from surviving estate accounts. For example, in 1795 he was described as 'Painter by the Great' (ie, paid by the piece)[6] and in 1801 he was paid £147 - 10s - 0½d and in 1802 he was paid £127 - 4s - 0¼d.[7] Among the more unusual jobs he did in that period were painting the estate coaches including the 'pheaton', two sloops and one boat, writing notice boards in connection with the Hemsworth Enclosure and writing two coffin plates. His son, Thomas, the subject of this study, was born on 18 June, 1778, and married Alice Moore of Chesterfield in 1800. The assumption is that Thomas worked as apprentice painter under his father. Thomas and Alice are known to have had five children, two of whom survived to adulthood, Elizabeth and Ann. Ann Salkeld married Robert Pepper in 1824 and their son, Robert, became apprentice painter to Thomas Salkeld with whom he was living at the time of the 1841 census. Thomas and Alice Salkeld died within little over a month of each other in the Spring of 1844 and they are buried in the graveyard at the old church at Wentworth.

Thomas Salkeld at work

The painters were, as we have seen, one of the smallest work teams on the estate. According to a set of job descriptions for the various officials and heads of departments on the estate issued in the early 1830s[8] the role of the principal painter – who was named as Thomas Salkeld – was to 'complete in a proper and workmanlike manner all the Painters Work which may be ordered by the Architect [,] Superintendent or Steward.' The work was to be done 'according to the Admeasurement and Valuation of the Architect' and payment was not to be made until the 'Quality of the Workmanship and the correctness of the charges' had been approved. The work of the daily painter – who in 1833 was another member of the Salkeld family, Solomon Salkeld – must have been repetitive and much less interesting than that done by the principal painter. According to the job description, he was 'to be kept constantly employed at daily wages in Out-Door Work when the Weather is fair; and in painting Gates, Garden Frames, Carts, Waggons, Implements of Husbandry, watering Pots, Garden Sticks etc in a Room or Shed at the Carpenter's Yard when the weather is unfavorable'.

The work that Thomas Salkeld, as principal painter, was asked to undertake reflected the large and complex organisation that employed him. He was constantly involved in maintaining the fabric of the estate and the agricultural and industrial enterprises attached to it. It was the responsibility of either the House Steward or the Estate Superintendent to keep a record of all the painting work. For the period 1827–30, the Estate Superintendent's record book, a small, leather-bound volume, with writing pages and blotting pages inter-leaved, has survived.[9] It records in the minutest detail all the work – done on a piecework basis – that was carried out during that period.

At the heart of the estate was the mansion itself (Figure 3). During 1827 Thomas Salkeld must have been engaged for a long period at the mansion. The record book shows that he painted most of the outside of the house: the chapel court, the south tower, the south wing, the front of the main part of the house, the northern end of the main front, the north wing, the north tower and the octagon skylight

Figure 3. The east front of Wentworth Woodhouse from the south-east showing the south tower, south wing and the main front of the building. *Pauline Bentley*

over the chapel. Inside, his jobs included painting the chintz and Red rooms, inside the north tower, the Pillared Hall door, the Saloon door, the Porter's hall door, the servants' hall and even the 'Cistern to Mrs Magts Water Closet'. The record book also states that he was engaged in papering Mrs Maggot's room. On other occasions between 1827 and 1830 he was back at the mansion and his jobs included painting the Clerk of Kitchen's bedroom, cupboards in Mr Hague's (the House Steward) room and Lord Milton's room.

Beyond the mansion itself he was busily engaged in painting new structures and repainting existing buildings and furniture in the gardens (Figure 4) and pleasure grounds. Among his commissions in the late 1820s were the 'New Conservatory', the door at the end of the 'stove',[10] the 'New Peach House', the orchard great doors, kitchen garden doors, the doors into the vinery, the seats in the botanic garden, the pleasure ground doors, the pump at the 'Melon Grounds' and the doors at the 'steam Calcutta' and 'Middle Calcutta' which were garden hot houses. No job was too small: it was recorded that he had painted the 'bee house legs'!

His job also entailed painting and refurbishing the estate monuments in the park and beyond. He painted the railings at the Mausoleum (Figure 5), the woodwork at the Grecian Lodge and Hoober Stand (the palisade, the door at the top, the rail inside, 38 transom lights, bottom door, frame . . .) (Figure 6). He was also regularly abroad in Wentworth village and other places on the estate painting and decorating the substantial houses and more humble cottages of estate

Figure 4. The entrance to the gardens at Wentworth Woodhouse. *Pauline Bentley*

employees. He is recorded as having painted the doors and cupboards in the kitchen at George Horsfield's (who was the cowkeeper), the inside and outside of Thomas Littlewood's cottage (he was the park keeper at Wentworth), Joshua Oxley's house, Mossy Myers' house, Mr Thompson's (he was the head gardener), and houses at Westfield and Lee Brook. He did several commissions at Benjamin Biram's house in this period. Benjamin Biram was the most important official in the Fitzwilliam establishment at Wentworth. He was superintendent of the estate and was in charge of all the local collieries, five in the early 1840s. He was one of the most well kown and respected mining engineers of his day. His family occupied a substantial house, Chesnut Cottage, on Cortworth Lane. On one occasion Thomas Salkeld was paid for painting 330 feet of spouting at Chesnut Cottage and on another he seems to have painted the whole of the outside of the house and ancillary buildings including the potato hole door, pighole door, hen hole door, duck hole door and, of course, the coal hole door. Wherever he went he was always painting privy doors, sometimes referred to euphemistically as 'necessary doors'.

His work took him into the far corners of the estate, to paint outlying estate buildings such as Swinton stables, Brampton Lodge, the carpenters' shop at Hood Hill. the 'door next Kimberworth Park', and a stable door at Tankersley Park. He also undertook some extremely tedious jobs, when he was probably assisted by the daily painter, for example, 937 yards of fencing to the 'New planta-

Figure 5. The Mausoleum erected to commemorate the life and achievements of the 2nd Marquis of Rockingham, 1730–82. *Pauline Bentley*

Figure 6. Drawing of Hoober Stand depicting what an observer might have seen when Thomas Salkeld was at work there in 1827. *Eric Leslie*

tion' and '1590 yards of posts to the farmyard'. Finally, he was sometimes engaged in doing jobs in the industrial establishments on the estate. For instance, he painted the door to the 'whimsey house' at New Park Gate Colliery and also five new houses there, and the counting house at Elsecar Iron Works.

Thomas Salkeld at home

According to the 1841 census[11] the Salkeld family lived in a stone cottage at the western end of Wentworth village on the north side of Main Street between Barrow Field Lane and Manor House Farm (Figure 7). At that time the Salkeld household consisted of Thomas, then aged 63, his wife Alice, 65, his sister Mary, 66, and his grandson, Robert Pepper, 17.

From Alice Salkeld's will made three years later,[12] we can say with certainty that their cottage was small. Downstairs it consisted of the 'house' (ie, the living room), kitchen and pantry; upstairs were three bedrooms, the house chamber, the kitchen chamber and the pantry chamber. What is equally clear from Alice's and Thomas's wills is that by the beginning of the 1840s they were financially secure and the house was comfortably furnished.

Surprisingly, Thomas was a property owner and company shareholder. In his will he directed that his wife should be the sole beneficiary of his 'Rents annual Profits and proceeds arising from my

Figure 7. Wentworth village at the end of the nineteenth century looking east along Main Street. *Chris and Pete Chapman*

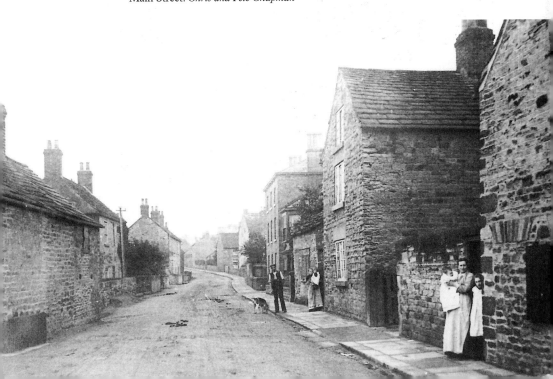

estate at Greasbrough . . . also . . . the Interest of my money securities
for money Dividends arising from my Shares in the Sheffield &
Rotherham Joint Stock Banking Company . . .'[13] He was also able to
bequeath £380 to his married daughter, Ann, (his other married
daughter, Elizabeth, having already received the same amount previously), and £100 each to two of his grandsons.

We can confidently describe the way the cottage was furnished
because in Alice's will she not only itemised the articles of furniture
and household possessions that she was bequeathing but in most cases
she said which room they were in in the cottage. The 'house' had a
carpet and on the hearth fire-irons, a fender and a hearth rug. The
family dined at a dining table sitting on 'six and two arm best
mahogany chairs'. This room also contained a 'mahogany round Tea
table', a sofa and a wardrobe. For use or display there were one silver
pint, one pair of silver salts and spoons, six silver tea spoons and two
silver table spoons. Although not located specifically in the house, the
six embossed china tea cups and saucers and the decanter and six wine
glasses were probably in this room. Decorating the walls were a framed
painting of the Marquis of Rockingham, five pictures in crayon, one
picture in a gilt frame, two engravings in gilt frames, a weather glass
and one pier glass (a tall mirror possibly over the mantelpiece). The
room also contained a clock but whether this was on the mantelpiece
or on the wall it is impossible to say.

The other two downstairs rooms were much more sparsely and
functionally furnished. In the kitchen there were an old dining table,
a round tea table and a sofa. This room also contained a tea tray, a
large metal tea pot, a small metal tea pot, a large box and two framed
election returns. The pantry contained a wash tub, one tub with cans
and a small tub.

Upstairs the house chamber was obviously the main bedroom occupied by Thomas and Alice. At the window was a set of 'moreen[14]
Window curtains, vallens and Cornice'. The main item of furniture in
the room was a 'four-post Bed complete'. Other items included one
square stand and possibly one washhand stand with pitcher and basin
(which is not located in the will), two miniature paintings in black
frames, one picture and frame (Miss Fitzwilliam), 'one oil painting
and frame of Charles' and one Burkett's testament. The kitchen
chamber contained a bed, a set of drawers and at the window were a
set of window curtains and a 'nice window blind'. There were also a
Brown's Dictionary of the Bible and a book on Human Nature in this
room. The only item that can placed with certainty in the pantry
chamber (which was probably Robert Pepper's room) is a swing glass,

although it is also likely to have contained the 'bed and bedding complete except posts' and a small camp bed, neither of which were located specifically in the cottage. Four other items were mentioned in the will: a desk, a bookcase, a spring cart and a family bible.

When all the other everyday household items not included in the will – 'all other items of Furniture and whatever I may die possessed of not herein before enumerated' as the will put it – are taken into account, then what is conjured up is a picture of comfortable Victorian domesticity, built on hard work and good management over a long number of years. The presence in the cottage of pictures of the Marquis of Rockingham, Miss Fitzwilliam (one of Earl Fitzwilliam's daughters) and two framed election returns (presumably showing the election to parliament of a member of the Fitzwilliam family) indicate a strong allegiance to the Fitzwilliam family, a circumstance to be expected in a family whose members were or had been long-standing, devoted and trusted estate employees.

References

1. Nunn, P., 'Aristocratic Estates and Employment in South Yorkshire, 1700–1800' in Pollard, S. and Holmes, C. (eds.), *Essays in the Economic and Social History of South Yorkshire*, South Yorkshire County Council, 1976, pp. 28–45.
2. Mee, Graham, *Aristocratic Enterprise*, Blackie, 1975, p. 24.
3. In the supplement to his *Sheffield Glossary* (1891), p. 13, Sidney Oldall Addy stated that on Collop Monday, the day before Shrove Tuesday, ' poor people go to their richer neighbours to beg a collop or slice of bacon, to supply fat in which pancakes are baked on the following day.'
4. Sheffield Archives (SA), Wentworth Woodhouse Muniments (WWM), WWM RA-42, WWM A-1543, WWM A-1412 - A-1424.
5. SA/WWM A-1412.
6. SA/WWM A-1535.
7. SA/WWM A-1634.
8. SA/WWM A-1389.
9. SA/WWM A-1359.
10. Stove – a hothouse for plants.
11. Microfilm in Rotherham Central Library, Archives and Local Studies Section, HO 107/2345.
12. The original will is in the Borthwick Institute of Historical Research, University of York.
13. Borthwick Institute of Historical Research.
14. Moreen – a stout woollen or cotton/woollen material used for curtains.

Acknowledgements

I am grateful to Olive, Countess Fitzwilliam's Settlement Trustees and the Director of Sheffield City Libraries for permission to quote from the Wentworth Woodhouse Muniments in Sheffield Archives and to reproduce Figure 2 from the original in the Wentworth Woodhouse Muniments. I also wish to thank Eric Leslie for drawing Figures 1 and 6 and the tailpiece.

John Salkeld, Thomas Salkeld's father, writing noticeboards in connection with the Hemsworth enclosure. *Eric Leslie*

4. THE PAYNE FAMILY OF NEWHILL: QUAKERS IN THE EIGHTEENTH AND NINETEENTH CENTURIES

by Alex Fleming

THE SIGNIFICANCE OF THE PAYNES is that their story illuminates so many areas of our national history while remaining so very deeply rooted in Wath and South Yorkshire. Furthermore, the telling of their tale also involves us in the story of the mass of ordinary folk; those people whose lack of education left them mute witnesses in history of the events which shaped their lives. Another facet to the family is that as their story unfolds we can see clearly how conventional 'wisdom' was challenged. For example, two extracts from the family's letters:

1771 Reputation is of such importance to a female it is very necessary to take proper means to secure it . . . I have heard by several hands that Nancy Tippen [of Doncaster] *has spent a week with thee lately* [at Newhill Grange], *poor Girl she is much to be pity'd indeed she's surrounded with complicated distress. I have often thought that the aptness of many females to scandal is the characteristic blemish of our sex, this is not a natural propensity, perhaps it may be the effect of Education or rather the want of a proper one.*

Mary Barnard to Elizabeth Payne.

1792 It is the practice of all decriers of the French Revolution to lower, vilify, and debase the human character; to treat the common people as if they were brutes, without feeling.

John Payne, Newhill Hall, *Sheffield Register*

Why did the Payne family and its friends have so critical an outlook on their world? In large measure the answer must be found in their Quakerism, which made them by definition dissenters. George Fox, born in 1624, was the founder of the Quaker movement and he taught that there could be no person, no priest, between the individual and God. Fox emphasised the importance of Christian scripture, but only as a guide to help individuals find the truth they already possessed within themselves. Such faith required no set form of worship; small groups could meet together seeking to find the presence of God by

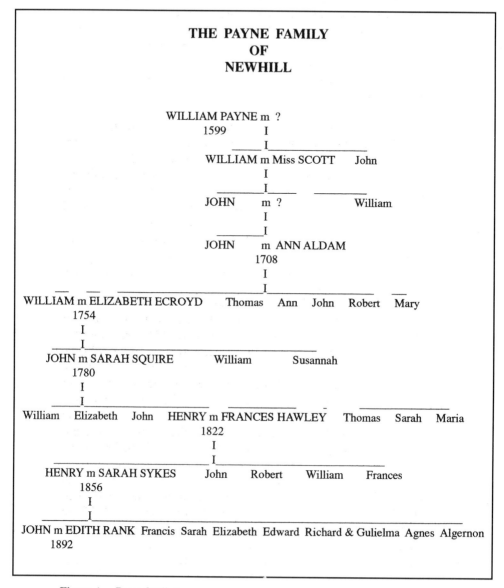

Figure 1.   Payne family tree.

prayer and meditation. Consequently, a questioning approach to life, emphasis on individual conscience and a scepticism of authority became second nature to Quakers. Why the term 'Quaker'? During one of his many court appearances Fox advised Justice Bennett to tremble at the word of the Lord and so Bennett referred to Fox as a 'Quaker'. Another valid explanation of the term is that it was given because of the trembling and spiritual stress which appeared sometimes in individuals during meetings.

In tracing the history of the Payne family the first name we have is William Payne, who lived in Hagnaby cum Hannah in 1599.[1] This Hagnaby is not even a hamlet today, surviving only as the name of a small parish to the south-west of Mablethorpe, Lincolnshire. Of the younger of William's two children nothing is known save the name John. The elder boy, also William, married a young woman named Scott and fathered two sons, again named John and William. It was John who moved to Yorkshire and with obvious regard for family tradition named his son John. Only with this fourth generation John Payne, born at Newhill Grange in 1651, does anything like a full picture begin to emerge (Figures 1 and 2).

For whatever reasons, John did not take a wife until very late in life. Consequently, his marriage in the Quaker meeting house at Warmsworth to Ann Aldam on 18 September, 1708, presented the unusual spectacle of a 57 year old groom and a 21 year old bride. Despite the considerable difference in age their marriage was fruitful, with six children being born. When, however, John died at the age of 72 on 12 February, 1723, he left his 36 year old widow to care for a very young family indeed, aged two months to 13 years. Given that both the Payne and Aldam families were established and prosperous farmers it is unlikely that the children would have been left in any material want, but the strain on Ann must have been considerable. The Aldams of Warmsworth were influential and highly respected in Quaker circles, with Ann's father, Thomas Aldam, being imprisoned in York Castle time after time for his religious principles. Nearly fifteen years after John's death Ann took another husband and died eventually at the remarkable age of 95 on 13 October 1782.

William, Thomas, Ann, John, Robert and Mary were the six children of the virile 'old man' of Newhill Grange. The youngest of them, Mary, married John Lever of Nottingham and bore him Ann, Mary and Dorothy. Robert and John remained single, with Robert dying in May 1742 when he was merely 19. His brother John died on 30 April, 1781, a month after his sixty-fourth birthday and judging by his bequests he was both a successful farmer and a wise investor. In cash

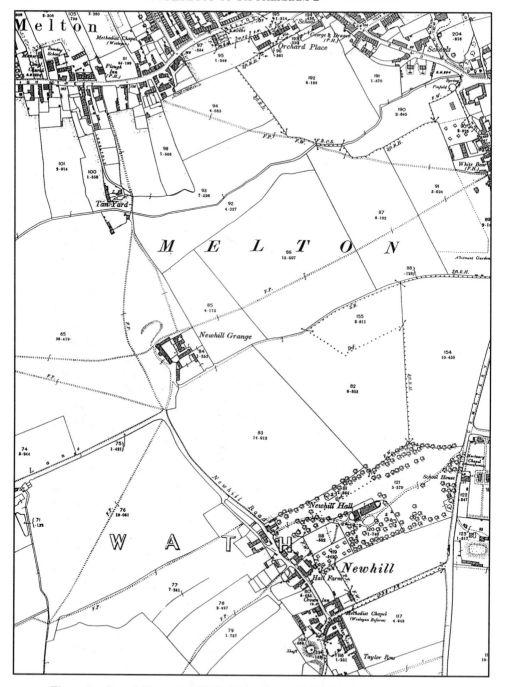

Figure 2. Part of OS map 1:2500, Yorkshire Sheet 283.07, 1903.

settlements alone he bequeathed £5,400 to his nephews and nieces. In addition he left to John, son of his brother William, all his household goods as well as lands and buildings in Newhill, West Melton, Brampton, Wombwell, Thurnscoe and Fishlake. Ann Payne married William Storrs of Chesterfield and they had one child, Joseph, who inherited lead mines, shares in lead mines and shares in the Chesterfield Canal Company from his uncle John. Thomas Payne's wife is unknown, but she bore three children: John, Calista and Mary.

William Payne, heir to Newhill Grange, was born there on 4 January, 1710 (Figure 3). Later in life documents described him as a 'tanner' and it was this occupation in combination with farming which added to the growing prosperity of the family. Located on the Brook Dyke, just north of Newhill Grange Farm, William's tanyard was an essential industry. Tanning was a vital first stage in the production of the mass of leather which shod the population and harnessed the horse power which moved the economy. Consequently, an efficiently organised tanyard was a profitable business, but though it provided a good return on capital invested, it was a long, expensive and foul-smelling process. Skins had to be soaked in a series of vats or pits containing solutions of urine and poultry manure, with the main process involving the soaking of hides in a 'liquor' produced from oak bark. Large, thick hides could take up to two years to be tanned.[2]

Figure 3. Newhill Grange Farm. The barn in the centre with the blocked-in doorway and upper window is believed to be the original farm house. *The Author*

In 1754 William had married Elizabeth Ecroyd of Edgend and a generation later, in 1784, it was to the tanning trade at Newhill that James Ecroyd of Edgend was apprenticed. By that time William had died and his son John was running the business. The 62 year old Elizabeth would have enjoyed the presence of her young nephew at

the Grange. James was seventeen and during his four year apprenticeship his friendly personality gained him many companions. For
example, his amiability and love of sport made him a favourite with
the Earl Fitzwilliam's shooting parties. We are, however, running a
little ahead of ourselves.

William Payne's wife was born at Lane House, Edgend, on 6 May,
1722. Edgend is in Marsden, which in turn is the southern part of
Nelson in Lancashire. Now engulfed by the urban sprawl linking
Burnley and Nelson, in the mid-eighteenth century it was an isolated
settlement. Even today it is still very much an area of isolated farms.
How then did William and Sarah become acquainted? The answer
must be found among the network of Quaker meetings they would
have attended. After all, Edgend lay in strong Quaker country only five
miles south-east of Pendle Hill, the very place where George Fox had
his 'vision' in 1652. Certainly there was a good deal of traffic between
Quaker meetings and it is possible the couple met at a Warmsworth
or even a York meeting.

When William married Elizabeth Ecroyd on 19 September, 1754,
he did so at Upper Haugh in Rawmarsh, the home of Joseph Clark
(Figure 4). The Clarks of Upper Haugh had been staunch Quakers
ever since the seventeenth century, beginning with Joseph's grandfather, also named Joseph Clark. With such a pedigree it was natural that
their home at Rawmarsh was licensed for Quaker marriages. Early in
their formation the Quakers laid down a procedure for marriage,
recognising the equal status and spirituality of men and women. They

Figure 4.   Upper Haugh, Rawmarsh, the home of Joseph Clark.

also emphasised the importance of individuals marrying someone belonging to the Society of Friends and took great care to ensure that prospective partners were 'clear of all others'. Consequently, the Friends were granted a rare exemption from Lord Hardwicke's Marriage Act of 1753, which required marriage to be publicly announced and celebrated in a parish church rather than in private houses.

In local folk memory at Rawmarsh there is a story that Quakers solemnised their union by climbing up a ladder and entering the house by the 'marriage window'! The truth is much more sober. We may reasonably suppose that at Joseph Clark's house William took Elizabeth by the hands and declared:

> *Friends, in the fear of the Lord and before this assembly, I take this my friend Elizabeth to be my wife, promising, through Divine Assistance, to be unto her a loving and faithful husband until it shall please the Lord by death to separate us.*[3]

Elizabeth would have responded in the same way. When they made their declarations William was 44 and Elizabeth 32, at a time when the average age at marriage was 26. In another way also they were not an average couple, producing only three children: John, born 12 February, 1757; William, born 12 July 1760; and Susannah, born 2 August, 1762.

This essay began with Mary Barnard's observation on 'the aptness of many females to scandal'. Her letter containing that observation was one of 29 written to Elizabeth Payne at Newhill Grange, between 1770 and 1779. Mary lived at Upperthorpe in Sheffield and though her relationship to Elizabeth is unclear it is obvious that they were close friends. Subsequently, Mary moved to Beverley as a Mrs Dickinson and her son married into the famous family of ironmasters, the Darbys of Coalbrookdale. Several of Mary's letters to Newhill were sent via Timothy Clark of Doncaster, the Clarks having moved from Rawmarsh to that town and securing a lasting place in history.

From Mary Barnard's letters we find that Elizabeth's three children were referred to as 'Jacky', 'Billy' and 'Sukey'. Also, that there was considerable movement between Newhill, Sheffield, Doncaster and North Lancashire. Indeed in March 1775 Mary Barnard's father rode nearly 60 miles from Marsden to Upperthorpe in one day, arriving home shortly after 11 p.m. The letters also reveal periodic concern about sore throats, colic, gout, rheumatism and smallpox. Amid the polite expressions and enquiries there are also intimations of scandal and tragedy. For example:

1772 I have received a letter from Cousin Sally Dillworth informing their safe arrival at Lancaster . . . The same letter brings a very melancholy account of the death of Joe Dillworth . . . it happened on 2nd day last. He was out shooting and in getting through a hedge his gun went off and wounded him in such a manner that he only lived a few hours. His parents got to see him about an hour before he expired, but he was then insensible . . .

Jacky Payne, the eldest of Elizabeth's three children, was moved to make a mark from his earliest days and I was fascinated to see how he had carved his name twice on the side of an oak wardrobe, 'John Payne 7th. 9th. month 1768'.[4] Three months after that assertion of individuality and just three days before Christmas, Jacky's father had a seizure while hoeing turnips. The poor man was carried into the house spitting blood and died within a few hours. No matter how uncertain life was in those times such a tragedy must have weighed heavily on the eleven year old.

Driven by the example set by his late father in developing the family's farming and tanning businesses, John was conscientious enough to keep a diary of agricultural observations and experiments. He began the record when he was twenty, entitling it

De Re Rustica
Observantia varia
&
Experimenta

A typical entry reads:

1780 July 11, A more remarkable winter than that of this year perhaps is not to be remembered the Frost was so severe that the turnips were all rotted & good for nothing by the middle of January & was the cause of Great Loss in my turnips this year. Did not make more than 18s per acre but it is very visible that their rotting on the ground has been attended with great benefit to the land as a finer Barley than the present growing never was known.

John was observing closely the effects of different kinds of manure and the efficacy of combining manure and lime to increase crop yields. The need for such careful husbandry was indicated by criticism from the leading farming journalist Arthur Young. In the summer of 1769

Young had toured South Yorkshire and subsequently published his findings in 1770 as volume I of his *Northern Tour*. He was not impressed by what he saw, observing that the system was '. . . deficient in numerous respects and the cultivation slovenly'.

The fact that John had no intention of neglecting his inheritance is further indicated by the memoranda he wrote to himself in his note-book, lest he forget the financial costs of wrong decisions. For example:

> *1779   In August refused to sell oates for 16s per qtr kept them while May then sold for 14s. It ought to be an invariable rule with the farmer to take the price of the times.*

> *1779   this year 3 acres of turnips kept more stock & better than 12 acres of hay did last winter.*

Under so watchful an eye business prospered, enabling John to marry in 1780 when he was 23. His bride was Sarah Squire from Hertford, north of London, and she bore seven children within eleven years, four boys and three girls. Perhaps it was the combination of marriage and the considerable bequest a year later from his uncle John which caused him to commission the building of a fashionable residence. Newhill Hall was built in 1785 and the architect was William Lindley of Doncaster (Figures 5 and 6).

After construction there were no signifcant alterations to the Hall and some idea of its internal layout is provided by John Payne's great,

Figure 5.   Newhill Hall front elevation, south. Contemporary copy of Lindley's drawing, 1785.

Figure 6.   Newhill Hall viewed from the east, *c.*1890.

great granddaughter Margaret Payne:

> *The main door opened into a large entrance hall containing a chandelier which you could pull up and down; to the right there was a very ancient piece of oak furniture with a flat top and with little cupboards in it. On your left was the breakfast room, then stone steps up with handrails. Straight in front when you went into the entrance hall was the door to the drawing room. On the right was the library, a long passage to the kitchens, then the dining room, next to the drawing room. You didn't enter the library from the hallway, you turned right into the passage leading to the kitchens and the first door on your right led into the library. As you went along the kitchen passage there were steps down into the wine cellars. On the left, half way down the passage, was a room used as a dispensary and the next room on the left was the butler's pantry. On the other side of the passage was the servants' hall, where people used to go if they wanted to pay rent or something.*
>
>   *Up the stone steps from the entrance hall you came to quite a large landing and the bedrooms off that. To the right was uncle Dick's bedroom, then there was the 'dressing room', which was used as a*

*nursery when they were children and had a nurse. Just as you got up
the stairs there was a bedroom on the left and then another small
'dressing room', then grandfather's bedroom, looking out over The
Grange to West Melton. Some stairs led into the attic where the servants
slept, they were proper rooms.*

*In the main rooms were Adam fireplaces and ceilings, the ceilings
were not coloured. In the drawing room the carpet had a blue background and the furniture was French style with spindly legs. The dining
room had a very long table and there was a glass cabinet with a lot of
stuffed birds. In the library the shelves were full of books.*[5]

The following is a small selection of the books which were in the
library:

Aristotle on Physics, 1638	*Analytical Review*, 1797
Antidote Against the Snake	
In the Grass, 1697	*Annual Register*, 1792–1799
Abbe Raynal's East and	
West Indies, 1788	*Ayliffe's Roman Civil Law*, 1734
Babington's Advice to	
Grand Jurors, 1692	*Bracken's Farriery*, 1745
Culpepper's Herbal	*Complete Attorney*, 1760[6]

Newspapers taken regularly at the Hall from its earliest days included,
*The London Chronicle, The Iris or Sheffield Advertiser, The Express &
Evening Chronicle, The Courier & Evening Gazette* and *The Observer*.
Except for *The Iris* such papers were London based and together with
the books and pamphlets in the library there emerges a picture of a
family with scholarly and radical leanings.

Using information from auction catalogues, together with a family
diary, we can be certain that some of the better furniture at the Hall
included mahogany pieces such as an early eighteenth century cross-
banded chest of eight drawers, a George III chest of five drawers and
an eighteenth century D-end dining table on twin triple-sabre
supports with brass paw feet. There was also a set of eight country-
made Chippendale dining chairs. Naturally, there was glassware and
crockery of appropriate quality: eighteenth century cordial glasses
and wine glasses together with Rockingham ware. Unfortunately,
shortly after Dr Henry Payne came to live at Newhill Hall a servant
carrying a tray of Rockingham fell and broke much of the set!

The hall was demolished in 1953 and only the family mausoleum
remains, on the eastern edge of Newhill Park (Figure 7). The first to

be interred was John Payne's wife Sarah, who died on 6 August, 1834, aged 78. John wrote a touching epitaph in Latin for Sarah (Figure 8). Inscribed in brass, the plaque still adorns the chamber in the mausoleum containing her remains:

Let Sarah Payne rest here
That which was mortal of the wife of John Payne
for fifty and almost four years
She departed from this life in peace on the
6th day of August 1834
in the 78th. year of her life
Justly and truly esteemed alas for her outstanding merits
and an example to her relations living and to come

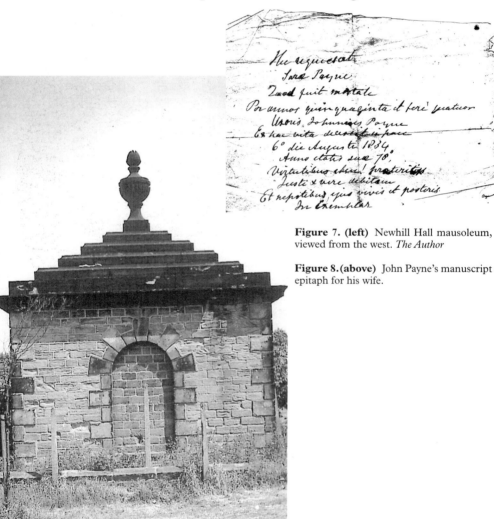

Figure 7. (left) Newhill Hall mausoleum, viewed from the west. *The Author*

Figure 8. (above) John Payne's manuscript epitaph for his wife.

Our excursion inside Newhill Hall above arose from a consideration of John Payne's wealth and further evidence of the family's prosperity is provided by this diary entry by John for 12 May, 1800:

I this year purchased of Thomas Halliday his estate at Loxley for the sum of £4,100. Consisting of a mansion house and barn and 22 acres of cultivated land and a large tract of uncultivated to the amount of 168 acres more. A great proportion of the whole seems adapted to the turnip management.

This estate was given by John to his son Thomas Aldam Payne (Figure 9). Thomas married Mary Parkin in 1810 and they set up home in some style at Loxley House, Wadsley, on the north-western edge of Sheffield.[7]

Thomas and his elder brother Henry were the only two of John and Sarah's seven children who married. Henry took charge of the family's corn mill at Newhill, which had been rebuilt by his father, but he wanted a more challenging career than that of a miller. Consequently, he was apprenticed to a Sheffield physician (Hall Overend) and after three years went to Edinburgh University to study medicine. After qualifying, Henry set up his practice in Nottingham.

It was in 1810 that John was one of ten petitioners for an enclosure award for Wath: a measure of his importance. In Wath township alone John owned 133 acres of land subject to tithes and he was the third largest landowner (excluding Earl Fitzwilliam). In the parish of Brampton, John was the fifth largest landowner (again excluding Earl Fitzwilliam). The rationale for seeking enclosure had been made clear by John's brother, William. William Payne is often quoted by Brown in his *General View of Agriculture in the West Riding*, published in 1799. For example:

Figure 9. Thomas Aldam Payne of Loxley House.

A considerable proportion of the arable land is unenclosed to the great obstruction of agricultural improvement . . . the liberal occupier of

*inclosed land . . . is completely master of his land, which in its open state
is scarcely half his own.*

Underlying this was the claim that enclosure would increase the rent
return by 30 per cent.

While brother John farmed at Newhill, William first farmed indepen-
dently at Bolton-on-Dearne, then he bought the Frickley Hall estate.
This was on a much grander scale than Newhill Hall and a visitor to
William at Frickley in 1797 wrote:

> *. . . in the morning I took a walk into the Park and through the plan-
> tations which are beautifully laid out with gravel and grass walks and
> into the gardens which are very large and adorned with reservoirs of
> water and seats and harbours* [sic] *also with great variety of trees,
> shrubs and plants all which with the neatness and elegance of the house
> . . . makes it a most beautiful and delightful place.*

After the turn of the century William's fortunes were eclipsed; he sold
the estate about 1815 and subsequently died in Paris in 1831. Of his
thirteen children by Barbara Arthington of Leeds, seven died before
reaching the age of twenty and of the remainder only three married.
Of those three only one produced children.

Susannah Payne, sister of John and William, married Jonathan
Peckover of Wisbech, Cambridgeshire. Born in Fakenham, Norfolk,
Jonathan moved to Wisbech in 1777 and in 1783 became associated
with the local bank of Gurney, Birkbeck and Peckover (which merged
with Barclays Bank in 1896). At the end of the eighteenth century
Jonathan bought the fine building in the centre of Wisbech to which
he brought Susannah; Peckover House is now a National Trust property.

The political backdrop to this period, which saw a blossoming of
the prosperity of the Paynes, was one of war and revolution abroad
and considerable fear at home. It speaks much of John Payne that
despite his affluence he was not blind to the great issues of his day.
Perhaps it was the combination of Quaker radicalism, personality and
family links with Philadelphia which made Jacky Payne of Newhill
Grange such a staunch supporter of the Americans in their fight for
independence. That war had begun in April 1775, with fighting at
Lexington and Concord. John subsequently condemned the
campaign waged by London as being contrary to natural rights and
ruinously expensive for the country. He obviously gave considerable
moral support to the American rebels because the Marquis de

Lafayette wrote to thank him for his work. John Payne's stand was not unusual, but we can only imagine what the authorities here thought of a young man who had been thanked by a commander who helped bring about the final surrender at Yorktown in October 1781! On that historic day British troops marched out to the tune, 'The World Turned Upside Down'.

While the disastrous outcome of the American war was still fresh in people's minds, John came into conflict with the authorities because of his outspoken sympathy for the French Revolution which had begun in 1789. The fear and revulsion felt in England at the terrible events in France are difficult to appreciate at this remove. Consequently, it is too easy to underestimate the risks courted by John Payne as he championed the cause of political reform.

In the spring of 1792 he was asked to quit land he rented from the Earl Fitzwilliam, who had been led to believe that John was a member of the 'Constitutional Society of Sheffield'. This was the largest of such groups in the whole of England and had political ideas far more radical even than similar groups in London.[8] Consequently, it was regarded as a nest of revolutionary vipers! John did, however, convince Fitzwilliam that the information was false and the matter was dropped. John was a marked man because a month or so previously, in February, a letter of his was published in the *Sheffield Register* in which he asserted:

In point of national prosperity, France is in a most enviable situation, the people have this consolation, they know that what they have is their own; the peasant reaps the produce of his labour.

This was not the type of sentiment expected from a man of considerable property and in the light of subsequent events in France, John was very exposed; within a year Louis XVI was executed and the 'Reign of Terror' was about to be unleashed.

Soon, John had enough political battles on his home front to keep him more than occupied. For example, in August 1795 James Montgomery was convicted of publishing seditious libel. He was a poet and hymn writer who was also a radical journalist, becoming editor of *The Iris* in Sheffield. Montgomery was innocent of the charge, but the authorities were desperate lest the plague of revolution spread to England from France. When he was sent to York Castle for three months, John championed his cause, as he did when the same thing happened again to Montgomery after release from York. From prison Montgomery wrote several letters to John. For example:

I had not been there above a week, when my neck began to swell in a very alarming manner, and a scorbutic humour [scurvy] *broke out so violently in my arms, that for several weeks I could not wear my coat . . . the Doctors here declare that it will be necessary for me to go to Scarbro' for the benefit of sea-bathing after my resurrection from this temporary grave.*[9]

John Payne perhaps first met Montgomery when the writer lived in Wath for a brief time, after fleeing the Moravian settlement at Fulneck. The persecution of Montgomery did not, however, turn John from his commitment to the defence of liberty. His sentiments are mirrored in an article in the *London Courier* of June 28, 1799 (this extract coming from an issue which was in the library at Newhill Hall).

The Allies have now nearly reached the frontiers of France . . . Will they invade France with views of dictating a Government to her, and dismembering her dominions? If they decide upon the latter . . . They will meet with an active and determined people; they will find the friends and foes of the Directory equally united against invaders, and they will experience this truth, that men who care not a farthing for the government, will still fight manfully for the ground.

Respect for the views of labouring folk and concern for their welfare is also reflected in letters from Newhill sent by Elizabeth Payne (John Payne's mother). Writing to her daughter Susannah Peckover in Wisbech on 15 December, 1800, she lamented the fact that

. . . the poor labour under common discourage not only in the excessive price of corn but in great stagnation in trade which deprives the poor of employ and is a great calamity.

A little later, on 14 January, 1801, Elizabeth wrote in greater detail to her brother, John Ecroyd:

The high price of provisions keeps increasing our bread meal is 5 shillings a stone and rice which has been much used is advanced lately, as everything is alike dear I know not how the poor are to get support as the want of employ is a sad thing and by the scarcity of the year before the poor are almost naked . . . rice 7 pence per lb sugar none under nine pence and bread corn was five shillings per stone last week and trade is in most branches declining. There is little business in the pottery and work scarce and the poor greatly distress'd . . .

What is so remarkable about Elizabeth is that she was aged 78 and in failing health when she wrote those two letters. How very typical that she devoted but a few lines at the end of her letter to her brother to say

> *have very little use of my limbs I cannot properly walk over the floor but am moved by castors in the chair to and from bed but enjoy a good degree of ease when I can be still which I esteem a good favour.*

A week later Elizabeth was dead.

In addition to the death of his mother, John had to carry the burden of increasing conflict with his fellow Quakers, for by this time his open sympathy for 'French principles' had led to him being disowned by the Society of Friends. There was the paradox that in following his own conscience he had become too radical for them! John reacted in 1802 by writing a pamphlet criticising the Society in which he asserted

> *. . . men have always been more ready to give up their purles than their opinions . . . Let not then the right of the society to disown its members for opinions ever be recognised by man. The power it may have, the right it cannot.* [10]

Perhaps this breach is what led him to become a Unitarian (regarded as the dissenting élite).

Another link with the events of that time is a workbox presented to John Payne by two French Catholic priests who were given refuge at Newhill Hall. Dr Henry Payne, John's grandson, spoke of the gift being

> *. . . made of boxwood and inlaid with Brazil and other curious woods, it has brass feet worked into lions heads and was made by French prisoners at Portsmouth.*

Perhaps the priests ministered to their countrymen before making contact with the Payne family? One priest was Vincent Louis Dennis, but the name of the other has been lost. Burland in his *Annals of Barnsley* recorded that Father Dennis 'officiated as private tutor to the children of John Payne Esquire'. The children in question would have been Sarah and Maria.

In 1814 Father Dennis was based at Burghwallis, near Doncaster and after a visit to France he wrote to John Payne describing conditions he had found there.

I have been to Paris, and travelled over nearly one third of France, and I have seen no disturbance . . . They cannot abide to hear they have been conquered; they will not allow of it; they maintain the Allies gained no battle in France nor taken any fortified town.

Commenting on the correspondence, Dr Malcolm Moyes has written:

The strongest impression given by the letters as a whole is pre-eminently of one cultivated mind addressing another. A set of shared assumptions lie submerged beneath the civilised surface of the prose . . .[11]

This observation by Dr Moyes is supported by what is written above about the literary quality of the books in the library at Newhill Hall. Father Dennis subsequently did much work in the Barnsley area to nurture the small Roman Catholic community there.

John Payne's keen sense of justice found a sharper focus when the European war ended in 1815 and parliamentary reform became more of an issue. Incensed by the tragic events at Manchester in August 1819, known as the Peterloo Massacre, John condemned the authorities when he addressed a great radical meeting in Barnsley. Large crowds gathered on Church Field on 8 November, 1819, to hear him and other speakers promote the notions of annual parliaments, universal suffrage and election by ballot.

An abhorrence of repression and a loathing for the denial of liberty did not, however, prevent John from pursuing a vigorous defence of his business interests. Indeed, fellow dissenters regarded Quakers as greedy, observing how new commercial opportunities led some to forget their old testimony against suing at law.[12] In 1822 Major Richard Henry Tolson laid claim in Chancery to substantial lands in Wath, offering 500 guineas reward for the return to him of leases proving his claim. Major Tolson subsequently accumulated many debts and one of his creditors was John Payne. By the end of 1833 John was prepared to accept security for the debt, with costs to be paid in six months. Unfortunately, Tolson by then was in the White Cross Street prison in London and could not make a settlement. Consequently, he wrote to his creditors asking for release on licence for two years. Apparently nothing happened, for in October 1838 we find Tolson still in the same prison and writing once more to John Payne. Tolson asked him to accept £30 in discharge of the debt, with costs, indicating that he would apply for bankruptcy, pointing out, 'For I beg leave to state, these walls never pay a debt, after being confined within them for five years and three quarters . . .'

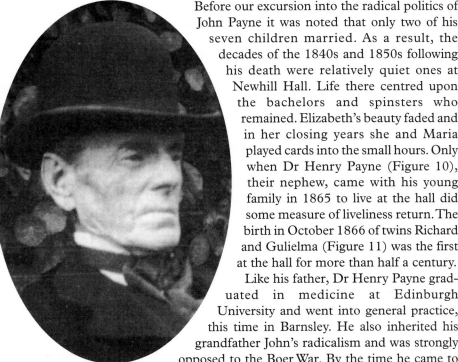

Figure 10. Dr Henry Payne at Newhill, 1901.

Before our excursion into the radical politics of John Payne it was noted that only two of his seven children married. As a result, the decades of the 1840s and 1850s following his death were relatively quiet ones at Newhill Hall. Life there centred upon the bachelors and spinsters who remained. Elizabeth's beauty faded and in her closing years she and Maria played cards into the small hours. Only when Dr Henry Payne (Figure 10), their nephew, came with his young family in 1865 to live at the hall did some measure of liveliness return. The birth in October 1866 of twins Richard and Gulielma (Figure 11) was the first at the hall for more than half a century.

Like his father, Dr Henry Payne graduated in medicine at Edinburgh University and went into general practice, this time in Barnsley. He also inherited his grandfather John's radicalism and was strongly opposed to the Boer War. By the time he came to Newhill the rural way of life which had been so characteristic of the area, typified in Figure 12, was beginning to give way to industrialisation as local coal reserves began to be exploited. Indeed, Newhill Colliery was sunk just across the road from the eastern edge of the hall grounds. However intrusive that may have been, the family continued to prosper as coal royalties began to overtake the income from farming.

We take our leave of the family with the genteel image of a tennis party in the Hall grounds, as shown in Figure 13. This has a poignancy because we know that the way of life it typified was

Figure 11. Richard and Gulielma Payne, twins, *c.*1876.

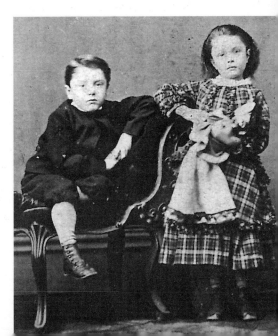

Figure 12. Making a haystack at Newhill, *c*.1885.

Figure 13. Tennis party at Newhill Hall, *c*.1883. Front row, fromleft: unknown, Gulielma Payne, Sarah Payne (née Sykes), Agnes Payne, unknown, unknown; back row, from left, Woodville Gray (later married Gulielma), unknown, Richard Payne. The unidentified individuals are believed to be members of the Sheffield branch of the Payne family.

destined to end. There was no catastrophic decline, no scandal, simply the inescapable erosion of time.

Notes and References

1. H. E. Smith, *Smith of Doncaster*, 1878, privately published. This is an invaluable guide to the Payne and related families.
2. B. Elliott, *The Making of Barnsley*, Wharncliffe Publishing, 1988.
3. Religious Society of Friends (Quakers) *Quaker Weddings*, leaflet.
4. Furniture auction, 1985, Outhwaite & Litherland Auctioneers, Liverpool.
5. Margaret Uttley (née Payne) interviewed by the author in 1989. Margaret was born in 1896, her father was John Henry Payne, and her grandfather was Dr Henry Payne.
6. Index compiled by Dr Henry Payne *c.*1865, Sheffield Archives, MD 6782.
7. In 1913 their descendants made a gift to the City of Sheffield of 75 acres of the estate, to be known as Loxley Chase, 'for the perpetual use of the public for the purposes of exercise or recreation'.
8. 'J. Wigley, James Montgomery and the Sheffield Iris', *Transactions of the Hunter Archaeological Society*, vol 10, 1975.
9. *Smith of Doncaster.*
10. John Payne, *Strictures On the Conduct of the Quakers as a Society*, Sheffield Local Studies Library, 289.6 ST.
11. M. Moyes, 'Reflections Upon the Revolution in France', *Transactions of the Hunter Archaeological Society*, vol.15.
12. W. R. Ward, *Religion and Society in England 1790–1850*, Batsford, 1972.

Acknowledgements

My debt to Pauline and Edith Uttley and to their parents, the late Margaret and William Uttley, is enormous. They have been unstinting in their hospitality and in allowing me unrestricted access to their family papers. Naturally, any errors are my responsibility entirely. As ever, I am indebted to the staff of Sheffield Archives, Barnsley Local Studies Library, Rotherham Central Library, Archives and Local Studies Section, and Doncaster Archives, for their unfailing courtesy and help.

5. 'THE SAPPER'S DREAM' – SIR DONALD BAILEY AND HIS BRIDGE

by Tony Munford

ANY OF THE INHABITANTS OF ALBANY STREET who called at number 24 on 15 September, 1901, to congratulate the occupants on the birth of their first child, would have had no inkling that, 40 years later, the child would be responsible for one of the great war-winning inventions of his age.

The occupants of number 24 were Joseph Henry and Caroline Bailey and the child in question was Donald Coleman Bailey (Figure 1). The Bailey family tree can be traced back to John Bailey who married Hannah Bailey at Rotherham on 17 January, 1796 (Figure 2). This John may have been the John, son of John Bayley who was baptised at Rotherham on 25 April, 1773, in which case he had a brother William, baptised in 1772. Hannah may be the Hannah, daughter of John and Hannah Bailey, baptised in Rotherham in 1777.

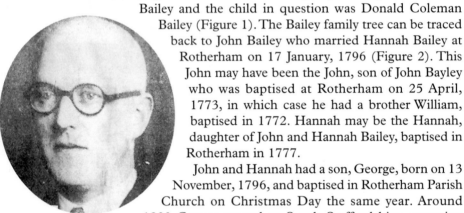

Figure 1. Donald Coleman Bailey.

John and Hannah had a son, George, born on 13 November, 1796, and baptised in Rotherham Parish Church on Christmas Day the same year. Around 1820 George moved to South Staffordshire, marrying Sarah Boot at St Chad's, Lichfield on 2 December, 1821. The couple set up home at Wichnor, on the River Trent, between Lichfield and Burton, where they had three sons, Joseph (1828), Thomas (1830) and William (c.1833) before moving back to Masbrough c. 1835. In Masbrough they had a daughter and another son, Sarah (c.1836) and Charles (c.1839).

The 1851 Census shows George Bailey as a 54 year old, widowed, steel melter, living in Stubbs Yard at the Holmes with his children Joseph, William, Charles (also steel melters) and Sarah. They were probably employed at the crucible steel furnaces in Peter Stubs's Warrington Works at the Holmes. The household also included John Bailey, widower, a labourer, aged 77. The Census lists him as George's brother but his age suggests that he was more probably his father.[1] The fourth son, Thomas, was living a short distance away in Rolling Mill Yard, Holmes, in the household of Thomas Tyler, steel forger. Also

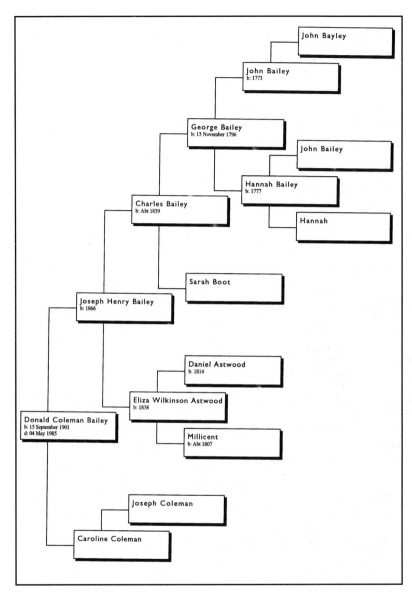

Figure 2. The Bailey family pedigree.

within walking distance lived Eliza Wilkinson Astwood. Eliza was born at Clarborough, Nottinghamshire, in 1838, the daughter of Daniel and Millicent Astwood. In 1851 she was living in Holmes Lane with her mother Millicent, her brothers Henry and Joseph and stepfather

John Duffield.[2]

Eliza Astwood became the wife of Charles Bailey, George's youngest son. Charles and Eliza's eldest child, Joseph Henry, was baptised at Masbrough on 18 March, 1866, when the family were living in Kimberworth Road and Charles was working as a steel roller. The 1881 census lists them at 59 Drummond St, Rotherham. In addition to Joseph Henry, then a 15 year old pupil teacher, the family had grown to comprise Frank (11), Walter (10), George (7), Annie (5), Ernest (2) and Edith (4 months) with Eliza's widowed mother Millicent Duffield.[3] The family soon moved to 9 Clifton Mount and were still living there at the time of the 1891 Census. By this time Charles had died and Eliza had remarried to foundry manager George W. Revill.[4]

Joseph Henry's ambition to be a teacher does not seem to have lasted long and in 1884 he entered the service of the British Wagon Company Ltd, wagon financiers and repairers, of College Street, Rotherham. As a sideline he also seems to have gone into partnership with his brother Walter, as Bailey Brothers, grocers. Their shop is listed at 2 Duffield Road in 1898 and 122–4 Fitzwilliam Road in 1912.[5] Joseph was possibly only a sleeping partner in the business, although he appears in the 1898 Sheffield and Rotherham Directory only as a partner in the grocery business. Frank Bailey also entered the grocery trade after a career as a commercial traveller, and became a partner in Cudworth and Bailey at 87, Masbrough Street. In 1895 Frank's home address was 5 Clifton Mount, the address at which Joseph is listed in 1898.

Joseph married Caroline Coleman, daughter of Joseph Coleman, a prosperous baker, corn and seed merchant from Margate, Kent, where he had been mayor in 1895–6. The marriage took place in Margate and it is unclear how the couple had come to meet. At the time of Donald Coleman Bailey's birth, the family were living at 24 Albany Street, Rotherham. This was one of a pair of small houses which had been designed by local architects Edward Hutchinson and Son for Joseph's stepfather, George Revill, in 1899[6] (Figure 3). The family did not stay long in Albany Street after Donald's birth and moved before September 1902 to 32 Godstone Road, where they were tenants of John Beckett.[7] Joseph seems also to have dabbled in property

Figure 3. Donald Bailey's birthplace, 24 Albany Street, Rotherham, as it is today. *Rotherham Central Library, Archives and Local Studies Section, ref 1358 – photo PB Littlewood*

development and it is probable that he was the J. H. Bailey of Rotherham who commissioned Edward Hutchinson to design seven houses for a site at the corner of Moorgate and Moorgate Avenue. Planning permission was granted in November 1901 but only the four houses on Moorgate Avenue were ever built.[8] Joseph must have disposed of his interest very quickly as the May 1904 rate book shows the owner of 1–4 Moorgate Avenue as John Baker (of John Baker and Co, railway wheel manufacturers).

In 1905 the family were on the move again. At this time suburban development was advancing along Broom Road, most of the houses being commissioned by William Mullet to designs by Edward Hutchinson with his hallmark bay-windows with shallow arched tops to the windows.[9] Joseph purchased a semi-detached pair of these houses, numbered 65 and 67 Broom Road, living in 65 and letting out number 67. The houses were named 'Rudston' and 'Melrose' respectively but it is not clear whether these names were chosen by the Baileys.[10]

Donald Bailey received his elementary education at a private school in Derbyshire. His secondary education was begun at Rotherham Grammar School in 1912 but he only remained for a year or two before his father sent him to the Leys School in Cambridge. The exact length of his stay at the Grammar School is uncertain. Writing in 1968, Sir Donald Bailey stated that he was at the Grammar School for 'just over a year'. The Leys School records, however, show that he did not start there until the autumn term of 1916. When he was interviewed by Brian Harpur in 1980, Sir Donald, who had by then suffered several strokes, could remember little of his elementary education, his period at the Grammar School or the reason why he was sent to the Leys.[11] The family were Methodists and the Leys School may therefore have been chosen because it was a Methodist school. His record at the Leys was undistinguished and he left little impact in the school records. One of the few early signs of his engineering genius was a disastrous attempt to build a raft from an old iron bed frame covered with sacking which proved to be less than waterproof. Another scheme, to build a gas powered engine, met with some success but was nipped in the bud before he could blow up the school.

Although he did not reach the sixth form at the Leys, Donald did achieve a leaving certificate of sufficient quality to gain a university place. Donald and his father discussed possible universities at which he could study engineering. Cambridge was discounted because the course was too theoretical and the journey from Sheffield involved a change of trains. Travelling to and from the Leys had given him an abiding dislike of waiting about on railway stations. They eventually settled on Sheffield University and Donald began an engineering degree course in 1919. Initially his academic career at Sheffield was as undistinguished as his years at the Leys and he failed his degree exams in 1922. Failure seems to have galvanised him into studying hard and when he re-sat the exam in 1923 he emerged with a first class Bachelor of Engineering degree and a recommendation as an 'attentive, capable and painstaking student'. His time was not all spent at his studies for he played tennis for the university, tried his hand at golf, cricket and hockey and earned a little pocket money mending watches. His engineering skills were put to use keeping his 500cc AJS running in local motorcycle races.

In 1914 Donald's parents had moved from Broom Road to another new house, 'Cranford', 33 Broomfield Grove.[12] In 1919 Joseph left the employment of the British Wagon Co after 35 years, having risen to the position of assistant company secretary. He was presented with a set of etchings by past and present members of the staff. The nature of his new post is unclear but it seems to have been occasioned by a desire to be near Donald at university. By the Spring of 1921 the Baileys had moved to 135 Rustlings Road, Sheffield, and early in 1924 they moved again, to 55 Woodholm Road. Joseph Henry Bailey is listed as 'secretary' in the 1921 Sheffield Directory with no indication of the company for which he was working. In the autumn of 1923, however, he applied for the post of secretary and superintendent of the Royal Sheffield Institute for the Blind, being successful from a field of 400 candidates. He remained with the Institute until he retired in June 1929, having worked part-time for the final nine months because of poor health.

After his graduation, Donald obtained a position with the Efficiency Department of Rowntrees at York and then gained practical engineering experience with the Civil Engineering Department of the London, Midland and Scottish Railway. His next post, with Sheffield City Council, gave him experience of dam construction which he later recalled as his 'first major challenge in a practical sense since I left University'. By 1928 he was feeling restless and thought of moving abroad. Instead he opted to become a civil servant and took a post as Civilian Engineer at the Experimental Bridging Establishment at Christchurch in Dorset. The new post was relatively poorly paid at £400 pa and it soon became clear that the Experimental Bridging Establishment was run on a shoestring. Although it was headed by a Royal Engineers officer, most of the staff were civilians, consisting of a single draughtsman, a crew of assorted mechanics, metal workers and odd job men with a gang of five or six labourers to manhandle heavy equipment and bridge sections. The EBE's remit extended from transportable bridges for the Army to anti-tank devices, amphibious warfare and water supply.

On 7 October, 1933, Donald Bailey married Phyllis Ann, daughter of Charles Frederick Andrew of Knightwood, Wick, Bournemouth at Christchurch Parish Church. The newly married couple initially lived with Donald's father who had retired to Bournemouth and were to have one child, a son whom they named Richard.

Even in 1936, the total manpower of the EBE was only 14 and throughout the thirties and the period of Appeasement there was a continuous threat over Bailey's position as Civilian Engineer.

The 1930s were spent tinkering with the design of the First World War vintage Inglis Bridge to adapt it to carry modern tanks. As early as 1936 Bailey had started to develop new ideas about the construction of transportable bridges but he was unable to interest anyone in authority in his ideas.

The British Expeditionary Force went to France in 1939 equipped only with the Inglis Bridge and a lightweight pontoon bridge. Most of the pontoon bridges were abandoned in France after Dunkirk. The Inglis Bridge was an intricate assembly of tubular members assembled into Warren girders. It suffered from a number of drawbacks – it was slow to erect and dismantle, particularly under combat conditions; it had to be assembled parallel with the bank, twice the length of the gap to be bridged, and then pivoted at its mid-point and it could not easily be adapted to take different loads. While it could carry a 26 ton Matilda tank it was clear that it would soon be outclassed by the larger tanks that would be coming into production. There was now a requirement for a bridge that could take the new 40 ton Churchill infantry tank. C. E. Inglis, by now a professor at Cambridge, was asked by the War Office to redesign his bridge to fit the new requirement. When he saw the new design, Bailey predicted that, when fully loaded, the top chord of the bridge (which would then be in compression) would fail. In December 1940, Bailey, together with Colonel F. E. Fowle and Captain S. A. Stair, commander of the Experimental Bridging Establishment, travelled to Cambridge to witness the testing of Inglis's new design. As predicted, the bridge failed the test. This left the Ministry of Defence with the serious problem of planning the Army's return to the Continent without an acceptable assault bridge. The problem was the main topic of conversation between Bailey, Fowle and Stair as they returned from Cambridge. Bailey had spent the years since 1936 developing his ideas for transportable bridges in the face of official indifference. In the back of the staff car, he pulled out an old envelope and, sketching his design on the back, used it to sell his idea to his companions.

A member of the staff of the EBE was later to recollect that, on his return to Christchurch, Bailey burst into the drawing office, brandishing the envelope and exclaiming 'This is going to take us into Germany'.[13] The EBE experts set to work refining the idea and checking the calculations. With the failure of the new Inglis design the authorities were now more amenable to innovative ideas and in February 1941 asked for a full-scale trial of the new design by 1 May. The work of a year was crammed into the next three months and the size of the EBE rose to 400 personnel.

As with most brilliant inventions, Bailey's was essentially simple and involved many of the elements of a child's construction set. The basic element was a single panel 5 ft [1.5m] high by 10 ft [3m] long. The top and bottom chords were constructed from 4 inches x 2 inches rolled steel channel, welded either side of vertical web and bracing members of 3 inches x 1½ inches rolled steel joist. The panels, weighing 570 pounds, were small enough to fit into a standard three ton Army lorry and light enough to be carried by six men (Figure 4). The side trusses or girders of the bridge were constructed by joining

Figure 4. An extract from the Bailey Bridge manual, showing a standard panel and the way in which it was carried. *From a copy held by the Rotherham Central Library, Archives and Local Studies Section*

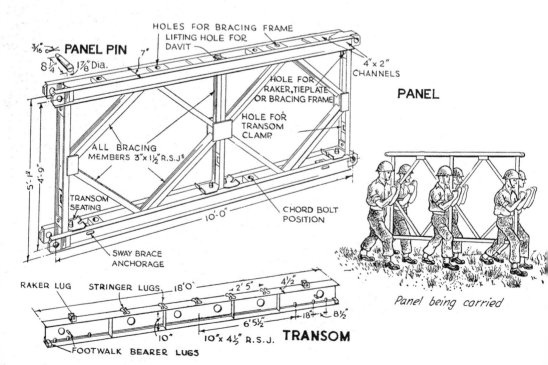

a number of these panels end to end until the required length was reached. A minimum of tools was required as the panels were joined with tapered pins secured with split pins. The two trusses were connected by cross-beams or transoms on which the road deck was laid. A big advantage of this modular construction was that bridges of different strengths could be built by building two or three lines of panels for each girder. Further strength could be added by constructing one or two more lines above each initial line (Figure 5). Another big advantage was that the bridge was constructed at right angles to the gap, with the first section, or nose, undecked for lightness. As construction progressed the bridge was pushed out over rollers until it grounded on the other side.

Figure 5. A section of a double triple Bailey Bridge, from the Bailey Bridge manual. *From a copy held by the Rotherham Central Library, Archives and Local Studies Section*

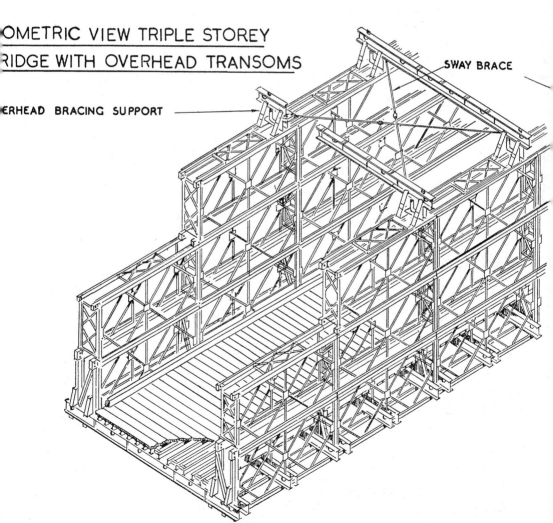

Enough panels to construct a 120ft double truss, double storey bridge were constructed by Braithwaite and Co and were subjected to exhaustive tests at Christchurch. To attain the 90 ton weight necessary to test the new structure fully a bridge was erected on a flat field some two feet clear of the ground with the centre supported on jacks. A Mark V tank of 1917 vintage was driven onto the centre of the bridge and filled with pig iron. Two more tanks were then driven up a ramp on top of the Mark V and the jacks slackened off and removed. To convince the authorities that the bridge could support the weight claimed by the EBE the Mark V was sent to the railway weighbridge at the Christchurch goods yard. The trial bridge also withstood an unrehearsed test when it was strafed by two passing Luftwaffe fighters. The final test before War Office representatives, using panels received from the manufacturers the previous day, saw the successful erection of a 70 ft [21m] bridge in 36 minutes.

The design, testing and approval was the easy part. The more difficult task was the organisation of mass production when all strategic materials were in short supply and the country's skilled workers were already involved in turning out vital tanks, aircraft and ships. It was therefore decided to use Britain's reserves of untrained workmen and women with work being sub-contracted to a wide variety of companies. In more normal times these companies had produced everything from bedsteads to confectionery. Even Littlewoods Pools played its part, turning out the pontoons used to float the bridge across wide rivers. There were to be a total of 650 firms concerned in the manufacture of the Bailey Bridge and it says much for the skill of the unskilled workforce that only 300 of the hundreds of thousands of panels made were rejected as faulty. Production started in July 1941 and the first panels reached the Royal Engineers in December the same year. The first ever Bailey Bridge to be erected in front line conditions, a 100 ft triple/single, was built by Royal Engineers during the night of 26 November, 1942, to replace a destroyed span of a bridge across the River Medjerda in Tunisia.

Among the local firms who were involved in the production of Bailey Bridge components were the Park Gate Iron and Steel Co Ltd who produced special high tensile steel and Robert Jenkins and Co Ltd who turned out over 1500 panels. In all some 500,000 tons of Bailey Bridge material was produced before the end of the War, including over 700,000 panels – enough for a single girder 1,400 miles long. The bridge was used in every theatre of war and received unstinting praise from all who used it, particularly from the sappers whose job it was to erect it, often under fire. General Sir Giffard

Martel, Director of the EBE, declared that the bridge had doubled the effectiveness of the Allied armoured and motorised forces. Thanks to the adaptability of the design it could be (and was) used as a suspension bridge, assault bridge and a pontoon bridge. The suspension bridge was developed especially for use in the Far East but was also used in Europe. Almost 2,500 Bailey Bridges were erected during the Italian Campaign of 1943–5, followed by over 1,500 during the advance across North West Europe in 1944–5. The longest of these was probably the pontoon bridge across the River Maas at Gennop, Holland, which totalled 4,008 ft including the approach viaducts. The most spectacular was certainly the 2,000 ft Bailey Pontoon Bridge across the Rhine. The immediate post-war period was to see the erection of a number of semi-permanent Bailey Bridges over the Rhine, including the twin Tyne and Tees bridges at Rees which reached 5,000 ft. The Patton Bridge at Cologne was not replaced until the 1960s. These bridges played an important part in Germany's economic recovery. In 1947 the *News Chronicle* described the Bailey Bridge as 'the Sapper's dream, the perfect reply to the enemy's orgy of bridge destruction'. The ease with which it could be constructed and its versatility is reflected in the regard in which its inventor is still held by Royal Engineers veterans today.

Donald Bailey's part in winning the war was recognised by the award of an OBE in 1944 and a knighthood in 1946. In the latter year he was promoted to principal scientific officer grade and appointed as Assistant Director of the Military Engineering Experimental Establishment (as the EBE had become). In 1946 he was also made a Commander of the Order of Orange Nassau in recognition of the part played by the Bailey Bridge in the restoration of communications in Holland. Sheffield University conferred an honorary Doctorate of Engineering on its old student in 1947. His work on the bridge design earned him a £12,000 award from the Royal Commission on Awards to Inventors in 1948. This was a recognition that much of the initial design and thinking had been carried out in his own time and not as part of his official duties. He gave his name to the Bailey Committee on House Interiors (1952–3) and was in demand to serve on other technical committees. 1962 saw him appointed as Dean of the Royal Military College of Science at Shrivenham, Berkshire, where he remained until he retired in 1966. Sir Donald's design had continued to be developed after the War and it was not replaced as the Army's main assault bridge until the early 1970s. It found a ready use in a wide variety of civil engineering situations and was even used to construct the launch gantries for the British 'Skylark' rocket programme in Australia. In retirement he continued to act as a consultant to Thomas Storey (Engineers) Ltd, one of the main civilian suppliers of Bailey Bridge components. A 1960s development of Bailey's design remains in widespread use for temporary bridging purposes.[14]

Sir Donald suffered the first of a succession of strokes in 1966. His wife Phyllis died in 1971. In 1977, after a further serious stroke, an advertisement was placed in *The Lady* seeking someone to care for Sir Donald in his Bournemouth bungalow. The advert was answered by a widow, Mrs Mildred Stacy. They obviously found themselves suited for, on 4 August, 1979, Sir Donald and Mrs Stacy (née Crees) were married at St Nicholas Church, Southbourne, Dorset. The second Lady Bailey was to nurse him devotedly through the ill health that marred his final years. One highlight of these years was the cake, complete with 1:20 scale replica of a Bailey Bridge, which Lady Bailey arranged for his 80th birthday. Sir Donald Bailey died in St Leonard's Hospital, Bournemouth, on 4 May, 1985, aged 83.

Christchurch, the town where he made his home, has two memorials to its adopted son. A Bailey Bridge section was erected on the Town Quay, in April 1989. In September the same year the town celebrated the 20th anniversary of the granting of the freedom of Christchurch to the Military Engineering Experimental Establishment (by then renamed the Royal Armament Research and Development Establishment). The celebrations included the unveiling of a plaque in memory of Sir Donald in Christchurch Priory.

Sir Donald does not seem to have paid many, if any, visits to the town of his birth after he left for University. Rotherham, however, has also considered him to be one of her famous sons although it was not until 1986 that there was any permanent mark of his connection with the town. When the Borough Council acquired the former Grattans building on Rawmarsh Road as offices for the Engineers' Department it was given the appropriate name of Bailey House. At that time it was not widely realised that for over 40 years local pedestrians had been daily passing over a physical reminder of Sir Donald's contribution to the war effort. In 1947 Rotherham Borough Council and Rawmarsh Urban District Council had jointly spent £300 on war-surplus Bailey Bridge parts which were then erected as a 100ft span footbridge over the Don, between Parkgate and Eastwood. Clerk-of-works for the erection of the bridge was Rotherham Corporation employee Matthew Melia, appropriately a former sergeant major in the 122nd Road Construction Company, Royal Engineers.

By 1992 the bridge was beginning to show its age. Rather than replace the bridge with a more modern construction, the Borough Council decided to keep the connection with Sir Donald, turning to the Territorial Army's successors to the Royal Engineers who had erected so many Bailey Bridges under combat conditions. The bridge was dismantled by 106 (West Riding) Field Squadron, Royal Engineers (V) from Somme Barracks, Sheffield, refurbished and re-erected on the original site (Figure 6). On 26 September, 1992, almost exactly 90 years after its inventor's birth, the Mayor of Rotherham, Cllr Jack Carr, unveiled a plaque on the bridge in honour of Sir Donald before an audience that included Lady Bailey, Sir Donald's son and his family, members of the Royal Engineers Association and their modern Territorial successors. The bridge was now fit to stand for another 40 years as a memorial to the son of Rotherham whose ingenuity, in the opinion of Sir Winston, had shortened the war by two years.

Figure 6. Rotherham's Bailey Bridge during the course of re-erection in 1992. *Rotherham Central Library, Archives and Local Studies Section, ref 1394 – photo PB Littlewood*

Bibliography

Harpur, Brian, *A bridge to victory*, HMSO 1991.
Hartcup, Guy, *The challenge of war*, David and Charles 1970, pp. 189–193.
Joiner, J. H., *The Bailey story: a tribute to Sir Donald Bailey*, Thomas Storey (Engineers) Ltd, 1987.
Military engineering, vol III, part III – Bailey Bridge: normal uses, 1944.
Munford, AP, 'Mrs Bailey's clever son', *Ivanhoe Review*, no 2, Rotherham Borough Council, 1992.

References

1. 1851 census return, ref. HO.107/2344/f136/p.15. Joseph Bailey had three children, Thomas, Sarah and Betsey by his first wife, Catherine, and another, Harry, by his second wife, Elizabeth Hudson, a widow who had been his housekeeper.
2. 1851 Census return, ref HO.107/2344/f131/p.5.
3. 1881 Census return, ref. RG11/4672/f67/p.4.
4. 1891 Census return, ref RG12/3846/f32/p.57.
5. It is tempting to speculate that Duffield Street took its name from Eliza Bailey's stepfather. It is more likely named after James Duffield of Workington, Cumbria, who was developing houses in St John's Rd and Watkin Rd *c*.1900.
6. Rotherham Borough Council building plan ref 3128, approved 15 February, 1899.
7. The 1903 Sheffield and Rotherham Directory lists the occupant as 'Harry' Bailey, clerk but the rate book lists him as Joseph Henry Bailey. Nos 30–32 were designed by the ubiquitous Edward Hutchinson and Son in 1898.
8. Rotherham Borough Council building plan ref. 3405.
9. Although William Mullet is described in contemporary directories as a 'warehouseman' he was responsible for building a number of houses in Gilberthorpe St, on both sides of Broom Rd and for laying out Broomfield Grove.
10. Rotherham Borough Council building plans ref. 3651, approved 16 November, 1904. The name 'Rudston' is now attached to 59 Broom Lane, while no 65 bears the name 'Rockside', the two houses having swapped names in the 1920s (see 'What's in a name' in *Ivanhoe Review*, no 2, Winter 1992). Rudston is a small village, five miles inland from Bridlington. J. H. Bailey also used it as the name of his house when he retired to Bournemouth to be near his son in the 1930s.
11. Brian Harpur, *A bridge to victory*, HMSO 1991, p.6. Harpur gives Sir Donald's date of birth incorrectly as 18 September.
12. Nos 31 and 33 were yet another design by Edward Hutchinson, this time commissioned by C. E. Cross of Wellgate (Rotherham Borough Council building plans ref 4768, approved 3 June 1914).
13. Harpur *op cit*, p.2.
14. At the time of writing a section of this modern development of the Bailey Bridge can be seen supporting a temporary road surface during the reconstruction of the Rotherway link from Junction 33 of the M1.

6. 'WAT TYLER WAS MY FRIEND': MIKE HAYWOOD, WRITER, 1934-1973

by Ray Hearne

EVERY OTHER YEAR for the last two decades, Rotherham and District Arts Panel has organised a writing competition. Its aim has been to provide a focus of support and encouragement for South Yorkshire writers and to offer a showcase for their work. The competition was instigated in conjunction with the Workers' Educational Association to commemorate the achievements of Mike Haywood and to ensure that his overall contribution to literature, in poetry, prose and drama might be celebrated and extended. What was the substance of that contribution? In December 1970, addressing the Hull Literary Club under the title 'Northern Voices', writer and broadcaster Alan Plater considered three such 'Voices': Leonard Barras, Barry Hines, and Mike Haywood, and felt confident enough about Mike's talent to speak of him in the following terms:

> *Professionalism is an attitude of mind . . . the dedicated professional does not write for his own comfort, joy or relaxation, though they may occur as by-products. He* [sic] *writes because of the endless search for some kind of truth and meaning, in the certain knowledge that he will not find it . . . This is what stimulates real writing – the urge to achieve the impossible. Nobody ever does it but some people get very close. Mike Haywood I am not sure about except that in essence I know he can produce, almost without realising it, two or three dazzling pages, and there is good reason to anticipate that one day he will produce a hundred or two hundred, all fastened together as a play, a novel, or an anthology and I hope there will be a publisher or producer big enough and bold enough to take him on.*[1]

Others thought along similar lines; throughout the late sixties his work was featured regularly on BBC North's celebrated arts magazine programme 'The Northern Drift' as well as its occasional forays into television; his play *A Hot Bath and Lemon* was broadcast in June 1973 on Radio Four; various productions of his plays were performed both at Rotherham's own Civic Theatre and at the newly opened Crucible Studio Theatre in Sheffield; amongst these were *Paddy's Cock, The Tiger in the Crow,* and *Man On A Donkey,* with music by Alex Glasgow, was produced by Theatre North in Rotherham and in Mansfield; and his poems were featured regularly in magazines and journals, and prose pieces appeared in such as *Tribune* and *Marxism Today*. Mike's tragedy was that this substantial burgeoning was cut short just as he was completing his artistic apprenticeship and maturing into his craft; illness stopped him in his tracks and cut him down at the age of thirty-nine before he was able to produce that major work envisioned by Alan Plater.

Shortly after his death, in 1975, Plater wrote the introduction to a collection of Mike's writings, *some poems, plays, stories and sketches* edited by Ted Hartley and published in a hardback edition by the Rotherham Central Library. Drawing upon this text and upon the four boxes of letters, papers and manuscripts which represent the Mike Haywood Archive[2] I shall try to offer a brief sketch of the writer who drew such earnest public tributes from his peers and whose example has continued to inspire so many others in these parts since.

Ted Hartley's foreword introduces Mike Haywood thus:

> . . . *born in Bramley . . . he attended a local junior and infant school and then Wickersley Secondary Modern, leaving at the age of 15. He became a painter's apprentice but left to join the Royal Marines; after four years he returned to Rotherham, married, and began work in the steel mills just as a labourer at Parkgate and then as a third-hand melter at Steel, Peech and Tozer . . . At this time he began to attend WEA classes, where a tutor, Derek Robinson, suggested he apply to Ruskin College, Oxford. From Ruskin Mike went to University College North Wales, Bangor and then to a full-time post as tutor/organiser with the WEA in Sheffield. At the same time he was working and helping to promote the Arts through the Yorkshire Arts Association. He died on November 10th, 1973.*[3]

That full and eventful life, short though it was, provided ample and wide-ranging material for an imagination as alert and restless as Mike's seemed to be. In retrospect it is perhaps too easy to interpret an all permeating sense of urgency that characterises the poems in particular, (what in *Journey to Sunday* is perceived in others as a universal 'restiveness',) as mirroring some deeply intuited intimation of his own mortality, or some unconscious anticipation of the short number of his own remaining days. Nevertheless, like those Jacobean writers he pitched into the hellish plague-ridden London of *The Tiger in the Crow*, he was himself undeniably 'much possessed by death' and frequently saw 'the bone beneath the skin'.[4] For me at any rate there

Mike Haywood, 1934–1973

are added resonances to many of his superficially straightforward images, witness the final verse of an old man's reminiscences of the General Strike; he and his brother, young, vigorous and energetic, 'getting the sun to their bones', kicking a tennis ball along the back lanes, running 'hard at the west wind'.

> *Until the buzzer rose again*
> *To send them home to the cage*
> *And swing them back*
> *To the waiting earth.*[5]

That 'waiting earth' is a stark motif which recurs intermittently throughout the work, but for all the darker asides Mike Haywood's affiliations are clearly and plainly with the ball-kickers; all those on the side of life and living, love, laughter and defiance, even in the looming face of 'dreadful night'.[6]

Mike's theme in general became South Yorkshire, the industrial heartland, and most specifically Rotherham itself; its landscapes and geography, main roads and snickets, factories and football grounds, parks, pubs and place-names; at one level his writing represents a literary acknowledgement, indeed a consistently robust celebration, in its own words, of the town's existence, at a time, in the nineteen sixties, when to many beyond its bounds Rotherham was little more than the stuff of music-hall jokes. And it was not merely the form and fabric of the town 'Locked in a charcoal cloud'[7] that Mike's writing sought to champion, it was essentially the people! His reading, his learning and his sense of application to his craft enabled him to develop a rigorously clear perception of Rotherham as a historical entity; a town 'Where tongues are round and proud'[8] whose population's great contribution to the wealth of the country, and to the Empire while it lasted, from even before the onset of the Industrial Revolution, in coal and steel products, but equally in terms of technological innovation and enterprise, has gone largely unrewarded and almost wholly unrecorded; as he reminded the readers of *Tribune* in 1967:

> *Rotherham is a place where monks first turned iron ore to a kind of malleable jelly, and . . . it was here . . . that the famous Walker family made their iron foundry and built the Southwark Bridge for transportation to London on the model of a design drawn by Tom Paine.*[9]

Mike Haywood's writings from beginning to end are redolent with that sense of mission; to record, to dramatise, and to make a song and dance about, *his* people and *his* town, and to create a Literature which would play its part alongside other progressive forces in transforming history for the betterment of the many rather than for the few, to create a future in which, as he unflinchingly saw it, the true generators of Society's wealth, '. . . the masses/Of mine/And mill'[10] would reap the rewards of their long and thankless labours. Such people are at the core of his vision; his family, his community; fellow-workers, local characters and personalities; enemies as well as friends; representative figures who played their parts in shaping the nature and identity of the town. Mike succeeded in discovering a down-to-earth, unpretentious language through which he was able to present images of his own experiences and those of his fellow townsfolk living and dead, and to explore some of the realities and struggles, economic, political and cultural, which defined and oppressed them, the rituals by which they patterned and ordered their lives, the myths and momentary pleasures which inspired and comforted them.

Like Charlie Brown, the central character in his well quoted short story *The Rose Garden*,[11] shoulder to shoulder with heroes of so many of his other works, Mike Haywood was, indisputably, 'a socialist of sorts'. At his most optimistic he remained an adherent of 'an old tradition' of dissent, non-conformity, collective pride, self-belief and dignity, stretching back to the Lollards and the Peasants' Revolt, down through the Diggers and Levellers, harmonised by poets such as William Blake and Sheffield's own Joe Mather;[12] by eloquent and courageous groups of South Yorkshire Jacobins and Chartists, and reverberating still through the dialectical materialist visions of Marxists of each and every 'sort' even up to the time of his death. Mike himself however, had seen too much of the greyness and casual brutality of what he could yet term 'the bourgeois world', to become over-intoxicated by his beliefs. His work rarely succumbs to sentimentality; both as a poet and as a political commentator, in his own community he was used to being thought of as 'crackers!' Sobriety and self-parody cool and sharpen the tendency to rhetoric; irony and understatement reinforce the sentiment; gloom and pessimism exist in endless opposition to his revolutionary optimism; 'a vision is well a vision'[13] and it needs to be weighed against the actuality of most folk's daily grind:

> *A dark shed*
> *And a pale long face*
> *A bus stop and a cold morning*
> *Clutching a newspaper*
> *And pulling a harsh cigarette*
> *For a lifetime.*[14]

'A life it is – of sorts' as he abruptly puts it elsewhere,[15] and we can begin to see that although the poet's sympathies are wholeheartedly with the so-called 'Proletariat' and against the 'big black combines' like 'Tube Investments/And United Steel'[16] the 'Double Barrel Metal Company/And their Electric Arc Furnaces,'[17] whose chimneys poison the very air folk breathe, he does permit himself the occasional expression of frustrated disappointment at the degree to which too many of

his fellow-workers in their fatigue-induced complacency so often
resign themselves to their fates, lulled by the unremitting routine of
shiftwork, or by the questionable truths of a Capitalist economy
proclaimed so religiously by even their own leaders:[18]

> *Among faces sad and disinterested*
> *Amid wheels that hum to the strum*
> *Of steel*
> *Machines work the mind*
> *To a gentle hypnosis*[19]

ordaining and rewarding a false 'ease' and a 'life of no questions'.
Again like the poet Blake, it is this kind of inhuman System and the
societies it creates in its own image that are clearly *The Enemy*[20]
throughout Mike's writings. His own heroes, his best drawn characters, like Milton's Satan, are those who dare to question and to
challenge; those who are naturally antipathetic to notions of masters
and gaffers; those who will not serve.

Much of what fuelled his opposition to the inexorably spreading
Machine State as he saw it, with all its attendant bleaknesses, seems
to stem from a keenly felt sense of the qualitatively different world of
his childhood in yet to be developed Bramley. In *Back to the Pond*, a
short story which confronts some of the results of preliminary 'developments', Mike recalls vividly the topography of his native village
which in those days, he writes, had been like so many others in South
Yorkshire:

> *A coal mine about a mile and a half either side, two farms, a church
> at one end and a chapel at the other, fields and lanes and what was left
> of a garage, two pubs and a working men's club, a backstreet bookie's
> and a welfare hall. The girls went to the chapel guild, the lads went to
> the church to join the scouts and the choir; we had concerts in the welfare
> hall as well as it being the place you could get free boots. But up past
> the allotments and down Sandy Lane towards one of the pits was a
> treasured place called Slacks Pond. It was in reality a small lake down
> by a farm. It was surrounded by tall trees and long grass on either side
> and the remains of an old boat house. Up at the top end of the lake was
> thick undergrowth and bush, with a maze of streamlets feeding into the
> lake and out of the lake running down to feed a duck pond was a
> shouting waterfall.*
>
> *We went there in the long summers by the hour, we stripped off for
> swimming in the lake, we caught coots' eggs by the bucketfull, we hunted*

for rabbits and stalked each other through the long grass with bows and arrows and sat and paddled long logs across the lake in search of gold and Tarzan.[21]

Mike's play, *A Hot Bath and Lemon* explores similar terrain, following the exploits and Hollywood-movie inspired adventures of a couple of wartime schoolkids, counting off the days till the anxiously awaited return of their Desert Rat father; a ring of authenticity characterises the whole text; the local idioms, the South Yorkshire speech patterns; Plater again has caught the tone:

His work had its roots in urban speech – you can hear the echoes of shop floor, bowling green and back yard walls – and he transformed this material into a poetry that spoke for the people with a rare tang.[22]

That transformation is apparent, as is the poetry, in snatches like the following, where the kids' mother, Ma Hogg, reminisces about her wedding-night:

...I had a nice blue suit on I'd made myself at night class on that owd treddle machine and your dad had to borrow a jacket...And then we all went off to a dance after. And we walked home arm in arm down the Back Lanes and stars was as clear, so clear you could reach out and touch 'em, and there was a full moon over the Grange. We sat on a hay cart and had a sup of beer we'd brought with us out of the dance, and we had a right old sing-song, I can tell yer. There were Sam from the cobblers. A miner, he were then, and he played a fiddle, and Old Tommy Riley, that's the dad of Jack and Stan, dead now God bless him, he played a mouth organ, and that was our honeymoon, up there in Back Lanes. I reckon yer got conceived up there our Connie.[23]

Moments after this scene the innocence of the kids' world is dashed; the dad they've all been waiting for is killed in the desert and an all too early adulthood is thrust rudely upon them. Interestingly enough, the only children's story in the Haywood collection, *The Silver Dustbin*, purveys a similar underlying message. Three kids discover a magic dustbin which can whisk them off to the destinations of their dreams; tired out after the third trip they forget to hide the bin away; in the morning they find to their sorrow that it has been filled up by adults with ashes and rubbish. Like the minds of children invariably are, seems to be the implication.

The story however, does end on a more cheerful note, with the possibility that some day other children might be fortunate enough to come across the dustbin and might find themselves able to fly away on similarly colourful adventures. As a metaphor for the human mind's ability to rise above the dross of the everyday, to imagine fresh perspectives, to envision new worlds, possibilities of communal delight and fulfilment beyond the individual litanies of disappointment and pain, this is both insightful and rewarding. Mike's choice of a brand spanking Council dustbin as the vehicle for imagination and vision is somehow all the more pleasurable! Throughout his plays, the most memorable figures are all possessed of this ability to imagine other ways of living and being; consistently the worlds presented in his drama are characterised by images of containment and oppressiveness. From his early trilogy *The Forest, The Field and The Factory* which charts the making of the class system in this part of the world, with its inbuilt conflicts and struggles, the drive towards enclosure and the imprisonment of a once free peasantry within walls, and into mines and mills is the overarching dynamic. Similarly in *Man On A Donkey* the whole play takes place in the debtors' prison in Sheffield in the period just following the French Revolution. The whole cast is literally imprisoned, including of course the deluded gaoler, as the cell becomes a microcosm of England itself in the reign of terror which succeeded the Sedition Acts, the Combination Acts, the Gagging Acts, etc. etc. much of which was recorded and damned in splendid South Yorkshire idioms by the real-life hero of the play, Joe Mather, in his songs and ballads.

The action of *The Tiger in the Crow* is equally static and restricted to one corner of a smelly London back alley. The stench of corruption is still detectable in the same city three centuries later where in *Here the Dance Begins* we are introduced to the pressure-cooker atmosphere of Karl Marx's extended family life as he struggles to complete his great life's work. People in Mike's plays are always, like Macbeth, 'cabin'd, cribb'd, confin'd', (sometimes ironically enough in snap cabins!) and this sense of oppression is often associated with, and enacted by, allusions to Hell and hellishness. It is probably a fairly obvious imagery to anyone who has ever worked in a steel-mill, and in *Inferno* Mike takes the notion beyond realism and into nightmare as it becomes clear at the end of the play that what started out as a furnace somewhere up Sheffield Road has somehow through diabolical means become transported with all its workers to the awful and inescapable pit of Hell.

Mike wrote another substantial trilogy, *Disciples*; a truly broad-ranging and ambitious piece based loosely on some of his own experiences as a mature student, moving between steelworks and residential college down south, where he had studied Politics, and ultimately on to university, where he had studied English and History. The central figure, named somewhat playfully Alec, (since he is so obviously 'smart'), has tried to overcome the trawls and trammels of proletarian life by getting an education. In the event, he discovers that the lifestyle of the bourgeois intelligentsia is if anything less rewarding and liberating than life in his home community. Such people are even more prone to delude themselves about the nature of the world and about the degree to which they are able to exercise their own freedom within it; even those whose philosophical stances or political perspectives make great claims for their own objectivity are often profoundly blinkered, and deeply entrenched within 'ideological shelters.'[24] Alec perceives ultimately that he has merely exchanged one kind of enclosure for another and thereby echoes Mike Haywood's principal message to his audience.

All these rebellious heroes of his, at various historical periods, by whatever ways and means, either possess or are helped by others to develop the vision to see through and beyond the delusions foisted upon them by Systems and their apologists; those 'mind-forged manacles' identified so lucidly by Blake back at the turn of the nineteenth century. Mike's plays become arenas wherein successive versions of these ideas engage in repeated battle, with varying outcomes for the protagonists involved; sometimes tragical, sometimes farcical; always linguistically exuberant, always challenging; invariably counterpointing the dream that once people perceive the reality of their situation, they find the will to act and to liberate themselves, and that what is obviously true on an individual basis is equally applicable at the collective level:

> *Now emerging nations bow*
> *And force between their own*
> *Traditional institutions*
> *The new idea*
>
> *Of how*
> *To construct a time*
> *When Sunday bends*
> *Beneath a strain of cars*
> *Going to goodness knows where*[25]

The 'strain' will always become too great; people will not 'bow' and scrape for ever. This is the consistently defiant moral to be drawn from so many of Mike's parables, small and large. This is most crudely stated in what is perhaps his shortest published piece *Two Women*; 'It was cold, the rain ripped hard.' Two women are caught picking coal on a local tip by an officious servant of 'the Company':

> *And he kicked them coal bags off the bikes all over the rotten lane. Charlie's mother started crying. But our Emma said nowt except to us: 'When you little sods grow up, think about it and remember him,' she said.*
>
>   *It took twenty years. But we got him one night after the boozer. When we were home from Suez. Proper troopers we were. Real red beret boys. Mr Churchill's lads. He wor a tough 'un. But we were fit lads then. Specially made to look after the oil interests. Funny how it works out isn't it. Proper funny.*[26]

Revenge is sweet, maybe, but for the reader a little depressing. The system has made the lads into identical copies of the tough old coal-bobby, they just work for a larger 'Company,' they have yet to learn to see through the ideological blindfolds though the extent to which the writer has perceived the global picture is penetratingly clear. In an unusual sister-piece *Two Marines*,[27] a much more subversive scenario is depicted. The two unpredictable heroes have reached the ends of their tethers; 'Commie Marines' they call themselves, and after a night out in exotic foreign parts the 'two bloody boozed bootnecks' do a bunk with two local girls:

> *Four pairs of eyes met, four pairs of arms embraced, jackets, caps, shoes thrown off. Four heads breathed into a long sleep. The Duty Officer paced the bridge. Lights winked from the shoreline telling him. The two had gone, this time – forever.*

People have to rely on themselves and believe in their own capabilities. The conclusion of *Great Rivers of Steel* is that leaders too often have a tendency to betray their own; the once legendary Cloggy Dick takes his place in the House of Lords alongside his long-time arch-enemy Mr. Smelt, Director of the mighty 'combine' Multi-Melt, to oversee the management

>   *. . . of the natural conflict which is inevitable in the system we have always had . . . of collective bargaining in this country.*

That 'inevitability' is the target for so much of Mike Haywood's artistic spleen. Though much of the rhetoric is now a little dated, the implications for us are as real as they ever were. In 1967 he was writing,

> *The South Yorkshire minefield is dying and the Steel plants are employing less men* [28]

and lambasting the casual use of euphemisms like 'natural wastage' which meant simply job-cuts. [29] One can only wonder what he could have made of 'There is no alternative,' though the likelihood is he would have recognised it as a variation on an old theme, and would have continued to imagine and construct just those alternatives, no matter how futile in the short term it might appear, hanging on to the vision like a man balancing on a plank, from the balcony of a skyscraper, [30] of the ancient climber and friend of Wat Tyler, swinging precariously by his fingernails from the cliff face of history. [31]

Perhaps the best place to leave Mike in this season of Rotherham United's great Wembley victory is back on the terraces at Millmoor where the significance of his sense of solidarity and oneness with the people of his town and his class is most apparent in his writing; colour, vigour, enthusiasm, excitement, skill, voices; all synthesised in a single great unconstrained drama of togetherness. One tiny poem in the archive carries two different titles; *Blake On The Spion Kop* and *Saturday Revolution*; Blake the Christian quietist for whom Energy was 'eternal delight' modulates into the Bramley Socialist who writes poems and plays, and for whom every Saturday afternoon

> *The struggle reasserts itself*
> *In dress rehearsal*

and even if your tongue is firmly in your cheek and people are not sure whether or not to take you seriously, what does it matter when you're up there on the terrace, and the sun beats down, 'the United lads going like mad' and they're 'up two nowt already'

> *And I shout, light a fag, feel the sun on my face. Look at the cranes in the scrapyard and the smoke belting out of the melting shop chimneys. . . .* [32]

References

1. *Northern Voices* by Alan Plater: manuscript in Mike Haywood Archive, Local Studies Section, Rotherham Central Library.
2. *Mike Haywood Archive*, Local Studies Section, Rotherham Central Library.
3. *Some poems, plays, stories and sketches*, Ed. Hartley, Foreword. This publication is henceforth cited as 'Ed. Hartley'.
4. *The Tiger in the Crow*, Ed. Hartley, p.68: (The line paraphrases T. S. Eliot's *Whispers of Immortality*).
5. *A Warm Summer*, Ed. Hartley, p.13.
6. *Steel Workers Walking*, Ed. Hartley, p.12.
7. *Spirit Of The North*, Ed. Hartley, p.25.
8. Ibid.
9. *Tribune*, October 27th 1967.
10. *Spirit Of The North*, Ed. Hartley, p.26.
11. See *Sweet and Sour*, Ed. Gervase Phinn, Bell and Hyman Short Stories, London 1986.
12. See Mike's play *Man On A Donkey*.
13. *An Old Tradition*, Ed. Hartley, p.14.
14. *Proletariat*, Ed. Hartley, p.21.
15. *Lines and Circles*, Ed. Hartley, p.23.
16. Ibid., p.24.
17. *When The Thing Gets Out Of Control*, Ed. Hartley, p.27.
18. See *Great Rivers of Steel*.
19. *The Enemy*, Ed. Hartley, p.25.
20. Ibid.
21. *Back to the Pond*, Ed. Hartley, p.136.
22. Ed. Hartley, Introduction.
23. *A Hot Bath and Lemon*, Ed. Hartley, p.56.
24. *Location*, Ed. Hartley, p.31.
25. *Journey To Sunday*, Ed. Hartley, p.33.
26. Ed. Hartley, p.146.
27. See *Spectrum*, Bangor University Arts magazine, 1966, in Mike Haywood Archive.
28. *Tribune*, October 27th 1967.
29. *Great Rivers Of Steel*.
30. *Get A Plank*, Ed. Hartley, p.145.
31. *The Climber*, Ed. Hartley, p.30.
32. *Saturday Afternoon*, Mike Haywood Archive, Local Studies Section, Rotherham Central Library.

Acknowledgements

I would like to thank Trudi Haywood for her kind support and for her permission to quote from all the documents in the Mike Haywood Archive.

In addition I would like to thank the staff of the Archives and Local Studies Section of Rotherham Central Library for carrying up the heavy boxes on a number of occasions.

7. 'LIFTING THE DARK VEIL OF EARTH: ROCHE ABBEY EXCAVATIONS 1857-1935

by Alice Rodgers

VERY LITTLE OF THE ONCE magnificent monastery of Roche survives to greet the modern visitor. Only the gatehouse and the transepts reach to any height, yet this is the abbey frequently favoured by text book writers in their elucidation of the mature Cistercian plan. It has even gained the somewhat dubious accolade of figuring largely in English Heritage's recent National Curriculum *Using Abbeys* guide for teachers. This situation is explained, in part at least, by the under-standing that, at Roche, an almost complete Cistercian plan is exposed. Unlike Meaux it is no mere cropmark: unlike Fountains or Rievaulx there are no surviving large ranges of buildings to restrict the view from one point to another. The remains now to be seen at Roche were deliberately and systematically brought to light over a long period. This article sets out to chronicle that process and to under-stand the factors which motivated Roche's excavators.

How the ruins came to be covered

Roche Abbey was dissolved in 1538 and there is strong evidence to suggest that much of it was rapidly demolished. For many years it was used as a source of building stone, the good square cut blocks being carted away and the carved and decorated material being discarded.[1] Buck's engraving of 1725 shows heaps of waste within the chancel and the transept chapels overgrown and beginning to sustain saplings.

When Lancelot (Capability) Brown landscaped the site in the 1770s he is said to have taken down further remains.[2] A comparison of the Dickinson Survey plan of 1724 and the Maltby Tithe Map *c.*1840 shows that Brown's main contribution was the alteration of the course of both Maltby and Laughton Dikes in order to create orna-mental ponds and waterfalls.[3] To do this he was compelled to raise the level of most of the abbey site by as much as two metres. Thus he covered up large areas of the ruins, smoothing over and planting as he went.

Roche before excavation

Hunter, writing in the 1820s, describes in some detail the effect of Brown's activities:[4]

> Of the fabric of the abbey only a gateway placed at the entrance and some beautiful fragments of the church remain . . . Much of the church has been carried away, but enough remains from which to collect its extent, its form and the age of its erection. A large mass of stonework at a distance westward from the principal portion which remains of the church, is evidently the base of one side of the great western entrance. This admitted to the nave, flanked by side aisles, the whole of which has disappeared. Advancing eastwards we arrive at the columns which supported the [crossing] tower. The eastern walls of [the] transepts remain and enough of the inner work to show that in each were two side chapels . . .
>
> On the north side of the choir may be discerned some rich tabernacle work, a part of which has been painted a red colour.

Hunter makes no reference to Brown, indeed he identifies Brown's ponds as those 'in which the monks were accustomed to keep their fish' (see Figure 1). In emphasising Roche's position as an important

Figure 1.   A view of Roche Abbey from the south-west prior to the excavations of 1884. In the foreground is one of Capability Brown's ponds which Hunter interpreted as a monastic fishpond. The piece of masonry on the right is a corner of the abbot's kitchen showing above the deep layer of soil and rubble with which Brown covered the site. *Lumley Archive*

abbey rather than a Romantic ruin he set the tone of the nineteenth century view of the site.

Dr James W. Aveling's Investigation c.1857–c.1867

In the preface to *Roche Abbey* Aveling expresses appreciation to the (9th) Earl of Scarbrough 'for allowing excavations to be made to determine the ground plan of the Abbey'. He also thanks Mr G. Naylor Vickers 'for assistance in carrying them out' and Mr W. M. Campsall 'for the service he rendered in preparing many architectural drawings'.[5]

Aveling, whose monumental work on the history, landholdings and architecture of Roche was published in 1870, makes no reference to the date of his excavations. Entries in the diary of Frederica, Countess of Scarbrough, however, reveal one period of activity:

> *24th February 1857*
> *. . . drove to Roche. Found Dr Avalyn and a Mr Campsall[6], archi-tect, excavating some of the ruins and making research for a history the former is writing of the abbey.*
> *4th March 1857*
> *Drove to Roche Abbey – met the Architect and Dr Avilyn. They have made some interesting excavations.*

Frederica's husband, the 9th Earl of Scarbrough, had inherited Roche (together with the rest of the Sandbeck Estate) on 29 October, 1856. He, unlike the 8th Earl, took a particular interest in his Yorkshire estate, so it seems likely that Dr Aveling's investigations of the site had begun after the 9th Earl succeeded. It is not clear over what period Aveling worked at Roche but in a letter to the 10th Earl written in May 1892 he observes that he had not visited Roche for twenty-five years. Thus it seems almost certain that he had ceased excavation by 1867.

References in *Roche Abbey* make it clear that Aveling's investigation was on a fairly limited scale and that it was confined to the area close to the abbey church. His detailed description (below) of the three west doorways compares interestingly with Hunter's 'large mass of stonework'.

> *The central and principal portal was of three orders with nookshafts, the bases of which have small foot ornaments. The side doors seem to be plainer.*

He also describes how fragments of 'three of the piers' (pillar bases) have helped to 'determine the extent and character of the architecture'.[7] His 'ground plan of the abbey church restored' indicates that these were the two pillars of the nave arcades nearest to the west door and the one on the north side next to the crossing. He seems also to have investigated a small section of the west wall of the north transept. Illustrations of decorative features in the chancel and transept chapels suggest he may have dug down a short distance in order to confirm their dimensions and form but the visible ground levels demonstrate that this investigation was superficial.

The only other reference to excavation in *Roche Abbey* is in Aveling's description of the chapter house.

> *. . . the chapter house . . ., in the early times of the erection of these abbeys . . . is always found in parallelogram form: and of this building again, vestiges have been disinterred here sufficient to verify this state-ment.*[8]

Aveling's general plan of the site (see Figure 2 and compare with Figure 12) shows a conjectural layout of the abbey buildings. This is based on the plans of Kirkstall and Fountains, adapted to include Roche's outlying areas of upstanding masonry. Although there are obvious misinterpretations, the plan demonstrates that by 1870 there was a substantially correct understanding of the abbey site.

In expressing his hopes for the future, Aveling makes reference to this and to the work of Capability Brown:

> *All true lovers of Architecture will . . . deplore the pulling down of detached fragments and the heartless covering up of the ground plan which we know still exists in great perfection. And for the present we must content ourselves by hoping that the noble owner will, ere long, enhance a hundred-fold the interest of the lovely spot he has the privilege to possess by lifting the dark veil of earth which has for a century hidden from all eyes innumerable objects of beauty.*[9]

An interesting footnote to Aveling's work is to be found in the *Sandbeck and Stone Parish Magazine* of February 1914. It reports that the heap of earth piled up by Aveling's digging out of the west wall of the abbey church had itself been found to be obscuring another feature.

> *He little knew as he cast up the mound outside that he was covering up*

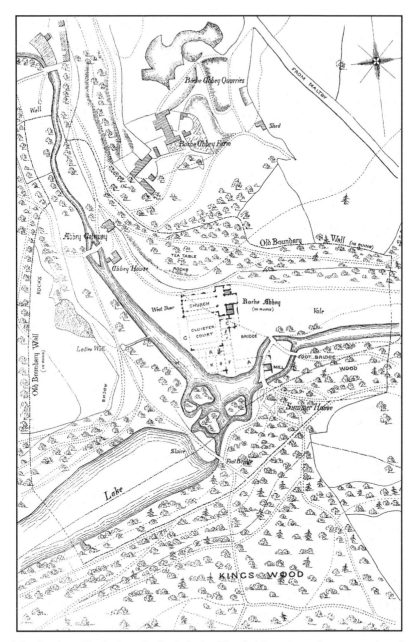

Figure 2. The site plan of Roche from Aveling's *Roche Abbey*. In his conjectural reconstruction of the abbey layout Aveling misinterpreted the function of four blocks of upstanding masonry away from the transepts. This led him to make his cloister too large and to place the lay brethren's range too far to the west.

a stone wall running the whole length outside the church. Some recent excavations have disclosed this fact. This wall, which is supposed to have formed part of the [west] *Porch is not marked on* [his] *plan of Roche Abbey.*

Enhancing 'a hundred-fold the interest of the lovely spot': Excavations 1884–1914

It was the 9th Earl's son who took up Aveling's challenge to begin to reveal the ground plan. In 1883 his father's failing health and loss of sight meant that the twenty-five year old Aldred, Viscount Lumley, had had to resign his commission in the army in order to return to Sandbeck to manage the family estates. A man of great organisational skill and enormous energy, he soon set about the task of excavation. In this he was helped by his younger brother Osbert, his sister Algitha's husband William Orde-Powlett later 4th Lord Bolton (who was a keen photographer), and by his chaplain William Travis Travis.

Viscount Lumley's excavation journal covering the period from 14 March, 1884, to 10 February, 1887, survives at Sandbeck together with personal diaries which give details of the investigation of the site. These reveal when activities began and say something of his motivation in undertaking the task:

12th March 1884

With Willy's help [William Orde-Powlett] *we have begun excavations at the abbey, our first object being to dig down to the foundations to see if the pavement of the church remains.*

14th March
  We have this week commenced excavations at Roche Abbey with a view to laying bare the ground plan . . .

and after describing Capability Brown's extensive covering over of the site:

Our object is to undo as far as possible his work, and to discover, we hope, the original plan of the building. We have commenced work in the chancel.

By 18 March the chancel floor had been reached and the lack of 'pavement' was recorded. A few odd floor tiles 'faced yellow' had been discovered together with the stones on which the high altar had rested and some finely carved masonry belonging to the decorated feature on the north side of the chancel.

On the 11 April Viscount Lumley drove his father to the abbey in a pony carriage. Continuing excavations were described as well as the problem posed by a large wych elm in the middle of the nave. Without this, it would have been possible to work directly towards the remains of the west doorways unearthed by Aveling. Instead Viscount Lumley decided to investigate further the interior and exterior of the east end of the church and to clear out the transepts.

By 16 April the diaries report that the large northerly pillar at the west end of the chancel had been cleared and two days later the excavation diary reveals the finding of fragments of the east window as the outside wall of the chancel was unearthed (see Figure 3). Burials in the centre of the chancel and below the decorated feature were discovered and Viscount Lumley speculated that the latter might contain the remains of Idonea de Busli. Others, in press reports, claimed this to be the grave of Maud Countess of Cambridge but no definite identification was ever made.

On 5 May the sloping off and turfing of the area outside the chancel

Figure 3.   The south-east corner of the chancel after excavation but before landscaping. Behind the stone marking the site of the high altar are fragments of the tracery of the east window. Photograph taken between 18 April, 1884 and August 1885 by W. Orde-Powlett. *Lumley Archive*

east wall was noted and about this time a possible vault beneath the crossing came to light. The area between the transepts was cleared by 23 May and June saw the clearance of much of the south transept (see Figure 4). Here a shallow stone basin in the form of a rose was uncovered (it remains even today, much effaced and its purpose not understood).

Activities appear to have been discontinued at this stage perhaps to allow the estate staff and their horses to attend to the hay harvest. Diary entries resume on 19 August when the site was visited by the eminent archaeologists and architectural historians J. T. Micklethwaite F.S.A. (of London) and W. H. St. John Hope (of Derby), the latter being from 1885 the Assistant Secretary of the Society of Antiquaries. The archaeologists attempted, without success, to reconstruct the east window[10] and began detailed investigations of the chapter house whose walls had been identified by Aveling. The diaries report that by mid-September the floor had been reached and much roof groining uncovered. Clearance of the chapter house continued until January 1885 but no traces of burials were found within it (see Figure 5). Whilst this work was proceeding there was a thorough investigation of part of the cemetery to the east of the transept chapels. Eighteen stone coffins were uncovered east of the south transept chapel (see Figure 6) and five were found next to the north transept chapel. These were carefully photographed, drawn and documented.

Early 1885 saw investigation of the north transept chapels and of part of the north aisle of the nave. On 6 April the personal diary records a further discovery.

> At Roche Abbey they have hit upon the culvert which is supposed to run under the kitchens, etc., the sluice of which we found in digging out the stream last spring . . . the depth of water at present in the culvert is 3ft 6in. It appears to be broken in and dammed up at the outlet as the water is stagnant.

On 9 April, St. John Hope revisited the site. The diary reports:

> Hope and self had a morning at the abbey. Settled to cover the tombs (east of the transepts) except the two with lids which are higher than the rest on the south side . . . Settled also the level of the chancel – to follow the course of the plinth about two inches below it, forming three steps, one near the altar and the other two near columns of the transept.

The following day the foundations of the refectory and the south end

Figure 4. View from the south transept looking north showing, in the foreground, the shallow stone basin in the form of a rose which had been uncovered by excavation. Note the large stones in the unexcavated area to the top right. Photograph taken after June 1884 by W. Orde-Powlett. *Lumley Archive*

Figure 5. The chapter house on 10 April, 1885. Next to the tree on the left are sections of roof groining discovered during its excavation. Photograph by W. Orde-Powlett. *Lumley Archive*

Figure 6. Stone coffins uncovered in January 1885 east of the south transept chapels. This print, based on a poor quality photograph probably by F. Royston Fairbank, was used to illustrate his article 'Roche Abbey and the Cistercian Order'. *Lumley Archive*

Figure 7. Investigating the ruins south of the cloister on about 10 April, 1885. On the left is Aldred, 10th Earl of Scarbrough and on the right is his chaplain the Reverend William Travis Travis. The man with the pickaxe is probably W. St. John Hope who advised on the excavation of this area. Photograph by W. Orde-Powlett. *Lumley Archive*

of the lay brothers' quarters were traced and arches were found above the culvert (see Figure 7). The consecration cross on the wall inside the west end, previously recorded by Aveling, was also identified. Investigation of the cloister buildings continued into the middle of the month the end of which was occupied by the covering up of the tombs. Excavation of the nave was under way at the same time leading to the discovery of two stone heads. This continued into August when the screen between the nave and the choir was uncovered. May had seen the remaking of the chancel steps, and the fencing of the east end with diamond pattern yew railing was completed by 10 August.

Work appears to have been left at this stage to be resumed in 1886. That year saw further investigation of the nave and the clearance of a ten foot roadway up its centre from the west door. Traces of fire, presumably dating from the destruction of the abbey, were found and on 8 November a stone reliquary was discovered on the north side close to the entrance to the choir.

The only diary entry for 1887, dated 10 February, details further clearance of the nave apart from two sections where large elm trees were growing. These areas remained undisturbed for a further quarter of a century. The diary painstakingly records the position and nature of the memorial slabs on the nave floor.

It will be observed that the rapid rate of progress in the unearthing of the site which prevailed in 1884 and 1885 was not sustained in the following two years. The 9th Earl had died in December 1884, and as his father's affairs were sorted out, Aldred (now 10th Earl of Scarbrough) was increasingly to devote his time to the reorganisation of estate matters. Excavation accounts reveal that between 21 March, 1884, and 6 February, 1885, £242-18-10 was expended on estate labour at Roche. It was a level of spending which could not be sustained indefinitely.

Following the first phase of excavations two articles on Roche were published by F. Royston Fairbank F.S.A. (of Doncaster) in the *Associated Architectural Societies Reports and Papers* for 1884 and 1885. The publication dates are misleading as the former concentrates on work not completed until 1885 and the latter gives details of monuments described in the diary for 1887.

From September 1887 to early 1891 the house at Sandbeck was let whilst the 10th Earl travelled extensively abroad. On 8 September the *Rotherham Advertiser* reported that the work of excavation

proceeded steadily considering the fact that experienced excavators have not been engaged upon the task, the men on the estate having to turn their attention elsewhere.

Work was supervised by the Rev. F. H. Valpy, successor in 1886 to William Travis Travis as chaplain to the Earl of Scarbrough.

Valpy's attention appears to have been directed to the clearance of the warming house, identified in contemporary reports as 'the kitchen'. Fragments of old pottery and glass 'which crumbled to the touch', an old weight believed to be part of a clock and a monk's jet cross belonging to a rosary as well as some animal bones were listed as finds. It is also noted that fragments of lead, apparently from the roof, had been found in every section of the building.

The only evidence traced of work continuing the following year is a plan of the west wall of the refectory dated 31 August, 1889. 1890, however, saw the return of estate labour to the work witnessed by a memorandum of the cost of excavations from 25 February to 5 July. A total of £77-11-10 was expended on excavation and on the formation of slopes and walks round the outside walls of the ruins.

A letter in the *Doncaster Gazette* dated 9 June, 1890, and signed FSA (probably written by F. Royston Fairbank, F.S.A.) details further work. 1890 had seen the south ends of the buildings on the south side of the cloister 'well exposed', the end of the refectory had been 'well cleared externally' with land nearby sloped down to its foundations. The south end of the day room of the monks had been cleared and the line of the culvert which passed beneath the day room and the refectory 'much opened out'. On the other side of the culvert the small extension of the day room with a semi-circular tiled fireplace had also been exposed. Here was discovered what was apparently a small, post-monastic limekiln.

On 11 August, 1891, the Earl of Scarbrough resumed occupation of the house at Sandbeck but no record of the recommencement of excavations can be traced until September 1896. It was then that the Rev. Valpy reported in the *Sandbeck and Stone Parish Magazine* that he and 'any other chance amateur navvies he may be lucky enough to enlist in the work' were digging out the foundations of what he described as 'the kitchen' on the west side of the refectory. A month later he added that 'the buttery', close by, had not yet been excavated. Valpy ceased to be chaplain shortly after this and his successor is not recorded as having been involved in excavation.

A detailed plan of 1903 measured and drawn by Harold Brakspear F.S.A. makes clear that little further work had been done by then but indicates that there was a clear and accurate understanding of the site north and just south of the main culvert. This plan includes information about submerged parts of the ruins gleaned by an Estate surveyor, Mr Dooley, when the ponds were drained for cleaning. No clearance of the western range or the cloister had taken place and the two trees left one on each side of the nave still prevented the removal of all the overburden from the abbey church. That the remains were fit to view is confirmed by a private visit made by King Edward VII during a brief visit to Sandbeck in 1904.

Whitsuntide 1910 saw the felling of the elm tree on the north side of the nave which permitted the removal of the stone and earth beneath it. Those reported to have 'assisted in the work' included Lord and Lady Scarbrough, the Duchess of Portland, the Marquis of Titchfield and Mr D. Milner. Two members of the Estate staff, J. Gray and Joseph Jepson, the latter having taken part in the 1884 excavations, were engaged to do the digging! The bases of two columns were uncovered as well as the remains of a pulpit or tomb with steps. Well preserved glazed tiles were found together with a fifteenth century coin. Colourwash lined out in black was found on some of the masonry.

The elm tree on the south side of the nave was removed in August 1913 exposing the tomb of Agnes Vincent of Braithwell. The 10th Earl's nephews Richard and Roger Lumley (later 11th Earl) joined Derek Milner, a cousin, in the clearance work (see Figure 8). Roger Lumley later revealed to his son, the present Earl, that he was less than enthusiastic about spending his summer holiday involved in spade work!

In February 1914 the *Sandbeck and Stone Parish Magazine* reported on the removal of Aveling's pile of debris from the outside of the west end of the church which exposed the wall of the western porch. By the outbreak of the First World War much clearance remained to be undertaken but Aveling's hope that the ground plan would be revealed had been largely achieved.

Securing the Future: Consolidation and Excavation 1919–1935

Work was suspended during the First World War but recommenced very shortly after the peace. In 1919 a local newspaper reported that 'a new piece of ground' had been opened up and 'the supposed domestic buildings' lying to the south of the main ruins were now exposed for inspection. Plans were being made to divert Laughton Dike and Maltby Dike into their medieval channels. The work would

Figure 8.   Excavation of the south side of the nave in August 1913. Roger Lumley (later 11th Earl of Scarbrough) stands on the left next to Richard Lumley (his elder brother killed in the First World War); Derek Milner is the figure on the right. The overburden of rubble and stone was some six feet deep at this point. *Lumley Archive*

involve the removal of a layer of earth 'upwards of ten feet thick'.

The proposed activity was, however, overtaken by negotiations about the guardianship of the Abbey. The Ancient Monuments Act 1913 had given powers to the Commisioners of Works to take into guardianship medieval sites of importance. The 10th Earl approached them early in 1920 offering to hand over Roche Abbey. Negotiations were protracted and Roche did not achieve its new status until late August 1921. Lord Scarbrough retained title to the site but the Office of Works now took over responsbility for both maintenance and exca- vation. Prior to the conclusion of the agreement, arrangements had been made for the Commissioners:

in view of the dangerous state of the vault of the eastern chapels of the south transept . . . to enter on the site . . . in order that such shoring as is needed may be put in place without delay.

The shoring was put up in 1920, the excavation required for it revealing a number of stone coffins (doubtless those which had been uncovered and recorded in 1885). These were photographed by the Office of Works and reburied. Work was suspended during the winter of 1920 but in May 1921 a Mr Bond from Kirby Muxloe was sent to take charge of activities under the direction of Mr J. H. Ball, the Office of Works superintendent for Yorkshire.

Throughout 1921 and 1922 attempts were made to secure the vaulting of the south transept which was greatly weakened because the supporting column of the east wall was sixteen inches away from the vertical in a height of twenty feet. Tons of liquid cement were poured into this section which was also supported by metal ties. The outer facings of parts of the transepts had become detached from their rubble core, the mortar of which had 'generally turned to dust'. Thin cracks were grouted, broad ones were pointed and a reinforced concrete beam was introduced to secure the east wall of the south transept chapel. Old stone was required for this work and in order to obtain some, a mound of waste in the cloister court was exposed. This revealed the stones of a late Norman arch.

In 1923 two elms in the cloister garth were cut down facilitating the clearance of this area. Seven or eight feet of overburden were removed and a few coins, fragments of tile, chards of pottery, scraps of coloured glass and a number of stones showing elaborate carvings were recovered. A local press report descrbed these as 'nothing of value intrinsically or archaeologically'! The cloister garth also revealed an unexpected grave, water chutes and a rectangular drain. Whilst the work of consolidation continued (see Figure 9) the outside wall of the nave was cleared to ground level and the bases of three buttresses and the whole of the plinth were revealed.

During the winter of 1924–25 'when unemployment was very rife in the mining district of Maltby'[11] the Office of Works received a grant from a relief works fund and spent it 'in maintaining some thirty men in spade work over the whole site'. The western range appears to have been largely cleared and a start was made on the excavation of the 'great' culvert (the main drain beneath the refectory and the monk's day room, rediscovered in 1885). Hundreds of tons of soil were

Figure 9.   Work in progress on the transepts about 1922. Note the use of light railway track to facilitate the movement of materials and waste. *Rotherham Central Library, Archives and Local Studies Section*

removed and wheeled away to fill up hollows near the stream. Investigation of the south of the site was also attempted at about this time but was prevented by 'water problems'. Fewer men were employed in the summer of 1925 and progress slowed. The masonry laid bare by the winter's spadework was 'straightened, cleaned and pointed' and excavation of the main drain continued. This was cleared at its western end to the level of its flagging.

During the investigation of the area south of the monks' day room, the culvert which had, in monastic times, brought the waters of Laughton Dike to join the main drain, was accidentally discovered by a workman whose crowbar disappeared between two stones. This culvert was traced for some twenty yards and brass pins were found in it.

Further examination of the east end of the main culvert revealed that what was thought to be a single arch carrying the path over the drain was in fact double, Brown having covered up the greater part of it. The clearance of this area brought to light brass book clasps, a dinner knife, some iron locks, a possible soldering iron, coins, pottery fragments and thousands of what were described as oyster shells. Most of the culvert was cleared out and in August 1926 water from the 'fishpond' close by was piped in to allow a modest flow in the medieval channel. An Aerofilms photograph (Figure 10) taken about this time shows the excavated main culvert. Also visible is evidence of clearance in progress of overburden from the kitchen, refectory and warming house area. Corners of the lay brethren's infirmary, the abbot's kitchen, abbot's lodging and the infirmary cloister had by this time been exposed.

Figure 10. Aerial view of Roche Abbey in 1926. Two thirds of the way down the picture are traces of the excavation work in progress close to the main drain. Capability Brown's diversion of Maltby Dike is visible across the left hand corner. *Lumley Archive*

The latter end of 1926 and the beginning of 1927 saw interest in restoration moving to the gatehouse. Vegetation was removed revealing well preserved vaulting. A large modern buttress supporting its south-eastern corner was taken away exposing an unexpected window. Amongst the rubble filling the north-western corner of the roof above the vaulting, a broken statue of the Madonna and Child was found complete with traces of its original colouring. The whole gatehouse was pointed and made safe.

It appears that activity went on at a slower pace until at least late 1929, although the discovery of a fourteenth century silver spoon in June 1928 indicates that it did not cease. Shoring is still visible on the south transept on pictures of Stanley Baldwin's visit on 24 May, 1928.

In November 1929 the Treasury authorised the spending of further monies on the excavation of historic buildings, as a means of relieving unemployment. Part of the fund was allocated to Roche and the Sandbeck Estate was approached with the request that both Maltby and Laughton Dikes be returned in total to their medieval culverts (see Figure 11). The 10th Earl, who had included in the 1921 Deed

Figure 11. Copy of an Office of Works rough sketch of November 1929 showing (dotted lines) the then courses of Maltby and Laughton Dikes and (solid lines) the proposed diversions to return them to their medieval channels. The effect of this work was to dry out the southern part of the site and thus permit excavation of the infirmarer's lodging, the abbot's house, kitchen and bakehouse and the lay brethren's infirmary. *Lumley Archive*

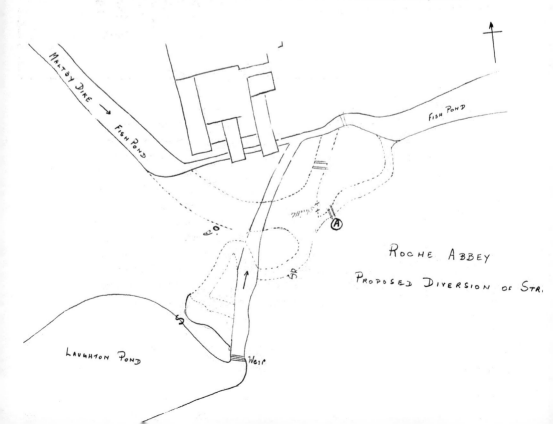

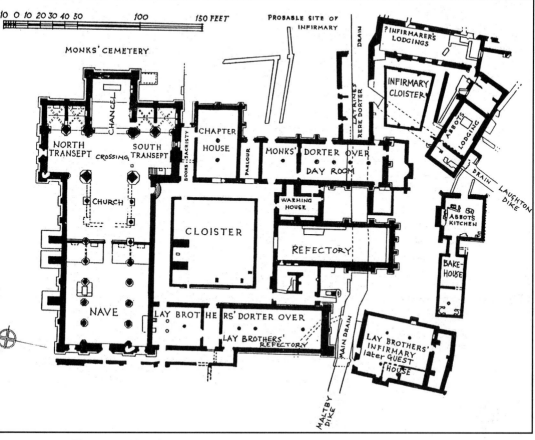

Figure 12. Plan of the abbey as excavated by 1935.

of Guardianship a provision retaining the then existing water courses, was less than enthusiastic about the proposals and negotiations were protracted. The delay meant that the offer of relief works money was not taken up.

The idea of diverting the streams was revived in October 1930 and this time it went ahead. Much overburden was removed and a weir was taken down. The effect of these works was to dry out previously submerged sections of the ruins and to permit the excavation of buildings now visible to the south of the site – the infirmarer's lodging, the abbot's house, kitchen and bakehouse and the lay brothers' infirmary (see Figure 12). The effects of the diversion were not wholly positive and, until 1940, letters were exchanged about flash floods and there were concerns about the stability of Laughton Dam.

As the last phase of excavation took place in an area beyond that already in guardianship, an additional deed was executed in 1932 extending this southwards towards Laughton Dam. A Hamilton Thomson's Office of Works Guidebook published in 1935 is the clearest indication there is that, at this stage, excavations were regarded as complete. After more than 75 years much of Capability Brown's work had been undone.

A Note on Sources

This article is based, for the most part, on uncatalogued family papers and memorabilia from Sandbeck Park including:

1. Diary of Frederica, Countess of Scarbrough, 1857.
2. Diaries of Aldred, Viscount Lumley (later 10th Earl of Scarbrough), 1884–1892.
3. Excavation diary of Aldred, Viscount Lumley 14 March, 1884, to 10 February, 1887.
4. The 10th Earl of Scarbrough's files of Roche material including photographs, correspondence, plans, guidebooks, newspaper cuttings and journal offprints.
5. Scrapbooks mostly assembled by Cecilia, Countess of Scarbrough, 1899–1932
6. Bound volumes and runs of *Sandbeck and Stone Parish Magazines*.

Particularly helpful in understanding the period 1919–1935 have been the Roche Abbey files in the Estate Office at Sandbeck (Lumley new catalogue 15/2 and 15/3) and books of newspaper cuttings in the possession of Maltby Local History Society. As the excavations were from time to time reported in newspapers in Sheffield, Rotherham, Doncaster and Worksop the use of cuttings files and scrapbooks has minimised the toil over microfilm readers! Other references are separately noted.

References

1. Alice Rodgers 'Water Powered Mills in Maltby' in *Aspects of Rotherham*, Ed. Melvyn Jones, Wharncliffe Publishing Ltd, Barnsley, 1995, p.63.
2. J. W. Aveling, *Roche Abbey*, Worksop, 1870, p.165.
3. Lumley EMS/5 and ET1/12 and plans.
4. Joseph Hunter, *South Yorkshire*, 1828–31, p. 271.
5. *Roche Abbey*, p. vi.
6. Mr Campsall assisted the architect William Burn in the alterations of the house at Sandbeck *c*.1856–58.
7. *Roche Abbey*, p.172.
8. *Roche Abbey*, p.167.
9. *Roche Abbey*, p.165.
10. Glass taken from the east window tracery was eventually used to make a small west window in Sandbeck Chapel.
11. As well as the depression, Maltby was still suffering the effects of the colliery disaster in 1923.

Acknowledgements

I am greatly indebted to the Earl of Scarbrough for allowing access to family papers at Sandbeck and to the Lumley Archive as well as for permitting me to reproduce photographs of the excavations. Thanks are also due to the staff of Rotherham M.B.C. Central Library, Archives and Local Studies Section, for their continuing practical help and encouragement.

8. THE MEDIEVAL DEER PARK AT KIMBERWORTH

by Melvyn Jones

JOHN SPEED'S MAP OF THE WEST RIDING of Yorkshire published in 1610 shows eight deer parks surrounding the town of Rotherham (Figure 1). They had all been created before 1320. The parks are not always precisely located and, although they are shown to vary in size, with the exception of the park at Conisbrough, they are all shown conventionally as being roughly circular in shape with a wooden boundary fence (called the park 'pale'). One of the parks is located between Thorpe Hesley and the town of Rotherham with Granesburgh (Greasbrough) apparently located just within the park's northern boundary. This is Kimberworth Park, the subject of this study.

Deer Parks Defined

The concept of the deer park, is probably of Roman origin but, although parks did exist in England before 1066, in Britain it was a tradition that flourished only after the Norman Conquest in the mid-eleventh century. In the Domesday Survey in 1086, twenty years after the Conquest, thirty-five deer parks were recorded; estimates of the number of parks by the year 1300 vary – one authority suggests 1,900, another puts the figure at over 3,000.[1]

Medieval deer parks were symbols of status and wealth. They were created by kings, by the nobility and by bishops, and they were also to be found attached to monasteries, nunneries and colleges. As all deer belonged to the Crown, from the beginning of the thirteenth century it was necessary to obtain a licence from the king to create a park. A grant of **free warren** was given which gave a landowner a general right to hunt on his **demesne** (the land surrounding his hall not in the hands of tenants), and this general permission was often converted into the creation of a specially enclosed area: the deer park. Among the places where grants of free warren were given in South Yorkshire in the thirteenth century were at Wortley in 1252, Aston in 1256–57, Thrybergh in 1259–60, Tankersley in 1303–04 and Treeton in 1315–16.[2] Figure 2 shows a particularly interesting example of a grant of free warren. The parks at Conisbrough and Sheffield predated the issuing of royal licences and so must have been of twelfth century

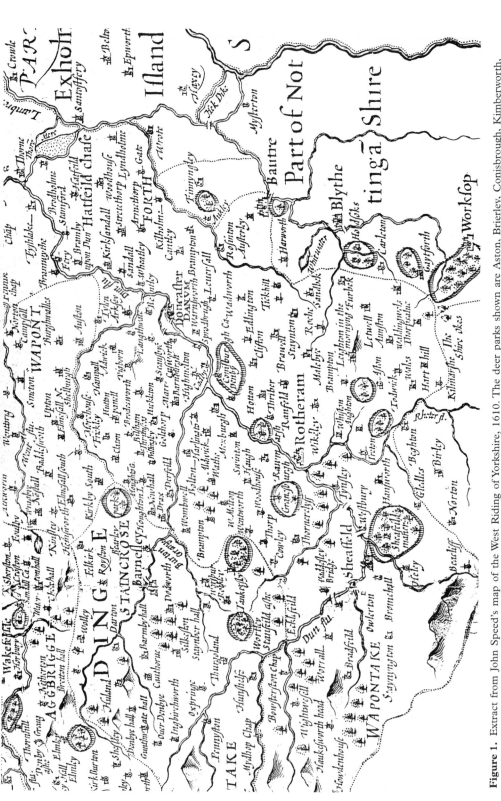

Figure 1. Extract from John Speed's map of the West Riding of Yorkshire, 1610. The deer parks shown are Aston, Brierley, Conisbrough, Kimberworth, Sheffield, Tankersley, Thrybergh, Treeton and Wortley.

Figure 2. A particularly fine example of a charter dated 1291 granting the right of free warren to Roger de Pilkington on his demesne lands in Lancashire. In the bottom left-hand corner is a huntsman blowing a bugle and accompanied by hunting dogs. Along the bottom are three pairs of deer (possibly meant to represent a male and female fallow deer (buck and doe), a male and female red deer (stag (or hart) and hind) and a male and female roe deer (buck and doe)), a fox and a wild boar. In the top left-hand corner are two rabbits. Along the sides and top of the document are a number of different bird species including a peacock and a woodcock. *Fitzwilliam Museum, Cambridge*

or even earlier – possibly Saxon – origin.[3] The creation of a park – called **emparkment** – involved enclosing an area of land with a fence to keep the deer and other game in, and predators (wolves) and poachers out. As has already been pointed out, the fence was called the **park pale** and consisted either of cleft oak stakes, often set on a

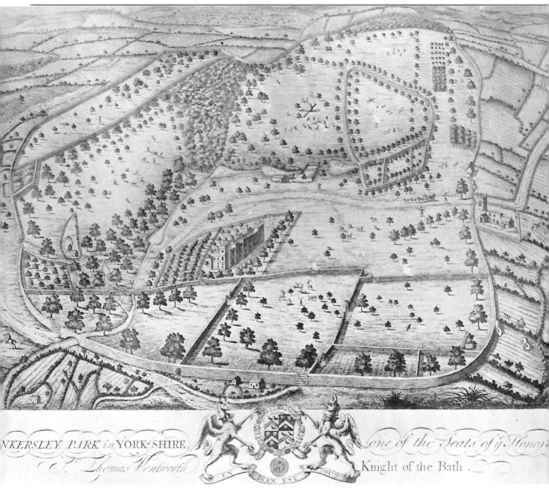

NKERSLEY PARK in YORK-SHIRE.

Thomas Ventworth

one of the Seats of ỹ Honor

Knight of the Bath.

Figure 3. An early eighteenth century engraving of Tankersley Park. Besides the Elizabethan Hall, among features shown are its encircling wall, launds with trees, enclosed woods, fish ponds, walled paddocks, and two keeper's lodges. Immediately beyond the three closely grouped fish ponds is a deer shed where the deer were fed with hay and holly in winter. In the adjoining large paddock deer are being hunted by a huntsman on horseback accompanied by a parker with four hunting dogs.

bank, or a stone wall. Tankersley Park, one of the longest surviving local medieval parks, is shown in an engraving of the 1720s completely surrounded by a stone wall (Figure 3). As parks could vary in size from under 100 acres to several thousand acres (Sheffield Park covered nearly 2,500 acres and was eight miles in circumference) fencing was a major initial and recurring expense. Because of this, the most economical shape for a deer park was a circle or a rectangle with

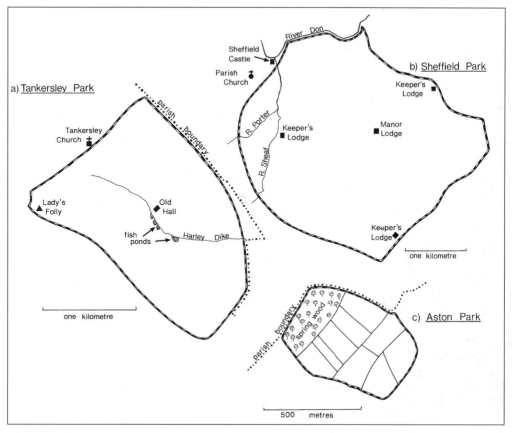

Figure 4. The outlines of three medieval south Yorkshire parks.

rounded corners. Figure 4 shows the outlines of the medieval parks at Aston, Sheffield and Tankersley. Park pales contained **deer leaps**, devices which allowed wild deer to enter the park but prevented the park herd from escaping (Figure 5).

Deer parks were not primarily created for hunting, although hunting did take place there. The first known documentary reference to Tankersley Park after its creation was in a law suit of 1527 when the owner, Henry Savile, was recorded as having been 'hunting at dere wythe hounds in hys parke of Tankersley'.[4] Besides their status symbol role, their main function was to provide for their owners and their families a reliable source of food for the table, and supplies

Figure 5. A deer leap. *Based on a drawing in E. P. Shirley's English Deer Parks, (1867), and another in Collections for a History of Staffordshire, v, pt i, (1884) in the William Salt Library, Stafford*

of wood and timber: they were, therefore, an integral part of the local farming economy.

There were three species of deer in Britain in the middle ages (Figure 6). The deer in most parks were fallow deer, which are not native to Britain but were probably introduced by the Normans. Fallow deer were much easier to contain within a park than the native red deer and roe deer. Locally both fallow and red deer were kept in parks. In his survey of the Manor of Sheffield in 1637, John Harrison recorded that the park there was 'not meanly furnished with fallow Deare, the number of them at present is one Thousand'.[5] Nearly a century later when Daniel Defoe rode through Tankersley Park he commented that he had seen '. . . the largest red deer that, I believe, are in this part of Europe: One of the hinds, I think, was larger than my horse . . .'.[6] There was still a herd of more than 50 red deer at Tankersley in the 1850s when they were relocated at Wentworth due to the reduction in the size of the park because of ironstone mining. Besides deer, wild swine, hares, rabbits (also introduced by the Normans and kept in burrows in artificially made mounds) and game birds were kept in medieval parks. Herds of cattle and flocks of sheep were also kept. Another important feature of medieval deer parks were fish ponds to provide an alternative to meat in Lent and on fast days.

Although there are records of parks without trees, deer parks usually consisted of woodland and areas largely cleared of trees. The park live-stock could graze in the open areas and find cover in the wooded areas. The cleared areas were called **launds** or **plains** and consisted of grass-land or heath with scattered trees. Most of the trees in the launds would have been **pollards**, ie, trees cut at least six feet from the ground leaving a massive lower trunk called a **bolling** above which a continuous crop of new growth sprouted out of reach of the grazing deer, sheep and cattle. John Evelyn in his book *Sylva* published in the second half of the seventeenth century recorded some massive pollards in the deer park at Sheffield. For example he recorded one oak tree in the park whose trunk was 13 feet in diameter and another 10 yards in circumference.[7] In the launds regeneration of trees was restricted because of continuous grazing and new trees were only able to grow in the protection of thickets of hawthorn and holly. Some of these unpollarded trees might reach a great age and size and were much sought after for major building projects. Evelyn recorded a large oak tree felled in Sheffield Park that was so big when it was lying on its side that two men on opposite sides on horseback could not see each other's hats! Even more impressive was his report that in an open area within the park called Conduit Plaine there was another oak tree

Figure 6. Animals of the medieval park.

whose boughs were so far spreading that he estimated (giving all his calculations) that 251 horses could stand in the shade of it.[8]

The woods within medieval deer parks were managed in different ways. Some were holted. A **holt** consisted of single stemmed trees grown for timber, rather like a modern plantation. John Harrison seems to be describing such a wood in Rivelin Chase in 1637 when he says:

> *Item Hawe Parke lyeth open to Rivelin ffirth . . . This peice is full of excellent timber of a very great length & very Streight & many of them of a great bigness before you come to a Knott in So much that it hath been said by Travellers that they have not seene such Timber in Cristendane.*[9]

Most woods, however, were managed as **coppices**, in south Yorkshire usually as **coppices with standards**. In a coppice with standards, in accordance with an overall plan, most of the trees would be cut close to the ground and from the stump or **stool** sprang poles. These were cut regularly according to a pre-determined **coppice cycle** ranging from just a few years in the case of a hazel wood to 20 or even 25 years. Among the coppice young trees were selected to become timber trees and therefore were not coppiced. These were the standards and they remained through a number of coppice cycles, depending on the demand for timber and were cut as the market demanded. Coppice woods within parks would have been surrounded by banks surmounted by hedges or by stone walls to protect them, during the early years of growth after the last felling, from grazing deer and rabbits and any other herbivores kept within the park. Once well grown the livestock would be allowed into the woods.

There was one other type of wood found in the deer parks in south Yorkshire and north Derbyshire. These were separate woods or compartments within woods in which the dominant tree was holly and which were called **holly hags**.[10] The holly was cut for winter fodder for the deer and other park livestock and must have been cut on rotation like other coppiced trees and then allowed to grow back. In a lease of Tankersley Park in 1653 it was stipulated that the deer had to be fed by ' serving them with holley to be cutt therein in winter.'[11] Early nineteenth century maps of the park show an enclosure in the south-east corner of the park called the Far Hollings and the early eighteenth century engraving of the park (Figure 3) shows a small walled wood in that location (the small diamond-shaped wood on the extreme left).

To summarise, most medieval deer parks comprised of a series of

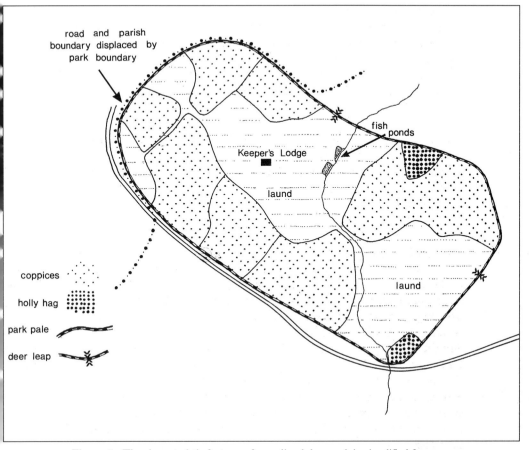

road and parish
boundary displaced by
park boundary

fish ponds

Keeper's Lodge

laund

laund

coppices

holly hag

park pale

deer leap

Figure 7. The characteristic features of a medieval deer park in simplified form.

compartments: periodically or permanently fenced holts, coppices and holly hags, together with permanently open launds or plains which might be treeless glades or dotted with thickets and pollards and other ancient trees. Man-made pillow mounds containing rabbit warrens would have almost certainly occupied part of one of the launds. There would also usually have been fishponds. Figure 7 shows these characteristic features in simplified form.

And finally, occupying the centre of the park or elsewhere commanding wide views would have been a parker's lodge. Large parks might have had several. Sheffield Park had three keepers' lodges (Figure 4).

Decline and Change

Between the late fifteenth and eighteenth centuries many surviving medieval parks either changed their function and hence their appearance, or ceased to be parks at all. Where a landlord was absent (his main country seat may have been in another county) or where his hall lay some distance from his medieval park, there was an increased possibility that the park may disappear altogether, the process being called **disparkment**. Well wooded parks often simply became large coppice woods, as locally was the case at Hesley Park, Cowley Park and Tinsley Park. By the time of John Harrison's survey of the manor of Sheffield in 1637, Hesley Park and Cowley Park, between Thorpe Hesley and Chapeltown, which together mark the medieval park of

Figure 8. Wentworth Woodhouse and its park in the early nineteenth century. The park was no longer a game preserve and source of wood and timber but an aesthetic extension to the country house. The animals were decorative. In the nineteenth century even buffaloes were kept in the park at Wentworth.

the de Mountenay family of Cowley, were coppice woods of 163 and 135 acres respectively. Interestingly the woods still contained deer at that time. The Earl of Arundel's tenant and employee at Hesley Hall at that time was Humfrey Northall, 'the keeper of Couley Woods',[12] and 27 years later in 1664 '£4 was paid to 'Henry Priest for lookeing to Cowley Woods and ye outlyeing Red Deer in Humphrey Northall's place . . .'.[13] Tinsley Park was another medieval deer park that had lost its former function by the mid-seventeenth century. In 1657 it was let by its then owner, the 2nd Earl of Strafford of Wentworth Woodhouse, to Lyonel Copley the ironmaster, for felling for charcoal making. It then covered over 400 acres and comprised 10 coppice woods and three holts.[14] Other parks simply reverted to farmland. The medieval park at Aston had become part of Old Park Farm by 1775 and, as Figure 4 shows, had been largely divided up into small enclosures. Even though Sheffield Park still contained 1000 deer in 1637, 971 of its 2,462 acres had been let to tenants.

While hundreds of medieval parks were disappearing, many others took on a new lease of life because the concept of the park was changing. Its primary function changed from being a game preserve and source of wood and timber to being the adornment to a country house. New residences were built within the boundaries of existing parks which were often extended. The concept of the park as an aesthetic extension of the country seat and garden began in the Tudor period and has gone through many fashions in the last 500 years. Some of the greatest changes and new creations occurred in the eighteenth century under the influence of landscape designers such as John Vanbrugh, Charles Bridgeman, William Kent, Lancelot 'Capability' Brown and Humphrey Repton. The parks at Wentworth Woodhouse (Figure 8) and Sandbeck Park date from this period.[15]

The Park at Kimberworth 1: the Documentary Evidence

In the light of what we now know about the history and characteristics of medieval deer parks, it is appropriate to turn to what known surviving documents can tell us about the park at Kimberworth.

The first known documentary record of Kimberworth Park is in the Feet of Fines (copies of agreements made after disputes over land ownership) for 7 December, 1226.[16] The proceedings record that the Abbot of Kirkstead Abbey in Lincolnshire and Robert Vipont, lord of the manor of Kimberworth, were in dispute over access to common land in Kimberworth for the Abbot's cattle. The Abbey had been granted access to the common under an agreement of 1161 when the monks were given permission to mine ironstone and set up forges. By 1226 the Abbot claimed that the lord of the manor had set up a dyke (wall) barring access to part of the common. The record of the proceedings makes it clear that the wall was a park wall of the 'park of Kimberwurth' and the final agreement was that the rights of the Abbey to pasture animals, to dig for ironstone coal and marl and work forges in the new park were annulled.

The next known record of Kimberworth Park is in the Hundred Rolls of 1276. These are the records of enquiries made on behalf of King Edward I about the privileges claimed by the nobility, clergy and others which diverted profits from the Royal coffers into private hands. They were called hundred rolls because the enquiries were conducted in every hundred (a group of contiguous parishes) throughout the country. In 1276 Robert de Vipont (lord of the manor of Kimberworth until his death in 1265), and his heirs, were accused of exceeding the bounds of their free warren in Kimberworth for the past ten years and of including within the deer park a portion of the king's highway, measuring one rood wide and 20 roods long.[17]

Following the initial investigations in the hundreds, the king sent out itinerant justices to conduct further enquiries and these became known as the *Quo Warranto* (What Right) proceedings. In 1292 Idonea de Leybourne, the daughter of Robert de Vipont and lady of the manor of Kimberworth, had to answer a number of questions about her deer park there. First she was asked by what right she claimed the privilege of having a free park and secondly she was charged with constructing a deer leap (in Latin *saltatorium*) to entice deer into her park which was to the disadvantage of the king because deer from the king's forest were likely to become part of the Kimberworth Park herd.

The jury was satisfied that she had not created a park unlawfully but that she had inherited an existing park from her father for which he held the right of free warren. In the matter of the deer leap the jury was satisfied it was not to the disadvantage of the king because his forest – presumably Sherwood – was more than 15 leagues away (more than 22 miles) and the Earl of Warenne's chase (Hatfield Chase near Doncaster) and Thomas de Furnival's chase (Rivelin Chase) were in between.[18]

Lady Idonea died in 1334 when she was 68. In 1313 she was granted another licence of free warren at Kimberworth.[19] She may have been extending her existing park.

The next known mention of the park at Kimberworth was 175 years later, in the late fifteenth century, by which time the manor of

Kimberworth was in the ownership of the crown. In 1487, on behalf of King Henry VII, Richard Byrley, who was connected with Archbishop Rotherham, was appointed bailiff and park keeper. The office was said to include herbage and pannage.[20] Herbage was payment for the right to graze animals other than swine in the park launds and woods and pannage was the payment for the right to graze pigs on fallen acorns and beech mast in September and October. Presumably Byrley was able to augment his income by letting the grazing.

In 1553, the Manor of Kimberworth was acquired by the 5th Earl of Shrewsbury and the park is referred to on three occasions in the so-called Talbot Papers which are letters to (and some from) the fifth, sixth and seventh Earls of Shrewsbury written between *c*. 1538–1617. The first of these occasions is particularly significant because a specific species of deer is referred to. This was in a letter from William Dickenson, the bailiff of the Sheffield estate, to the sixth Earl on 31 July, 1586, telling him that a deer has been killed in Kimberworth Park, that it was thought the culprits were known – two men called Hurt and another called Francis Greaves – and begging the Earl to arrange for them to be kept in Sheffield Castle.[21] A further letter of 11 August confirmed that the poachers were by then imprisoned in the castle.[22] The significant point about the first letter is that it referred to the dead animal as a **stag**. Different names are used for the males and females of the different deer species. Male fallow and roe deer are referred to as **bucks** and the females as **does**. In the case of red deer the males are called **harts** or **stags** and the females **hinds**.

The third occasion on which Kimberworth Park is mentioned in the Talbot Letters is in an undated letter to the seventh Earl (who became Earl in 1592 and died in 1616) from the 'collyars of kymberworthe' requesting that he will not press them for the overdue rent for the Earl's coal pit in Kimberworth Park. They said they had paid their rent regularly for the last thirty years, so that we know there was a coal pit in the park from at least 1586.[23]

Another undated document dating from the time of the seventh Earl is a list of his coppice woods in south Yorkshire. The document states that in Kimberworth Park there were 300 acres of coppice wood 'all redie to be coled', ie, the coppice would have been 20–30 years old and ready to be made into charcoal.[24]

Seventeenth century records of the park are much more frequent and much fuller than in previous centuries and show that the deer park was still functioning as such until at least the mid-1630s, but that soon after that in the aftermath of the Civil War the park began to be dismembered and its function changed.

In the seventeenth century the park and the manor were still the property of the descendants of the Earls of Shrewsbury (the earls of Arundel and Norfolk) but in the first part of the century the park was leased to the first Earl of Strafford of Wentworth Woodhouse (d. 1640). While Viceroy of Ireland, he wrote a letter to a Mr Greenwood, rector of Thornhill, which contains interesting details of Kimberworth Park:

> *I appoint my cousin Rockley master of the game at Tankersley; desiring him he will now and then look into the house, to see that it be kept from decay; that the woods be preserved without cutting, or lopping, which is almost as bad; that the park be sufficiently maintained; the deer increased till they come to three hundred; that the ponds be from time to time kept in repair and maintained. In like manner, I appoint my brother Hutton master of the game at Kimberworth; always provided that you have the liberty to command in either park what deer you list; and that I would have venison sent to my cousin Wentworth of Wolley, to my cousin Wentworth of Elmsal, and to my brother Rodes, every season; and that any of them may command a piece of venison when they have occasion to desire it. Sir Richard Scot hath power to dispose of a buck in either park in summer, and a doe in either park in winter; and soe I pray you let him know, that if he hath any friend, he may pleasure them therewith, as he likes best himself.*[25]

The letter confirms that Kimberworth deer park still contained deer in 1635 and if we take the references to bucks and does at face value then fallow deer were being referred to. The reference to the privileges that Sir Richard Scott (of Barnes Hall in Ecclesfield parish) enjoyed suggests that deer hunts were still a feature of the park.

However, by the middle of the century momentous changes were beginning to take place. By 1649 the first steps had taken place leading to the park's eventual total disparkment. In a rental of 1649 part of the park had become a farm, called Park Gate Farm, later records showing it to be of about 140 acres. By 1671 the whole of the park had been leased, the farm as in 1649, and the rest, amounting to over 600 acres, to a local ironmaster whose main interest was in the iron-stone and coal that could be mined and the coppice (spring) woods that could be felled and made into charcoal. The entry in the rental book is as follows:

Mr Lyonnell Copley ye pke	605-0-24	[acres]
ye springwood in ye pke	98- 1-38	
Mr Lyonnell Copley the coalpitts in Kimberworthe pke . . .		
. . . Park-gate		
Mr Tho Barnsley & Rich Elam	141-0-04 [26]	

Between 1671 and 1732, when a survey of the manor of Kimberworth was undertaken for its then owner, the Earl of Effingham, the parkland, with the exception of the surviving woodland, had been divided into farms and the park had disappeared.

The Park at Kimberworth 2: Map and Landscape Evidence

Although there are large gaps in the documentary evidence we know that a deer park was in existence at Kimberworth by the beginning of the second quarter of the thirteenth century and that it continued to function as a deer park until some point between 1635 and 1649. Complete disparkment took place in the century after 1635. But where exactly was Kimberworth Park? What shape was it? Were its boundaries formed by banks or were they stone walls? Where were its coppice woods and launds? Were rabbits kept in warrens? Were there fishponds? Was there a keeper's lodge? To attempt to answer these questions we need to turn to maps and the landscape itself.

Some areas in the park may have been fenced by hedges or walls at a relatively early stage in the park's development as breeding areas, to separate stock of different species, gender or age, or to grow a hay crop. It would be expected that as the remaining open launds were enclosed as farms in the period between 1635 and 1732, the new farms and farmland would display a relatively high degree of uniformity of layout and that the farms and their constituent fields might be given names reflecting their former location within a deer park. Figure 9 shows the area stretching eastwards from the farm that had become known as Park Gate Farm by 1649. To the west lay the extensive Thorpe Common so we must assume that the park to which it led – assuming that gate in Park Gate means entrance – lay to the east. The map shows the field pattern as depicted on maps made in 1802 by the Fairbanks for a 'General Survey of Kimberworth Park the property of the Earl of Effingham' and shows farms and, using different kinds of shading, fields which included the elements, *park, warren and plain* in the 1802 survey.[27] According to the 1802 survey the park extended from the western extremities of Kimberworth township, for almost

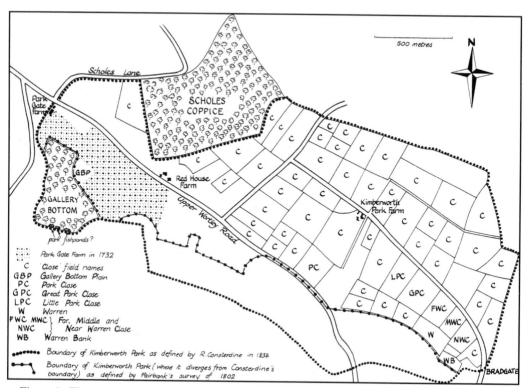

Figure 9. The medieval deer park at Kimberworth: the map and landscape evidence.

two miles at least in a south-easterly direction to Bradgate. The use of
the name 'Park Lane' for the southern part of Scholes Lane near the
cottage called Nether Fold in a deed of 1699[28] suggests that Scholes
Coppice, which at that date may have extended westwards right up to
the lane, may have been within the park. This issue is taken up again
below. The large size and relatively uniform layout of the fields in the
area north of Kimberworth Park Farm suggest that the park may have
extended to the boundary between Kimberworth and Greasbrough
townships.

    It will be noted that in the south-eastern corner of the park is a
group of five enclosures including in their names the element *warren*.
Much of this area was a dry, sunny, south and south-easterly facing
bank (parts of which still survive beside Wortley Road as a bracken-
strewn slope where not quarried or covered by housing). This type of
site was much favoured for rabbit warrens, which needed to be shel-
tered from prevailing winds and free from the risk of flooding.[29]

Another noteworthy feature of the area between Park Gate Farm and Bradgate is the remarkable lack of variety in the field names. In the Fairbank survey of 1802, out of 101 parcels of land (excluding housing plots, gardens and lanes) included in the survey in the area between Park Gate Farm and Bradgate, 55 were *closes* mostly concentrated in the area radiating from Kimberworth Park Farm (see Figure 9). 'Close' simply means enclosure and was a name used over a long period but one that is often associated with the late enclosure of previously unenclosed land such as common fields, commons, chases and parks. The concentration of such a large number of closes adjacent to each other suggests a planned process of enclosure over a relatively short period, exactly what would be expected when a park was deliberately and quickly dismantled and converted into farmland.

The total acreage of the 1802 survey was just under 618 acres. If Scholes Coppice and Gallery Bottom Wood are added, this makes 749 acres – just three acres more than in the 1671 rental book entry for that part of the park leased to Lionel Copley and Park Gate Farm.

The final piece of map evidence is a map of the Earl of Effingham's (Thundercliffe) Grange Estate, by R. Consterdine dated 1834.[30] The cartographer shows by a coloured line the 'Ancient boundary of Kimberworth Park'. It is significant because a test can be made: does the field name evidence cited above fall within Consterdine's boundary? The evidence is problematic because it is not known on what basis Consterdine was able to identify the boundary with such confidence. Consterdine's park boundary is shown by the bold dotted line on Figure 9. Park Gate Farm, Kimberworth Park Farm, the fields with the elements *plain, park and warren* and the many closes about Kimberworth Park Farm all fall within the park limits as defined by Consterdine. Moreover the extent of the park as defined by Consterdine is about 800 acres, not very much different from the acreage of 746 acres of the 1671 rental quoted earlier.

Three other features are worthy of note in relation to Consterdine's map. First, the map adds weight to the suggestion made earlier, based on field layout and the distribution of fields called closes, that the long northern boundary of the park coincided with the boundary between Greasbrough and Kimberworth townships. Figure 9 shows that according to Consterdine the park boundary coincided with the township boundary for almost a mile between Scholes Coppice and Bassingthorpe Spring.

Secondly, it may be significant that four lanes run alongside stretches of the park boundary. In places park boundaries must have followed existing features such as lanes and, as we have seen, parish

or township boundaries; in other cases if routes had been displaced by
the creation of a park it would be expected that they would be re-
established as near as possible to the original routes. There were
ancient lanes running south from Bradgate (Bradgate Lane); running
north from Bradgate (Low Lane), and running in a north- east–south-
west direction south of where Dropping Well Farmhouse was built. In
addition, as has already been pointed out, the southern part of Scholes
Lane was called Park Lane and, if we take the 1802 survey and
Consterdine's map at face value, it appears that Scholes Lane south
of Scholes village has been displaced by the presence of a 'no-go area'
– the deer park. For what other reason should the lane take a sudden
right-hand turn after leaving Scholes?

Thirdly, lying in a small narrow valley on the southern edge of
Gallery Bottom Wood are three silted-up ponds (see Figure 9). All
three ponds are shown on Consterdine's 1834 map, but only the lower
pond is shown on OS maps published between 1854–1956. The ponds
are not shown at all on the most recent OS maps. Stone-built sluices
are still in place in the dam walls (earthen banks) of the lowest two
ponds. The bottom pond is 30 metres long, the middle pond 38 metres
long, and the top pond, which is more difficult to define is more than
60 metres long but much narrower than the other two. The ponds lie
within the boundaries of the park as defined by Consterdine and to
the south are the remains of a stone wall. The ponds may be the park
fish ponds and the old stone wall the remains of the park wall.

There is one other puzzling feature of the park. Upper Wortley Road
(the modern A629) goes right through the the middle of the park,
however defined. In this section the road follows the top of an escarp-
ment for much of its course and is likely to be an ancient route in
existence before the deer park was created. It is believed to have been
an important salt route in the past.[31] So we must ask the question: what
would have become of this important transport route during the existence of the park? There is no obvious alternative route without a long
diversion. We have already seen that Robert de Vipont was accused of
exceeding the bounds of his free warren in 1276 and including within
it a portion of the king's highway. One possibility is that the road went
through the park and that walls prevented the escape of animals and
the entry of poachers. In his study of medieval parks published in
1988, Paul Stamper includes a map of Willey Park in Shropshire which
was crossed by the road from Much Wenlock to Broseley. Stamper
describes this as 'an unusual but not unique feature'.[32]

Conclusion

Deer parks were common features of the English medieval landscape. A minority have survived intact, substantial numbers have been converted into landscaped parks but many have disappeared following disparkment, with their features ploughed out by modern agriculture, destroyed by mining activity or buried under suburbia. In the case of Kimberworth Park all three of these developments have contributed to its disappearance from the landscape. Now, to the general observer, nothing is left – other than the name Kimberworth Park on a map denoting a suburban housing estate – of what must have been a magnificent sight at the height of its development with its deer and other park animals, its woods and launds, and the lord of the manor and his (or her) guests and a retinue of servants enjoying the sport. But with the fragmentary evidence well deployed, with the right questions, and informed speculation, we can still piece together a coherent, if incomplete, outline history of the park and its landscape. We know it was in existence by the beginning of the second quarter of the thirteenth century and that it continued to function as a deer park until well into the seventeenth century, until disparked and converted to farmland and also systematically exploited for its minerals. We also know, if we accept the historical evidence at face value, that at various times it contained red and fallow deer, and that the latter were still being hunted in the park in the 1630s. Moreover, if we accept the park boundaries as indicated on Fairbank's survey of 1802 and Consterdine's 1834 map on the grounds that they are generally confirmed by other historical evidence, then we know the park's location, its general extent, its shape and the positions of some of its component features (Gallery Bottom Wood, a nearby small *plain*, an area called the Warren (where the park rabbits were reared?), short stretches of the park pale in the form of stone walls, and possibly the park ponds).

Having said that, there is much more to learn about this particular park. Two unresolved questions will illustrate this. First, was Scholes Coppice once part of the park? Consterdine's boundary excludes it. However, the alignment of Scholes Lane, the nature of Consterdine's boundary (zig-zagging instead of the smooth curve it would have if it followed Scholes Lane and the boundary of Scholes Coppice itself) and comparison of the 1671 and 1802 acreages all suggest that the wood may have been a park woodland. I have found no documentary evidence of its existence before the 1680s which is very late for an old woodland. It may not have been named before that date because it was part of the extensive woodland – 300 acres in *c.* 1600 – within the park. A second puzzle is where was (or were) the park lodge(s)? It is interesting to speculate about whether Park Gate Farm (now Kirkstead Abbey Grange) fulfilled this role at some point in the park's history; or Red House Farm (which was located where the Tarmac offices are now sited next to Upper Wortley Road) which was on an eminence within the park.

References

1. The lower figure is proposed by L. M. Cantor and J. Hatherly in 'The Medieval Parks of England', *Geography*, Vol 64, 71–85 and in *The medieval parks of England: a gazeteer*, Loughborough, 1983, and the higher figure by Oliver Rackham in *Ancient Woodland: its history, vegetation and uses in England*, Edward Arnold, 1980, p. 191.
2. The information on Treeton is from J. Hunter, *Hallamshire* (1819), p. 492; that on Aston and Thrybergh is from J. Hunter, *South Yorkshire*, Vol 2 (1831), pp. 161 and 38 respectively; for Tankersley and Wortley, D. Hey, 'The parks at Tankersley and Wortley', *The Yorkshire Archaeological Journal* (YAJ), vol. 47, 1975, 109–119.
3. Hey, *YAJ*, p. 109.
4. Hey, *YAJ*, p. 111.
5. John Harrison, *An exact and perfect survey and view of the manor of Sheffield 1637*, transcribed and edited by J. G. Ronksley, Robert White & Co., Worksop, 1908, p. 3.
6. Daniel Defoe, *A Tour through the Whole Island of Great Britain*, Vol 3, Folio Society edition, 1983, p. 59.
7. John Evelyn, *Sylva or a Discourse of Forest-Trees*, 4th edition, 1706, p. 230.
8. Evelyn, *Sylva*, p. 230.
9. Harrison, *Survey* p. 152.
10. For a general discussion of the use of holly as a fodder crop see M. Spray, (1981), 'Holly as a Fodder in England', *Agricultural History Review*, Vol. 29, 97–110; and for information on the local use of holly in the past see M. Spray and D. J. Smith, (1977), 'The Rise and Fall of Holly in the Sheffield Region' in *Transactions of the Hunter Archaeological Society*, 10, 239–251.
11. T. Walter Hall (1937), ' Tankersley Old Hall and Fanshawe Gate' in *Incunabula of Sheffield History*, J. W. Northend Ltd., p. 181.
12. Harrison, *Survey*, p. 39.
13. J. Eastwood (1862), *History of the Parish of Ecclesfield*, Bell and Daldy, London, p. 360.
14. Wentworth Woodhouse Muniments, D 778–782, in Sheffield Archives.
15. See Melvyn Jones (1995), 'Rents, Remarks and Observations: The First Marquis of Rockingham's Rent Roll Book' in *Aspects of Rotherham: Discovering Local History*, Wharncliffe Publishing, pp. 113–128, and Tom William Beastall (1995), 'Sandbeck Hall and Park' also in *Aspects of Rotherham*, pp. 89–98.
16. J. Parker (Ed) (1921), *Feet of Fines for the County of York*, from 1218 to 1231, Yorkshire Archaeological Society, Record Series, Vol LXII, p. 93.
17. Hunter, *South Yorkshire*, Vol 2, p. 27.
18. John Guest (1879), *Historic Notices of Rotherham*, Robert White, pp. 583–84.
19. Hunter, *South Yorkshire*, vol 2, p. 27.
20. Hunter, *South Yorkshire*, vol 2, p. 28.
21. Calendar of the Talbot Correspondence in the *Catalogue of the Arundel Castle Manuscripts in Sheffield City Libraries* (1965), Sheffield City Council, p. 195, letter 2/86.
22. Calendar of Talbot Correspondence, p. 195, letter 2/87.
23. Calendar of the Talbot Correspondence, p. 216, letter 2/260.
24. Shrewsbury Papers in Lambeth Palace Library, ' A breife estimate of the [word indecipherable] springe woodes [word indecipherable] belonging to His Lo[rdship's] forges besides hedggerows and timb[e]r trees not included, Ms 698, Fol. 3.
25. Hunter, *South Yorkshire*, Vol 2, p. 303.
26. Arundel Castle Manuscripts in Sheffield Archives, ACM S131.
27. Fairbank Collection in Sheffield Archives, 'General Survey of Kimberworth Park the property of the Earl of Effingham', 1802; maps: Rot 45R and Rot 46 L, Field Book 91, pp. 31–43 and 75–86, Field Book 94, pp. 7, 11, 30–51, and Miscellaneous Book 382.

28. Bagshawe Collection in Sheffield Archives, 163.
29. J. Sheail (1971), *Rabbits and their history*, David & Charles, p. 39.
30. In Rotherham Central Library, Archives and Local Studies Section.
31. D. Hey (1980), *Packmen, Carriers and Packhorse Roads*, Leicester University Press, p. 158.
32. S. Stamper, 'Woods and Parks' in G. Astill and A. Grant, eds, (1988), *The Countryside of Medieval England*, Blackwell, p. 142.

Acknowledgements

I wish to thank Bob Warburton for drawing the final versions of Figures 4, 5, 6, 7 and 9.

9. ROTHERHAM'S ROLE AS A MARKET TOWN AND THE PROPOSED ROTHERHAM TO BAWTRY RAILWAY

by Tom William Beastall

FAMOUS FOR MANUFACTURING and heavy industry, Rotherham as a market centre for a productive and varied agricultural region is less well known. Near to the lower reaches of the Pennines with their pastoral farms, Rotherham is also within reach of agricultural communities to the east on the sandstones and shales of the coal measures, on the magnesian limestone belt running north to south through South Yorkshire and on the alluvial soils beside the rivers Torne and Idle beyond Tickhill and Bawtry.[1] The countryside is today still visible from every approach to Rotherham and, although they are no longer in private ownership in many cases, the town is surrounded by country estates whose tenant farmers have looked to it for centuries as a market centre for their produce and as a source of labour and as

Figure 1. Rotherham's medieval market place.

Figure 2. The Crofts Cattle Market, Rotherham. *Rotherham Central Library, Archives and Local Studies Section*

a supplier of essential implements and services.

Evidence of Rotherham's role as a market occurs in the early medieval period (Figure 1). Its church, mill, fair and market were recorded in pre-Conquest times.[2] In 1306 Edward I gave permission for a Friday market, a privilege confirmed in 1308 by Edward II who conferred it upon Robert de Waddesley. In 1315 the Abbot of Rufford was given the right to hold the market and fair.[3] A beast market near Wellgate existed in 1777 and in 1801 an Act of Parliament provided for improved market accommodation with the building of the Shambles near the Butter Cross.

During the Civil Wars of the seventeenth century Rotherham's importance as a consumer of malt for its brewers was evident.[4] When after the battle of Marston Moor in 1644 the Royalist cause in the North lay in ruins, Tickhill Castle surrendered and the town was occupied by Scottish Parliamentary troops. The soldiers led by their officers extracted cash from the unfortunate farmers of the town. They soon appear to have understood that a source of ready money lay in the malt trade with Rotherham and Doncaster brewers. Far from home, ill-disciplined and lacking regular pay, the troops threatened the forcible sale of confiscated malt confident, it seems, that there were ready local markets for it in nearby towns.

By the mid-nineteenth century Rotherham, with its growing population, was a notable market town. It had a weekly Monday market and every second Monday a fair for fat stock cattle, sheep and hogs. A market for butter and poultry on Fridays was followed by a Saturday vegetable market. Evidence before an enquiry suggested that on Friday nights 20 or 30 carriers' carts left Tickhill laden with vegetables for Rotherham.[5]

Cattle were displayed in pens in the south side of the town at the Crofts (Figure 2). Rotherham's market arrangements for cattle sales had been taken as a standard when, in the 1790s, 29 Lincolnshire gentlemen, graziers, farmers and land agents met in Lincoln's Guildhall to establish a fat stock cattle market. They decided that pens should be laid out and charged for at 'the same sum as is now paid at the like markets in Rotherham'.[6] It is significant too that in promoting improved road communication by the establishing of turnpikes some Lincolnshire initiatives such as the Wragby to Bawtry and the Stainton to Bawtry schemes had easy access to Rotherham as an objective.[7]

The droving of cattle and sheep from the farms of north and west Lincolnshire to the markets of South Yorkshire was important until well into the nineteenth century before railways killed the trade. By 1845 the lack of a railway through settlements to the east of Rotherham was thought to diminish their value. When William Downes, a land agent and valuer from Dedham in Essex surveyed and reported upon the Yorkshire estates of the 8th Earl of Scarbrough he made a number of observations on the need for a railway to revive the agriculture of the district. In the eye of this independent observer from a distant county the importance of 'railroads' and the value of Rotherham's market potential are clear.

> *The nearest Railroad is at present the North Midland at Maresborough [sic] or (Rotherham) but there is one projected which if carried will pass through the Estate at Stainton and Tickhill within two miles of the Mansion and which may prove in several ways beneficial to the Property.[8]*

He had no hesitation in placing Tickhill in relation to Rotherham rather than to Doncaster as a '. . . small Town in Yorkshire situate upon the Road from Rotherham to Bawtry'.

When he reported upon individual properties he wrote of the former Black Swan Inn in Sunderland Street, Tickhill:

> *This occupation comprises a Public House called the Scarboro' Arms with extensive stables and some valuable meadow land . . . The House or Inn affords comfortable accommodation but it is not the principal*

Inn in the place . . . The Trade of the House since the Introduction of Railroads and the withdrawal of droves of Stock from the Roads, has been decreased and as a Public House the Value has become lessened.

When in 1862 another survey was undertaken, this time for the 9th Earl of Scarbrough, by a Lincolnshire valuer, it was reported:

The trade of Tickhill appears to have gone down of late, in consequence of the establishing of Railways in the neighbourhood which have diverted Traffic formerly passing through Tickhill to a considerable extent in other Channels; it is not therefore an improving place . . .[9]

The Scarbrough Arms by then with stonework and tiles in bad repair was a victim of railway development having taken away, '. . . the Droves of cattle which used to pass thro' Tickhill, and by which it was mainly supported'.

Rotherham appeared early on the railway map of northern England. Well before either Sheffield or Doncaster had stations on a main line, Rotherham's Masborough station gave the town a place on the network connecting London with York. When the eastern counties lines from the capital to York were established, Retford, Doncaster and Bawtry became important points on the route to the North and Scotland from London. By 1870 the great age of railway expansion was over, leaving settlements to the east of Rotherham untouched by a branch line, let alone a main one. To the north and west railways followed the Dearne and Don valleys, to the east the Great Northern ran from Retford to Doncaster. To the south the Manchester, Sheffield and Lincolnshire company linked Sheffield with Worksop and Retford through Kiveton Park and Shireoaks. Thus a large area was left lying within a triangle of main lines. It is not surprising that a number of schemes were advanced to link Rotherham with Bawtry so bringing within cheaper travelling distance the markets of the town and the agricultural districts to the east (Figures 3 and 4).

Of all the schemes proposed, perhaps the Rotherham and Bawtry railway, 1880–81, illustrates best the aims and beliefs about the agricultural, geological and industrial potential of the district entertained by the promoters in the late nineteenth century.[10] Led by the 9th Earl of Scarbrough, twenty promoters launched the project. They represented landowners in the main though they had support from local industrialists. Viscount Lumley, Lord Scarbrough's heir who became the 10th Earl in 1884, was joined by the Reverend H. G. Jebb of Firbeck Hall, W. F. Hoyle of Hooton Levitt, Thomas Grey Fullerton

Figure 3. Bramley, one of the villages to the east of Rotherham, which retained its rural aspect well into the twentieth century. *Rotherham Central Library, Archives and Local Studies Section*

Figure 4. Whiston, although no more than three miles from Rotherham town centre, was by the time of the Rotherham–Bawtry Railway proposal, little affected by the heavy industry and urban expansion of the nearby town. *Rotherham Central Library, Archives and Local Studies Section*

of Thrybergh Hall, Captain R. A. Hall of Lindrick, Tickhill, B. H. Brooksbank of Sandrock, Tickhill, F. J. Leather of Tickhill Friary, the Reverend G. M. Athorpe of Dinnington Hall, Thomas Marrion of Thurcroft Hall, P. H. C. Chrimes of Plumtree, Bawtry, the Reverend Philip Schofield of Maltby Hall and W. H. Crossley of Maltby. Sheffield was represented by W. P. Milner of Meersbrook Hall. Messrs. Guest and Chrimes of Rotherham were also promoters, with Hugh Hoyland of Rotherham, George Eskholme, Wickersley's rector, the Reverend F. Freeman, S. Skinner of Throapham Manor House, and George C. Revill of Doncaster, a wool merchant, completing the list.

Bankers for the promoters were the Sheffield and Rotherham Joint Stock Banking Company and the London and Westminster Bank. Their engineer was R. E. Wilson of Delahay Street, Westminster, who had been the resident engineer for part of the Settle to Carlisle railway. Rodgers and Thompson were the promoters' agents in Rotherham and three brokers one each in London, Sheffield and Rotherham acted for them (see Figure 5).

As one would expect the promoters advanced confident claims for the district's potential once the railway was in operation.[11]

> *The proposed Railway is intended to supply a want of communication long felt to be desirable and to place the districts of Whiston, Wickersley, Maltby, Roche Abbey, Tickhill and Harworth, Plumtree, Bawtry and Scrooby and their rich mineral wealth, in direct communication with the systems of the Trunk lines of Railway on the east and west.*

The need for such communication had been felt for a long time but '. . . from one cause or another little has been done . . .' The present plan was presented for:

> *. . . the development of the local resources; and, perhaps, no district in the United Kingdom offers, within a length of 15 miles, so many distinct and natural sources of wealth.*

Figures 6–8 show details of the route of the proposed line.

The promoters pointed out the advantages of placing Sheffield with its population of 'about 400,000' in communication with the villages of the region. Rotherham's population had increased in some 30 years to 50,000. The line would help the cattle market there, adversely affected by the cattle plague thirteen years ago, to regain its status as '. . . the most important in the north midland counties'. As a great

ROTHERHAM AND BAWTRY RAILWAY.

CAPITAL £250,000, in 25,000 SHARES of £10 Each.
Deposit 10s. per Share.

Promoters.

The Right Honorable the EARL OF SCARBROUGH.

THE VISCOUNT LUMLEY.

REV. H. G. JEBB, J. P., Firbeck Hall, Tickhill.

W. F. HOYLE, Esq., Hooton Levitt, Maltby.

THOS. GREY FULLERTON, Esq., J.P., D.L., Thrybergh Hall, Rotherham.

CAPTAIN R. A. HALL, Lindrick House, Tickhill.

B. H. BROOKSBANK, Esq., J.P., Tickhill.

THE REV. G. M. ATHORPE, Dinnington Hall, Rotherham.

THOS. MARRION, Esq., Thurcroft Hall, Rotherham.

P. H. C. CHRIMES, Esq., Plumtree, Bawtry.

F. J. LEATHER, Esq., J.P., The Friary, Tickhill.

THE REV. PHILIP SCHOLFIELD, Maltby Hall.

W. H. CROSSLEY, Esq., Maltby.

W. P. MILNER, Esq., J.P., Meersbrook Hall, Sheffield.

MESSRS. GUEST & CHRIMES, Rotherham.

HUGH HOYLAND, Esq., Rotherham.

THE REV. F. FREEMAN, Rectory, Wickersley.

GEORGE ESKHOLME, Esq., Beechen-hurst, Rotherham.

S. SKINNER, Esq., Manor House, Throapham, Rotherham.

GEORGE C. REVILL, Esq., Doncaster.

Bankers.

THE SHEFFIELD AND ROTHERHAM JOINT STOCK BANKING COMPANY LIMITED.
(At Sheffield and Rotherham.)

AND THEIR LONDON AGENTS,

THE LONDON AND WESTMINSTER BANK LIMITED.
(41, Lothbury, London.)

Engineer.

MR. R. E. WILSON, C.E., 8, Delahay Street, Westminster, S.W.

Solicitors.

MESSRS. BIRCHAM & CO., 46, Parliament Street, Westminster, S.W.
MR. WALTER B. STYER, 5, Royal Exchange Avenue, London, E.C.

Agents in Rotherham.

MESSRS. RODGERS & THOMPSON, Rotherham and Sheffield.

Brokers.

MESSRS. MANNERS-SUTTON & GRAHAM, 7, Finch Lane, London.

MESSRS. F. E. & S. SMITH, George Street, Sheffield.

MESSRS. HART & MOSS, Rotherham.

Figure 5. Introduction to the proposed Rotherham to Bawtry Railway's prospectus.

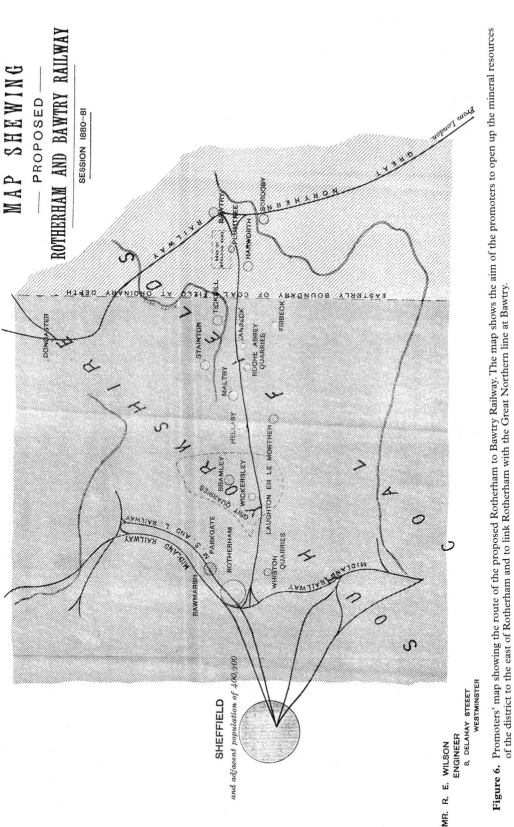

Figure 6. Promoters' map showing the route of the proposed Rotherham to Bawtry Railway. The map shows the aim of the promoters to open up the mineral resources of the district to the east of Rotherham and to link Rotherham with the Great Northern line at Bawtry.

centre of manufacture the town was almost built up to meet Sheffield as there was '. . . only one mile of road not built on at the extent of the two towns'. At Whiston a siding or tramway to the line would open up markets for the Rotherham Red sandstone found there in beds; a stone so useful for 'ornamental building'. Wickersley's famous grindstone or 'Wickersley Grit', valuable for the cutlery industry and exported to America would no longer carry heavy transit costs. Roche Abbey's stone quarries would, it was claimed, have supplied building material for the Houses of Parliament but for the cost of transport. The new line would lead to unlimited development of the magnesian limestone quarry there.[12]

Apart from freight traffic the health and recreation of thousands of town dwellers would be enhanced by better access to the open air of the Roche Abbey valley and the picturesque village of Maltby (Figure 9). Already visited by holidaymakers in their hundreds, a railway would open them up to thousands.

Probably there is in South Yorkshire no more attractive spot than the district of Maltby . . . many now resident in those towns [Rotherham and Sheffield] *will avail themselves of the opportunity that will be offered for acquiring land for building purposes in that district, and will reside there and travel to and from business daily.*

The vegetables of Tickhill and district as well as its farm, garden and dairy produce would reach Rotherham and Sheffield both quickly and cheaply. The best red moulding sand found between Tickhill and Bawtry would be brought within easy reach of customers in the iron industry. Coal was known to lie beneath the villages through which the line would pass. At present Rotherham's demand for timber was supplied more cheaply from woodlands at a greater distance than Maltby where there were extensive woods.

Minutes of evidence taken before a House of Commons Select Committee in March 1881 as well as correspondence to the Earl of Scarbrough's agent, H. V. Tippet, show support for the railway both within and outside Rotherham itself and an awareness of the significance of the town's influence on the villages lying east of it. Edwin Kelsey, a Rotherham house builder, Alderman member of the Market Committee and chairman of the Waterworks Company, thought that Wickersley stone, vegetable produce, livestock and timber would be conveyed on the line. James Clifford Morgan, a former Mayor and now an Alderman and chairman of the Sewage and Health Committee, believed, as a grindstone manufacturer, that the

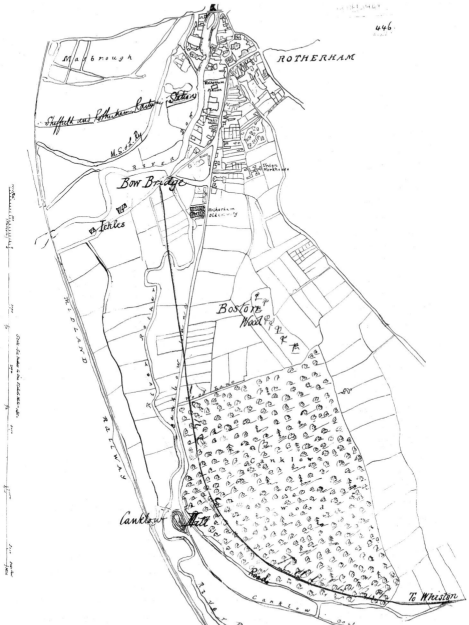

Figure 7. The proposed Rotherham to Bawtry Railway's entry to Rotherham through Canklow Wood.

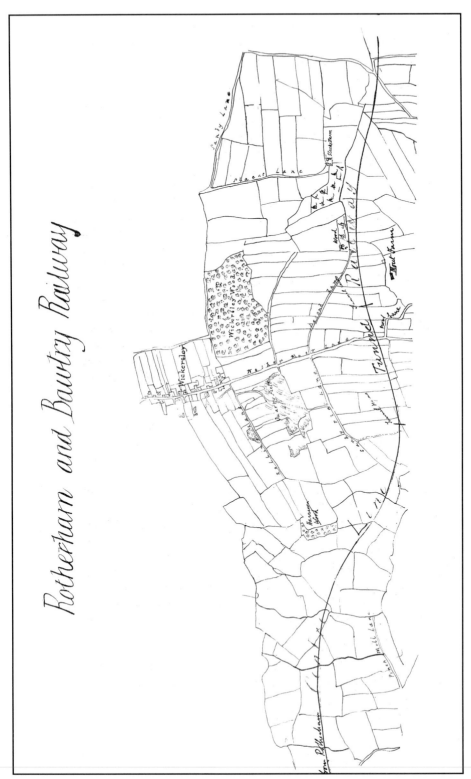

Figure 8. The route of the proposed Rotherham to Bawtry Railway near Wickersley showing its relationship to the quarries there.

Wickersley trade would benefit. He sent grindstones north to Newcastle and south to Devonshire and to many other parts of the Kingdom. Henry Saxton, Guardian of the Poor of Wickersley and for 25 years a quarrymaster, thought that the present output from the two quarries in the parish would increase from between 10,000 and 14,000 tons per annum to 20,000 tons and that the line would be worth £2,000 a year to the quarrymasters in selling hard stone for metal grinding and soft stone for saw grinding. George Neill, owner of steam rolling mills and Chairman of the Highways Committee, also supported the scheme.

Farmers gave evidence in favour. John Foster, tenant of Newhall Grange, farmed 300 acres, 200 arable and 100 pasture. He claimed to be familiar with the agriculture of Bramley, Laughton and Firbeck as he had lived 50 years in the locality. Potatoes yielded six tons to the acre, turnips fifteen tons an acre. Wheat, barley and fodder crops were all productive and would be carried by the railway. The district was hilly therefore '. . . you cannot put a very heavy load on a horse . . .' He estimated that from the three parishes about a quarter of all turnips, nearly all the barley, beans and wheat would be put on the rail. Much straw was sent by road to Rotherham at a cost of 5/- to 6/- a ton but the railway would take it for perhaps as little as 2/- a ton. Mr Fretwell Hoyle the owner of 500 acres 'opposite' Maltby at Hooton Levitt said, 'We are out of the world without it [the railway] at present'. There was a belief expressed by witnesses that general merchants, shopkeepers, house builders and coal merchants, especially those in Tickhill, would benefit as coal was relatively expensive in such rural areas at a distance from a railhead. Development of the eastern reaches of the coalfield lay some 25 years in the future and in the 1880s Shireoaks was the most easterly colliery.

Cheap transportation of guano, imported from Peru via Liverpool docks, would be possible on the railway while night soil from Rotherham and Sheffield would be brought to the agricultural districts beyond the towns. Most farmers, however, were interested in swift movement of cattle and sheep to Rotherham so avoiding having to drive stock to market two days in advance of sale during which they lost condition. William George Hagger an implement maker and iron merchant said that cattle from Bramley, Tickhill, Maltby, Roche Abbey and Braithwell would arrive in a more marketable state having been moved by rail.

On 17 March, 1881, J. D. Styring of Whiston Manor House, an auctioneer and tenant under Sir George Sitwell, was questioned about the railway's potential. He gave an illuminating answer about

Rotherham's cattle market.

What do you say about the Rotherham Cattle Market?

The Rotherham Cattle Market is one of the oldest cattle markets in Yorkshire, and ever since I can remember, it has been one of the best markets and it is one of the easiest to get to. I have one gentleman, Mr Marriott Hall, that farms something like 1,200 acres of land, and I have sold off on his farm £14,000 of the stock in three years, and to prove that Rotherham Cattle Market is the best market for making the best prices, he sent from Kiveton Park to Sheffield and through Sheffield to Rotherham Market (that is 6 miles further) on purpose that I might sell those cattle at Rotherham, and a great deal of the cattle that I sell comes from Tickhill and Maltby on the line of rails, and many of my customers complain that they cannot get their stock because they have to send them on the Saturday, and stock that leaves home a day or two before shewn in the market, deteriorates in value, and they do not shew so well, and on a Monday now, I should think, on an average I sell from £2,000 to £3,000 worth of stock.

At Whiston have you any of your population, your working men, who work at Rotherham?

Yes, I should say there are near upon half of the population at Whiston that work at Rotherham.

How do they get to their work now?

They have to walk backwards and forwards.

The farmers of Whiston, Ulley and Brampton, it was also argued, would use the line for the movement of artificial manures from Sheffield and district.

Michael Joseph Ellison the Duke of Norfolk's agent who had known the estates since 1834 believed that the 250 acres of Canklow Wood needed a railway to move timber to customers. Further east interest in the proposed line seemed positive. William Hallifield of Misterton near Gainsborough, a large cattle dealer and farmer-landowner, bought and sold stock in the Wakefield and Rotherham markets. He sent about 1,000 head a year and would have found a direct line to Rotherham an advantage as he could have moved the cattle within the day instead of having to put them on the line the night before. Thomas

Figure 9. Maltby at the end of the nineteenth century. *Rotherham Central Library, Archives and Local Studies Section*

Smith, a farmer of 1,000 acres at Gringley-on-the-Hill, wanted a line for Sheffield, Rotherham and other 'western markets' for manures, corn, market garden produce and livestock. The Chesterfield canal was of some use to him but it lacked regularity of service and he could not use it for moving livestock.

Another interested user would have been Thomas Cocking who ran two brickyards on 90 acres of land near Gringley-on-the-Hill. His customers were in Sheffield and Rotherham. He supplied them from the excellent Walkeringham claylands unequalled, he claimed, for brickmaking. His production of two million bricks a year would, he thought, increase to four millions with better transport facilities. He even hoped for an opening in the London brick market if the Rotherham to Bawtry line was linked with new railways then being proposed for the Trent ports. Nearby at Stockwith, George Willows, who farmed 500 acres, hoped such connections would speed his celery and potatoes to Rotherham.

The Rotherham to Bawtry promoters faced oppostion from the established railway companies. Resenting competition from another line they were in a strong position to thwart its development as it would depend upon them for running rights into main lines and stations. Locomotives and rolling stock would have to be leased or otherwise provided by the great companies as the proposed railway would not be able to finance its own. The Mayor and Corporation of Rotherham were concerned about the effect of the line on the town's water supply works, about a new bridge causing flooding on the low-lying Sheffield road and about the inadequate provision for passengers and sidings for manufacturers. There was apathy too from local potential shareholders some of whom though supporting the line in principle were reluctant to give financial backing. Mr T. G. Foljambe, MP, of Osberton Hall, Worksop, favoured the scheme but would not attach his name to the prospectus. The land agent for the Fox estate in Tickhill, W. E. Watson, approved of the scheme but would not appear as a promoter. Henry Jubb, JP, of Rotherham thought it 'would not answer' and A. K. Evans of Moorgate thought the line should run through Dalton, not Whiston. The vicar of Harworth would give no support and even the Rev. G. M. Athorpe of Dinnington only allowed his name to appear on the prospectus as long as he had nothing to pay![13]

Sadly, for its promoters, lack of capital began to affect the enterprise. A double track line, though desirable, would have strained the promoters' resources. By 1882–83 it was being suggested that a merger between the Rotherham to Bawtry Railway and plans for a line between Bawtry and Stockwith would benefit all concerned. On 25 April, 1882, the *Sheffield Telegraph* discussed railway links between Rotherham and Sheffield and the Trent ports. Stockwith had enough water as Goole for 'foreign trade'. Coal, iron and general merchandise could then go by rail and steamer directly to Rotterdam, Antwerp and the French Channel ports. Bringing the two projects together would, it was argued, improve the financial prospects of both within 'one purse'. The great companies remained unenthusiastic, however, and capital failed to materialise. A further problem was the depressed state of the coal trade and the belief then current that no more pits would be sunk.

Coal was to be the deciding factor in further railway development rather than the attraction of Rotherham as a market for agricultural produce. Nevertheless, local interest and pressure continued to keep Rotherham's role in mind. Demand for an east–west railway connection expressed itself in the remaining years of the century with the 1891 scheme for a Rotherham, Blyth and Sutton line with a Great Northern connection at Retford. In 1893 there was a plan to build a Retford, Rotherham and Barnsley railway, while 1900 saw the

Rotherham, Tinsley and Tickhill light railway proposal, followed in 1901 by the Rotherham and Laughton light railway. In 1902 there was a Sheffield, Rotherham and Bawtry proposal.

Given these speculations Lord Scarbrough's agent and J.Whittaker, a Tickhill landowner, wrote to parish councils in the district and to Tickhill Urban District Council warning them that the coal trade would dictate the direction of lines and that local effort was needed to advance the claims of passenger and agricultural traffic.[14] Development of the coalfield was once again profitable. On 8 June, 1900, the *Doncaster Chronicle* reported a meeting at the Guildhall about light railways near Tickhill where the need for more land to be put under market garden crops was expressed with the hope that any new railway would take account of such a demand. Although agriculture was at last recovering from the collapse of cereal prices experienced in the 1870s and 1880s, farmers were looking to dairying and market gardening to keep their farms viable and so good, swift transport to urban centres like Rotherham figured in their calculations.

Even so when the South Yorkshire Joint Railway was built, the Great Central, the Great Northern, the Lancashire and Yorkshire, the Midland and the North Eastern companies saw to it that it had a north-east to south-west orientation designed to move coal to customers through the Humber ports in one direction and to industrialists in the north Midlands in the other. The needs of the agricultural interest were given little consideration though the line was used for livestock and bulk crops like turnips and sugar beet.

Rotherham's markets were to be supplied increasingly along the routes of the old Bawtry to Tinsley turnpike road and the Barnby Moor to Rotherham turnpike using lorries as the internal combustion engine brought about a revolution in road haulage in the second decade of this century.

Although the railway schemes to link Rotheram to the villages on its eastern side came to nothing, the evidence left behind by their promoters' efforts affords the historian with a view of the district as seen by local people at the time. That so many schemes were put forward before the internal combustion engine re-established the importance of road transport in the local economy at least illustrates Rotherham's impact on those who, living in nearby villages, looked to it as a source of income and economic advantage.

Notes and References

1. Derek Holland, *Changing Landscapes in South Yorkshire*, 1980, has a perceptive description and analysis of the four topographical regions of the county.
2. John Guest, *Historic Notices of Rotherham*, 1879, p. 26 and p. 33 and George Gummer, *Reminiscences of Rotherham*, 1927.
3. *Yorkshire Archaeological Journal*, Vol 13, p. 220 and Guest, p. 411.
4. Tom W. Beastall, *Tickhill: Portrait of An English Country Town*, 1995, p. 102.
5. *Collections for the History of Tickhill II*, 1973, University of Sheffield, p. 77.
6. Lincolnshire Library, Lincoln, 5020.
7. Tom W. Beastall, *Agricultural Revolution in Lincolnshire*, 1978, pp. 100 and 147.
8. Lumley Mss. EMS/41/1.
9. Lumley Mss, EMS/45.
10. Lumley Mss, Box 2, 58, 12.
11. Lumley Mss, Rotherham and Bawtry Railway Prospectus and evidence before the Select Committee of the House of Commons, 1881.
12. Lumley Mss, Box 2, Letter from the Earl of Scarbrough to Lord Colville, Chairman of the Great Northern Railway Company, 1883.
13. Lumley Mss, Box 2. Correspondence to and from H. V. Tippet, the land agent at Sandbeck.
14. Lumley Mss, Box 2. Correspondence, S. Coetmore Jones, the estate agent at Sandbeck, press cuttings and miscellaneous material relating to proposed railways 1891–1902.

Acknowledgements

I am indebted to the Earl of Scarbrough for access to the Lumley archives at Sandbeck, for permission to quote from them and to reproduce plans of the route of the Rotherham to Bawtry railway. My thanks are offered to Kay Casey of the Sandbeck estate office whose helpfulness to research workers is appreciated by all who study there. Thanks are due to Alice Rodgers for her assistance and for many useful conversations about the railway papers at Sandbeck and to Tony Munford and his staff in the Rotherham Central Library, Archives and Local Studies Section.

9. Some Dovecote Sites in the Rotherham Area

by Brian Elliott

Please note that all sites are marked on the distribution map (Figure 1) and listed in the gazetteer towards the end of the study.

FOR ANYONE INTERESTED in dovecotes[1] a visit to the pleasant village of Letwell, about nine miles (14km) SSE of Rotherham, is a good place to start. By calling at South Farm, Barker Hades Road, access can be gained to a nearby field containing a splendid showpiece example (Figures 2.1 to 2.4). Built of hand-made brick, with a Magnesian Limestone base and door surround, its octagonal fabric and tiled hipped roof has a central lantern, cupola or louvred *glover* (allowing access for the birds) which in turn supports an attractive weather vane in the form of a pigeon. The latter is an example of modern local craftsmanship, indeed the entire building was carefully

Figure 1.   Distribution of dovecote sites referred to in the text.

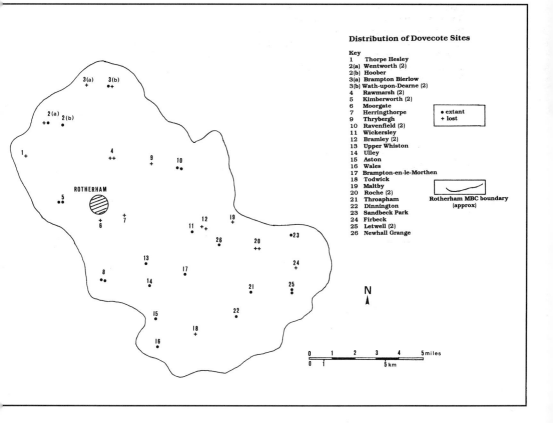

Distribution of Dovecote Sites

Key
1   Thorpe Hesley
2(a) Wentworth (2)
2(b) Hoober
3(a) Brampton Bierlow
3(b) Wath-upon-Dearne (2)
4   Rawmarsh (2)
5   Kimberworth (2)
6   Moorgate
7   Herringthorpe
9   Thrybergh
10   Ravenfield (2)
11   Wickersley
12   Bramley (2)
13   Upper Whiston
14   Ulley
15   Aston
16   Wales
17   Brampton-en-le-Morthen
18   Todwick
19   Maltby
20   Roche (2)
21   Throapham
22   Dinnington
23   Sandbeck Park
24   Firbeck
25   Letwell (2)
26   Newhall Grange

● extant
+ lost

Rotherham MBC boundary (approx)

ROTHERHAM

N

0   1   2   3   4   5 miles
0   1   5 km

restored by villagers in 1984, with assistance from the Council for the Protection of Rural England. Today the dovecote serves as a proud village logo. A stone 'rat ledge' encloses the middle part of the exterior walls like a neat trouser belt. String-courses, often architecturally pleasing, were also used for combating vermin. The ability of rats to scale the smoothest of walls was attested by several farmers interviewed in this study. Above the ledge, on each face, there are arched recesses, several having ventilation holes.

Inside, there is a central post with a revolving ladder or *potence* (Figure 2.5), an ingenious device used in round and polygonal dovecotes which allowed relatively easy and efficient access to the eggs and young birds. The nest boxes, originally made from red clay, are arranged in three sections (5 per row & 15 rows deep) on each complete face (Figure 2.6). Allowing for the doorway and ventilation areas there are about 470, a relatively modest number compared with other examples. Nevertheless, when parent birds were present – with fledglings or *squabs* as they were called – the capacity could approach a thousand.

The Letwell dovecote, probably a late eighteenth century replacement of an earlier example, is an architectural feature as well as being of utilitarian purpose. It may have been associated with either the Knight family of Langold who held the manors of Letwell and Firbeck, keen and fashionable builders, or the Staniforths of Firbeck who had marriage links with the Knights. Dovecotes at Firbeck Hall and Letwell are mentioned in a deed recording the sale of Firbeck to Jonathan Staniforth, in March 1676/77.[2]

Figure 2.1. Letwell's restored octagonal dovecote stands in a field at South Farm, and can be viewed by visitors – a superb example of what can be achieved where a rural community is proud of its historic buildings.

Figure 2.2. Letwell: detail of the louvred cupola or glover with access holes for the birds – and fine pigeon weather vane.

Figure 2.3. Letwell: detail of commemorative plaque on the entrance door, awarded to the village by the Council for the Protection of Rural England.

Figure 2.4. Letwell is rightly proud of its showpiece dovecote which is portrayed in a very attractive village sign.

Figure 2.5. The revolving potence with attached ladder at Letwell was a traditional device that enabled efficient and effective access for collecting both squabs and eggs. It is the only surviving example in the area.

Figure 2.6. Detail of the interior of Letwell dovecote showing restored nest boxes, Notice the continuous protruding tile alighting ledges under the middle niches and linear pattern of the nest holes.

Figure 2.1.

Figure 2.2.

Figure 2.5.

THIS·OTHER·EDEN
THIS·BLESSED·PLOT
CPRE
DEMI·PARADISE
THIS ENGLAND

MERIT AWARD

Figure 2.3.

Figure 2.6.

Figure 2.4.

LETWELL

Nearer to Rotherham, another relatively accessible and reasonably well-preserved pigeon house can be seen in the former grounds of the seventeenth century Kimberworth Hall or Manor House. Probably contemporary with the hall (1694), it is a small two-storey square structure, misleadingly so from the higher level of the hall where access into the building is via four steps and a typically low door with a dressed stone surround (Figures 3.1 to 3.3). Of local rubble Coal Measure Sandstone, with a stone slate roof, access for the birds was via two first floor openings, one at the front, now converted to a window, and another (now blocked) on the right side. Both have typical 'alighting ledges', providing a platform for the birds to land prior to entering the interior. The wooden lantern which has three pigeon holes at its base is a replacement of an earlier glover. Inside the compact interior which measures approximately 4 x 4 metres square and has a timber-framed roof structure (Figure 3.6), there are about 320 L-shaped stone nesting holes (Figures 3.4 and 3.5), adjacent pairs being served with crude stone alighting ledges built into the stone walls, the earliest in the area.

Figure 3.1. The Kimberworth Hall dovecote with the Manor House in the background. The large ground floor opening, with boarded doors, is a later addition. Remains of rendered plaster are visible on the sandstone walls.

Figure 3.2. Kimberworth Hall: At higher ground level a flight of four steps to a typically low doorway entrance into the compact square interior. Notice the wooden glover and blocked opening at right gable with alighting ledge still in place.

Figure 3.3. Kimberworth Hall: detail of 'security' doorway – low and narrow, limiting possible egress of the birds – and in sight of the main house in case of unwelcome visitors. The louvred door is also an interesting feature.

Figure 3.4. Kimberworth Hall: dovecote interior: part of the left gable wall showing arrangement of nest boxes with crude stone ledges inserted as perches for the birds.

Figure 3.5. Kimberworth Hall dovecote interior: detail of L-shaped stone nest holes. Nesting material still present in many of them.

Figure 3.6. Kimberworth Hall dovecote interior: view looking up into the central roof timbers into the glover.

Figure 3.1.

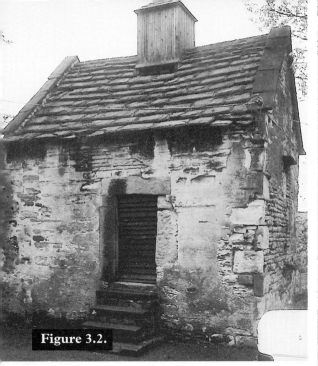

Figure 3.2.

Figure 3.3.

Figure 3.4.

Figure 3.6.

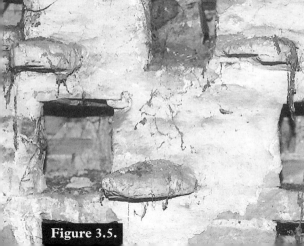

Figure 3.5.

Such examples are fairly well-known and are listed buildings but there are others that few of us recognise. Less than 400 metres from Kimberworth Manor, between the *Green Dragon* public house and St Thomas's Church Hall are the former buildings of Old Hall Farm. Above the principal range is the remains of what would have been a most elegant dovecote, complete with palladian 'window' (Figures 4.1 and 4.2).

Figure 4.1. 'Dovecote Range', Old Hall Farm, Kimberworth.

Figure 4.2. Detail of dovecote, Old Hall Farm, Kimberworth showing Palladian window (central part blocked with brick) which has louvred side lights and stone alighting ledge. Notice the rat course on right, fol-lowing the apex of the adjoining range

This study attempts to record extant and some lost examples set within the present Rotherham MBC area but it is an enthusiastic rather than an exhaustive survey. More sites will exist and further documentary research will throw up numerous other locations. The great joy of such work is locating hitherto 'undiscovered' dovecotes, especially those at more inaccessible farmstead locations or 'hidden' among former farm buildings. If we return to Letwell, just across the road from 'the dovecote', an early nineteenth century square example – with an attractive hipped pantile roof – towers over the Magnesian Limestone barn of North Farm (Figure 5), but is very much a forgotten feature. By this time many farmsteads had a dovecote, usually within a dual or multi-purpose building.

Figure 5.   Dovecote over former barn at North Farm, Letwell. The shelter shed to the ground floor has clearly been added later.

Dovecotes are often regarded as relatively minor vernacular buildings, though it is pleasing that a short chapter is devoted to them in the 1987 edition of R. W. Brunskill's *Traditional Farm Buildings of Britain*.[3] They are in fact fascinating structures, especially when their interiors are reasonably intact. To view the inside of a good 'new' example is a lasting experience. Even for better known examples there are always some features of interest as rarely are two dovecotes the same.

Rotherham is a particularly useful sample area of study because of the variety of local geology – from the undulating Coal Measure Sandstones of the North and West and the striking Magnesian Limestone belt that breaks the central landscape to the low lying brick and clay-making Marls in the South and East of the area – providing contrasting building materials, as we have already seen by reference to Letwell and Kimberworth.

The Rotherham area also has a variety of dovecote types – from simple holes in walls to distinctive free-standing single cell examples. In between there is a variety of forms where the keeping of pigeons was combined with other farm or ornamental functions. Although most of the surviving dovecotes in the area date from the Georgian era, some earlier, lost examples can be identified in documents.

Until relatively recently dovecotes have been a somewhat neglected and undervalued source of study.[4] The writer's interest began more than two decades ago when visits were made to a number of Barnsley and Wakefield area examples. Obtaining a rare copy of Arthur Cooke's *A Book of Dovecotes*, published in November 1920 (T. N. Foulis), only confirmed the fact that there was great scope for local fieldwork. Cooke's Yorkshire chapter has less than ten pages of text and no South Yorkshire examples are mentioned – although the pigeon holes in the tower of the Victorian church at Monk Bretton are cited in another chapter.[5] Ironically, an interesting late eighteenth century dovecote exists in the village and the base of a fine round medieval example was located at Monk Bretton Priory.[6] However, despite such limitations (which Cooke was right to acknowledge) – the book remains a classic study. In recent years the research, promotion and publications of enthusiasts such as Alan Whitworth and members of the Yorkshire Dovecote Society have helped to give a more balanced view of our region in relation to other parts of the country.[7] Clearly, much more research and recording work needs to be done, and quite quickly in view of the number of buildings at risk through deterioration, demolition and conversion.

Pigeons were once an integral part of the rural economy, through the privileged individuals and religious communities allowed to keep them. The birds' dung was a potent form of manure and had a history of use in the making of gunpowder, medicines and for tanning. Pigeons were used for falconry and, much later, for shooting. To sleep on a pillow of pigeon feathers was even believed to promote longevity. But the main purpose of keeping pigeons was to provide fresh food, including eggs, especially in the winter and spring when alternative sources of meat were scarce and monotonous, the four to six week old squabs in particular being regarded as a tasty addition to the diet.

However, the pigeon house was also a very convenient larder for unexpected guests and birds could be culled 'on demand' throughout the year. In 1552 an Essex dovecote provided 1,080 birds for the table between Easter and Michaelmas, the heaviest 'drawing' of 'three score pair' being taken in August.[8]

In medieval times the right to keep pigeons was limited to barons, abbots and manorial lords; and later extended to the clergy. By the seventeenth century feudal restrictions had waned and smaller landlords built dovecotes. It has been estimated that there were 26,000 dovecotes in England, about one or two per parish. But the distribution obviously varied from region to region and this oft-quoted figure, probably conservative, serves only as a very rough guide.[9]

Although dovecote building continued to take place throughout the eighteenth century changes in agricultural practice as well as fashion offset the demand for the birds. Yet it was this period when most of our extant dovecotes were made, hand in hand with waves of interest in architecture. The local landowner or smaller tenant farmer could express good taste in a relatively cheap project that still had some functional use. Dovecotes therefore were often the most graceful and decorative of farmstead buildings. Their recent listing, as with other vernacular buildings – either singly or for group value – has certainly helped to combat complete demolition but, Letwell apart, a wider appreciation is urgently needed if what remains of these fascinating buildings are to survive as meaningful, interpretative features of our local landscape.

Nationwide there has been a trend to convert dovecotes into dwellings and the Rotherham area is no exception. In fact the earliest example, at Herringthorpe Hall, now demolished, appears to have been used as a cottage featured in picture postcards from about 1910 (Figure 6). When executed 'sympathetically', especially to fast deteriorating examples, owners, public and planning authorities appear satisfied. Yet the inevitable obliteration and reshaping of exteriors – and especially the destruction of unique interiors – is a desperately sad state of affairs. In the course of research for this article only eight dovecotes with reasonably intact interiors have been found, and one of the most significant is undergoing conversion. Others are at risk. The demise of the dovecote is well-illustrated by reference to several local examples, though there are also instances of good practice by local owners, architects and builders. The relatively remote freestanding dovecote at Vessey Close Farm, Hardwick, near Aston-cum-Aughton (Figures 7.1 & 7.2) dates from the early to mid-eighteenth century. Made of coursed dressed sandstone, with a stone

Figure 6. Herringthorpe Hall dovecote, from an old picture postcard, converted into a cottage but the glover remains a distinctive roof-top feature; also notice the continuous rat course. *Rotherham Archives & Local Studies Photographic Collection (ref 2704)*

Figure 7.1. The Vessey Close Farm dovecote at Hardwick, near Aston.

Figure 7.2. (right) Vessey Close Farm dovecote: detail of opening in right gable showing displaced mullion, alighting ledge, and part of rat course; two iron 'tangs', anti-poaching rods, are still in place guarding the entrance.

slate roof, it has an attractive though deteriorating exterior. The original doorway was located at the base of the right gable, now blocked and hidden within a later outbuilding whilst bird access was via a two-light mullioned window (the mullion now displaced). Under the window, which has a wider than usual alighting ledge, two (of four) arrow-headed anti-poaching spikes or *tangs* remain in place. The exterior also has a distinctive rat course running around the upper walls. Inside, the lower half of the two-cell structure has about 100 nest boxes, without ledges or perches, arranged linear fashion and set within a brick lining. Above, also in brick, there are no nest boxes but instead, and somewhat unusually, a series of protruding brick ledges, used as perches by the entering birds. Although listed, this interesting building is clearly at risk having little use by the present owner.

Yet disused dovecotes are appreciated. Little more than a mile to the south of Hardwick – at *The Beeches* – is a small late eighteenth

Figure 8.1. (Top)   The attractive stone and brick dovecote at *The Beeches*, Wales. The stable range to the right is a later addition.

Figure 8.2. (Right)   The front of the Wales dovecote. The blocked central doorway can be clearly seen. Elegant hipped and pantile roof, hand-made red brick first floor with arched boarded opening with entrance holes for the birds.

Figure 8.3. (Below)   The Wales Dovecote: detail of arched opening with dual-purpose alighting ledge/rat course.

century stone and brick dovecote, once free-standing, with a hipped, pantile roof and stone ridges (Figures 8.1 to 8.3). It has a blocked central doorway, replaced (*c*.19C ?) by an entrance with an ashlar surround. As at Hardwick there is a continuous ledge to deter vermin which doubles as an alighting ledge under the central opening. The latter has ten pigeon holes in wooden boarding and is an attractive feature. The ground floor may have been used for hens or as a store but, via an open trapdoor, about 320 brick nest boxes are visible. Listed 'for group value', it is indeed a very pleasing architectural asset in the grounds of the house and regarded as such by the present owner.

The dovecote once associated with Moat Farm, near Wickersley, on a medieval site, is one of the most interesting in the Rotherham area (Figures 9.1 to 9.4). Built over a two-bay cartshed and dating from about 1780, the first floor has a double round-arched blind arcade with a door and window with projecting sill on the north side, both recently unblocked. Above the door is a single row of five pigeon holes in a wooden board but at the apex of the stone slate roof once stood a graceful glover, protected by iron spikes, glazed

Figure 9.1.

Figure 9.1. Moat Farm dovecote: front elevation in 1972. *Alan Whitworth, Yorkshire Dovecote Society*

Figure 9.2. Moat Farm dovecote: Front elevation in May, 1996.

Figure 9.3. Moat Farm dovecote: Interior detail showing arrangement of nest boxes and perches. *Rotherham MBC, Department of Planning*

Figure 9.4. Moat Farm dovecote: interior detail showing timber construction of mud and lath nest boxes. *Alan Whitworth, Yorkshire Dovecote Society*

Figure 9.2.

Figure 9.3.

Figure 9.4.

with 60 (15 per side) small panes and having a lead roof and elegant carved oak ball finial. Whoever added this had an eye for architecture. Inside, the upper floor (measuring *c.* 17 feet square) incorporated over 600 nest boxes of mud/plaster and wood lath construction with distinctive wooden perches strategically arranged to the lower right of each niche. Such composition appears to be quite unusual for the north of England but, as we shall see, there may have been a highly localised fashion for this style, almost as though a jobbing craftsman had moved from one site to several others in close proximity to each other. The exterior of the building began to deteriorate several years ago and the roof was removed, therefore exposing the interior to the weather. Conversion work had just begun prior to the sale to the present owner who, at the time of writing, has been granted planning permission for the building to be converted into a dwelling. Fortunately the owner appreciates the value of retaining the general character of the dovecote, including restoration of the roof and its glover, though the now delisted nest boxes are in too poor a state to be saved.

Two dovecotes, one sited just four miles to the north of Wickersley – at Old Ravenfield – and the other three miles to the south at Brampton-en-le Morthen also had plaster and lath nest boxes but both interiors are now gone. The Ravenfield example (Figures 10.1 to 10.4) was associated with Oak House/Farm which has a 1682 date-stone but was probably altered on several occasions, beginning in the eighteenth century. Architectural details suggest that the building of the dovecote, which has a centrally placed circular window near the eaves of the east face, and an attractive arched opening, with protruding ledges (for bird access) high on the south side, was probably contemporaneous with early alterations to the farmhouse. Of three storeys, the brick-lined middle and top spaces were used for accommodating the birds. Very unusually, extra capacity was catered for by the cramming of central partitions consisting of what appear to be identical plaster and lath boxes as per Wickersley. There appear to have been well over 1000 nest boxes. All the interior has now gone as the building, apparently in an otherwise deteriorating condition, was converted into a dwelling a few years ago. Fortunately photographs were taken at the time of conversion. Interestingly, the building, and other renovated properties, are reached by a back lane which has been known as Dovecote Lane for at least 60 years. Today, assuming that the few remaining Moat Farm nest boxes will soon go, the only remaining plaster and lath nest boxes are at a private location in an octagonal dovecote just outside the RMBC area.

Figure 10.1 Oak House (facing) and dovecote (with circular window), March 1996 (*Author*) & prior to conversion *c.* 1986 (*T Lynskey*).

Figure 10.2. Oak House dovecote ('Rear' view), 1996 & 'Dovecote Lane' sign.

Figure 10.3. Oak House dovecote: Interior detail prior to conversion showing timber roof, brick-lined wall and plaster & lath nest boxes. *T Lynskey*

Figure 10.4. Oak House dovecote: detail of plaster and lath nest boxes during demolition *T Lynskey*

Figure 11.1. Ravenfield Hall dovecote is a striking central feature of this former range of farm buildings.

Figure 11.2. Ravenfield Hall dovecote: interior showing detail of brick nest boxes and alighting ledges still to be seen in the loft of the converted building.

Returning to Ravenfield, a range of listed farm buildings, formerly belonging to Ravenfield Hall, only 100 metres from stables designed by the popular Yorkshire architect, John Carr, includes an integral dovecote, changed to residential use about eight years ago (Figure 11.1). Here the conversion – by an architect/builder with experience of local period properties – has retained some or all of the brick nest boxes (Figure 11.2) which now form the loft of the central projecting bay. It is a feature that is of interest to the present, and hopefully future owners since it was the very reason why the building was created. There are several similar 'courtyard' examples in the Rotherham area, where the dovecote formed a central feature or focus for a 'model farm'; or was placed over an entrance archway. This trend was part of the general process of 'agricultural improvement' of the late eighteenth century when landowners were encouraged to improve their farm buildings or 'offices'. Some employed architects and, with an eye on neighbours (or from the benefit of travel) selected from pattern books a suitable style. Such schemes took place when the traditional purpose of keeping of pigeons overlapped with decoration and ornamentation. A few score of specially bred doves cooing in one's architect-designed courtyard was more a civilised prospect than an economic necessity.

As we have seen, pigeons were subject to pilfering and theft, especially during the nineteenth century when shooting parties required – and were prepared to pay for (sometimes no questions asked) – a few score birds. A local case of cunning poaching – at Maltby – was reported in 1849, the owner being left in a distraught condition:

About the middle of last week [c. 7.1.1849], *some thieves of expert character, entered the farming premises of Mr. Jonathan Hazlehurst of Maltby . . . They* [the thieves] *removed a ladder to the pigeon house, and having ascended it picked the lock, and removed 200 pigeons therefrom, without molestation, leaving the owner 5 as a sample. So clean was the work performed, that Mr. Hazlehurst could perceive no loose feathers about the yard the following morning.*[10]

The report advised 'our agricultural friends' to be vigilant, 'as pigeon shooting is now in its zenith', and thieves could expect to obtain one shilling for each bird.

The following illustrated **gazetteer** provides brief details of all recorded sites. *Please note most are private property and permission is required prior to any visit.*

Kirkstead Abbey Grange: from the *Sheffield and Rotherham Independent,* 1887. *Melvyn Jones*

1. Thorpe Hesley
Kirkstead Abbey Grange

A series of 20–22 square pigeon holes arranged in linear fashion were extant in the late nineteenth century. The birds may have entered an enclosed loft or cavity. Possibly late-medieval and if so a very interesting early site associated with monastic ownership. *Lost.*[11]

2(a). Wentworth
Home Farm

Combination farm building, part of former model farm of Wentworth Estate. Dovecote over shelter shed (openings now blocked). Dressed sandstone with hipped Welsh slate roof. Single storey bays on either side of showpiece centre. Boarded opening served as original bird access; underneath a small timber box with five arched pigeon holes (modern). Inside, nest boxes apparently intact, access via trap door to first floor. Mid-nineteenth century, one of last fashionable examples in the area. Ground floor used as a workshop for Wentworth Pine Furniture. *Listed.*

Dovecote at Home Farm, Wentworth.

Wentworth Woodhouse

A rectangular dovecote is shown on a sketch by Samuel Buck c.1720. *Lost.*[12]

2(b). Hoober

Hoober Hill Farm (Wentworth Estate).
Combination farm building, three-storey, upper projecting over courtyard, stabling below. Local sandstone rubble with brick on N upper storey. Centrally-placed square opening under eaves on E face and on W face (now blocked), both with alighting ledge, at the W gable end almost gone. Interior not inspected but appears to have been brick-lined. Good example of an unpretentious farm dovecote of mid-eighteenth/early nineteenth century date. *Disused.*

Dovecote at Hoober Hill Farm.

3(a). Brampton Bierlow

The field-name Dovecote Ing (a wet or marshy area) occurs in 1773. *Lost.*[13]

3(b). Wath-upon-Dearne
Brook Farm.

Dovecote over former cow house. Probably early eighteenth century but interior roof lines suggest that the structure was heightened on two later occasions. A tall, eyecatching part of a small but prestigious range of farm buildings. Hipped stone roof, small elegant Palladian window to first floor. Central door, originally boarded. Interior housed *c.* 400 nest boxes, with alighting ledges, built into brick-lined first-floor walls. Converted into a dwelling mid-1980s as part of Brook Farm Mews. Lost interior fortunately photographed by Alex Fleming. *Listed.*

Manor House ?

Earliest medieval reference, 1307, to a dovecote in RMBC area; owned by the late William Fleming who held the manor of Wath: 'A dovecote worth 2s, therefore so little because it is poor country'. *Lost.*[14]

Dovecote at Brook Farm, Wath: detail showing interior nest boxes 1985.
Alex Fleming

4. Rawmarsh
Rectory

A dovecote 'belonging to the Parsonage of Rawmarsh' was erected in 1749 by Christopher Stephenson, rector and 'cost upwards of thirty pounds'. *Lost.*[15]

Rawmarsh Hall

An elegant three-storey free-standing rectangular dovecote with glover, sited near the house, is shown on Samuel Buck's drawing of *c.* 1720. Possibly 17th century. *Lost.*[16]

5. Kimberworth
Kimberworth Hall/Manor House

Free-standing square dovecote (see main text) formerly belonging to the Hall. Late 17th century. Interior intact. Now owned by Manor Barn Inn. *Listed.*

Old Hall Farm

High Street. Towers over farm building (see text). Sandstone. Palladian window. Mid to late eighteenth century. Interior not inspected. *Disused.*

6. Moorgate
Moorgate Hall

Faint outline of what appears to be a free standing dovecote on Buck's sketch of *c.* 1720. Associated with the Tooker family. *Lost.*[17]

7. Herringthorpe
Herringthorpe Hall

Free-standing, with glover, converted to cottage as per Edwardian and later picture postcards (see text) when owned by Pashley family (earlier Jubbs). Shown (but not identified) on a sale plan of 1905 but referred to as 'quaint old pigeon house'.[18] Sandstone rubble with quoins, 2/3 storeys. Square plan with access stairs to rear. Early eighteenth century? After some debate the Hall was demolished in *c.* 1977. *Lost.*

8. Treeton
Spa Well Farm

Interesting unpretentious dovecote in coursed dressed sandstone, incorporated in three-storey farm

Dovecote at Spa Well Farm, Treeton. The right side of the building has been added later.

building, ground floor used as a harness room with integral fireplace & chimney. Later addition to farmhouse side; may originally have been free-standing. Square opening, with ledge, on gable end. Early nineteenth century? Wooden nest boxes removed 'many years ago' by present owner. 'Paddy' Logan, a pigeon fancier, apparently used the building in late Victorian period. *Disused.*

Old Flatts Farm

Good late example of a pigeon loft or 'pigeon hoile' in small enclosed space over late 19th century stable range. Coursed dressed sandstone. Probably built by present farmer's grandfather. Inside a small number of large wooden nest boxes, partitioned, with wide open entrances. Single square window to loft, modern oblong opening for birds, outer stone ledge removed. Used by occasional visiting pigeon!

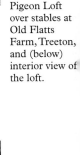

Pigeon Loft over stables at Old Flatts Farm, Treeton, and (below) interior view of the loft.

9. Thrybergh

Medieval place-name reference to 'the Dovearne' (v. dufe, aerarn 'house'); a field-name, 'Dovecote Close' occurs in 1543. *Lost.*[19]

10. Old Ravenfield

Oak House (Main Street/Dovecote Lane)
Very interesting 18th century dovecote (see text). Brick-lined interior used for nest boxes with later plaster and lath boxes providing further accommodation for the birds. Now converted to a private dwelling. May have been listed for group value.

Ravenfield Hall

One of two main groups of buildings associated with the demolished Hall. Fine tall centrepiece of range of designed farm buildings (see text). *Converted* but brick nest boxes left in situ in loft ensures much of the character of the building being retained. *Listed.*

11. Wickersley

Moat Farm.
Very elegant 18th century dovecote with graceful glover (see text) but allowed to deteriorate in recent years. Plaster nest boxes mostly ruined by weather and structural damage at time of writing. Now in the process of *renovation and restoration* – to a private dwelling – by an interested owner. *Listed* (but not interior).

12. Bramley

Bramley Hall
What appears to be a dovecote with cupola was sketched by Samuel Buck when he visited Henry Eyre's Elizabethan house in *c.* 1720. *Lost.*[20]

Bramley Grange

Also sketched by Buck. Faint outline of detached dovecote in grounds of 'the Seat of Mr Spencer Esqr' ?[21]

13. Upper Whiston

Old Manor House Farm/The Poplars
Combination farm building but dovecote originally detached?

Dovecote over stables. Three-storey. Late 18th century, later heightened (?), rubble sandstone with (new) pantile roof. Modern

Dovecote over stable with farm range to left at Upper Whiston, partly converted.

dormer window inserted plus two modern windows to first and ground floor. Nest boxes (plaster & lath?) removed late 1960s. *Disused/part converted.*

The Ulley Hall dovecote has a prominent flight of steps leading to the access door and an attractive string/rat course. The bird entrance appears to have been via a mullioned opening at the left gable.

14. Ulley
Ulley Hall

Single cell dovecote with attached outbuilding to right, forming part of the Hall. Late 17th/early 18th century. Coursed squared sandstone rubble, stone slate eaves to pantile roof. Stone kneelers and substantial quoins make it an attractive building. Protruding rat course which rises up above gable of outbuilding. Entrance door to first floor reached by flight of 13 stone steps. Blocked two-light mullioned window centrally placed over string course on left gable where stonework suggests that heightening has taken place. Interior not inspected, no nest boxes apparently. An interesting example, *listed for group value.*

15. Aston-cum-Aughton (Hardwick)
Vessey Close Farm

Square dovecote of early 18th century, one of most interesting local examples but gradually deteriorating (see text). Interior intact. *Listed.*

16. Wales
The Beeches (Manor Road)

Very interesting 18th century dovecote, about 20 metres N of the house, half Magnesian Limestone and half hand-made brick (see text). Nest boxes in situ – in upper storey. *Listed for group value.*

17. Brampton-en-le-Morthen
Holme Farm

Mid-18th century combination farm building; tall, three storey structure, dovecote over granary and barn, attached to right end. Coursed square sandstone with later sheet asbestos roof. Quoins, dovecote

possibly heightened. Entrance to granary via ladders to first floor doorway and then to dovecote via trapdoor. Elegant arched semi- circular opening with alighting ledge for birds. Square opening at apex of right gable. Blocked opening to dovecote to rear ? with protruding iron spike in place. Interior has 'remains of lath and plaster nest boxes' according to listing information of 6.1995 but all had gone on inspection. *Listed.*

18. Todwick
Todwick Hall

Pigeon holes are evident at the gable end of a range of buildings belonging to Todwick Hall and sketched by Samuel Buck in *c.* 1720. *Lost.*[22]

19. Maltby

Theft of pigeons from farm dovecote in 1849 (see text).

The dovecote over granary and cartshed at Brampton-en-le-Morthen has some fine exterior architectural features but the interior has been lost.

20/23. Roche Abbey & Sandbeck

Most monastic houses had dovecotes and Roche appears to have been no exception. A 'dufcoate and seaven orchards whereof two ly upon the east side of the monastarie' are mentioned in a document dated 23 June, 1546. *Lost.* 'Dovecote yard' appears before 'Churchyard' in 'a particular of the lands and grounds of the Right Honorable Nicholas, Lord Viscount Castleton at Roche' of 1628 – possibly E of the Abbey? Later in the same survey there is a reference to 'Woodyard meadow with a new Dovecote' associated with the Grange House in the occupation of John Hunt. *Lost.* Interestingly there are small modern-style wooden dovecotes set in the rock face near to the custodian's house at Roche, apparently used 'well into this century'. Limestone dovecote with stables at Sandbeck Park.[23]

The once detached Throapham dovecote now forms the right-hand side of a range of former farm buildings.

21. Throapham
Throapham Manor Farm

Most interesting, 'newly discovered' example, probably originally free-standing, of rubble limestone with pantile roof. 18th century. No string course evident. Single cell dovecote, ground floor later converted to stable. Bird access via square opening facing house and also via gable end openings, now blocked. Spectacular brick-lined interior housing linear arranged nest boxes with protruding brick perches/ledges to right of each. Nest boxes begin about five feet above ground floor level (away from vermin). Total capacity *c.* 600, making it one of the larger local examples. Disused. 'Dovecote Close', is named on the 1841 Tithe Award.[24]

The dovecote over the carriage entrance formerly leading to the courtyard and stables of Dinnington Hall.

22. Dinnington
Dinnington Hall

Dovecote over arched carriage entrance to courtyard/stabling, formerly belonging to the Hall and associated with the Athorpe family. Probably contemporary with the Hall, *c*.1780–1800 and architect-designed (John Carr?). Local dressed limestone with hipped *c*. 20th century cement-style roof, Quoins with continuous string course, mainly for decoration. Glazed, oval *oeil-de-boeuf* window with two pigeon holes in small timber extension. No nest boxes apparently remaining, though not inspected to confirm. Used as a store by veterinary practice. *Listed*.

24. Firbeck
Firbeck Hall
A dovecote is recorded at Firbeck Hall in a sale document of 1676/7 (see text). *Lost*.

25. Letwell
South Farm
Showpiece late 18th century octagonal dovecote (see text) with cupola, red brick, with hipped tile roof, restored by village with support from CPRE *c*.1984. Interior retains potence and all nest boxes, many of them restored. Best complete example in RMBC area. *Listed*.

An earlier dovecote may have existed, contemporary with Firbeck (**24**). *Lost*.

North Farm
Farm dovecote over large barn; ground floor converted to stables and shelter shed built on to right front. Square opening under hipped pantile roof, towers over yard. Rubble limestone. Interior not inspected. *Disused*.

26. Newhall Grange
Fine centrepiece dovecote in courtyard block. Late 18th century. Sandstone with modern tile roof. Small central window and two round 'pitching-eye' windows for ornamental purposes. *Converted* to private dwelling and received civic award in 1987.

The Newhall Grange dovecote is a fine centrepiece example, either architect-designed or a local builder's pattern book commission.

Notes and References

1. These buildings are also known in England as pigeon houses, columbaria (Roman) and culver-houses (Saxon); in Scotland as 'Doocots'; archaically as 'duffus' (and variations); and in parts of S Yorks as 'pigeon hoiles' (dialect).

2. Courtesy of Alan Whitworth, Yorkshire Dovecote Society (hereafter YDS); and in J. Hunter South Yorkshire, II, 1828, p. 301.

3. Chapter 4 ('Accommodation for Birds'), pp. 82–88, also includes brief details of poultry houses. Victor Gollancz Limited.

4. The most recent general works are by Jean and Peter Hansell: *Dovecotes*, 1988 (Shire Publications Ltd, No.213); *Doves and Dovecotes*, 1988 (Millstream Books Ltd of Bath) and *A Dovecote Heritage*, 1992 (Millstream). Also useful are G. A. G.Peterkin, *Scottish Dovecotes*, 1980 (William Culross & Son Ltd) and T. Buxhaum *Scottish Doocots*, 1987 (Shire Publications Ltd, No. 190).

5. Chapter VIII, 'Pigeons of the Church', p. 22.

6. Located S of 'prior's house' in angle formed by its S wall and wall of the cellarium. It collapsed in *c*.1880. A drawing is reproduced in J. W. Walker 'An Illustrated and Archaeological Description of the Priory of St Mary Magdalene of Monk Bretton', *Yorkshire Archaeological Society*, Extra vol V, 1926.

7. A. A. Whitworth, *Comprehensive Bibliography of Dovecotes*, 1995, YDS. A touring exhibition by the YDS appeared at Cusworth Hall, near Doncaster, in 1995. For membership details of the Yorkshire Dovecote Society please contact Alan Whitworth at Linden, 10 The Carrs, Sleights, Whitby, YO21 IRR. Also A. Whitworth 'Yorkshire Dovecotes and Pigeon Lofts: A Preliminary Survey', *Yorkshire Archaeological Journal*, Vol. 65, 1993, pp. 75–89.

8. Peterkin, *op cit*, p. 7.

9. A. O. Cooke *A Book of Dovecotes*, 1920, p. 36. The original source for this figure appears to have been Samuel Hartlib (d.1670?) who published pamphlets on education and 'husbandry', said to be a friend of Milton.

10. *Doncaster, Nottingham and Lincoln Gazette*, 12, January, 1849, (Doncaster Local Studies Library). I am grateful to A. Whitworth for drawing my attention to this reference.

11. Information from Melvyn Jones.

12. *Samuel Buck's Yorkshire Sketchbook* (hereafter SBYS), Wakefield Historical Publications, 1979, p. 118.

13. A. H. Smith, *The Place-Names of the West Riding of Yorkshire*, English Place-Name Society, Vol..xxx, Pt I, p.110 (Fairbank).

14. Information from Alan Whitworth, Inquisition Post Mortem 35 Edw.I, No. 28.

15. Rawmarsh Parish Register, PR 80/4, Rotherham Local Studies & Archives: I am grateful to Tony Dodsworth for drawing my attention to this source.

16. SBYS, p.117.

17. SBYS, p.110.

18. Rotherham Central Library, Archives & Local Studies Section.

19. Courtesy Alan Whitworth.

20. SBYS, p.78.

21. SBYS, p.77.

22. SBYS, p.86.

23. Information from Alice Rodgers & courtesy of Lumley Archive (Earl of Scarbrough).

24. Tithe Award reference from Alan Whitworth.

Acknowledgements

As well as acknowledgements cited in references and in captions I would like to express my appreciation to Tracey Ingle, Conservation Officer, Planning Department, Rotherham MBC, Tony Munford and staff at Rotherham Central Library, Archives and Local Studies Section, Alan Whitworth and the Yorkshire Dovecote Society, Alice Rodgers and the Earl of Scarbrough (Lumley Archive) and Alex Fleming.

This study would not have been possible without the help and co-operation of many owners of dovecotes sites. My thanks are therefore due to Mr & Mrs R. Collier, Wentworth Pine Furniture, Richard Longley & Geoff Copley, Roger Hirst, John Moody, Mrs L. Rotherham, T. Lynskey, Jill Jesson, Mr & Mrs P. Leverick, Mr L. Taylor, Mrs Longford, Mr Horsely, Mr A. Palmer & Mr L. Ketley, Mr B. Brightmore, Mr & Mrs S. Gerrity, Mr J. Hollingworth of South Farm & residents of Letwell, and Mrs Alton.

Picture Credits: All photographs are by the author unless otherwise stated.

11. Rawmarsh Common: A Study in Landscape History

by Tony Dodsworth

JUST OVER TWO HUNDRED YEARS AGO Rawmarsh Common ceased to exist as a result of an Act of Parliament. It was divided up mainly amongst seven of the largest landowners in the parish of Rawmarsh as part of the process of enclosure. The name of Rawmarsh Common survived on the 1854/5 Ordnance Survey Six Inch map but its link with, and use by, many of the inhabitants of Rawmarsh over a period of hundreds of years had ended in the early 1780s.

To explore the history of the great changes that affected the Common in the eighteenth century it is necessary to explore two key sources available in Rotherham Central Library's Archives and Local Studies Section. One is a copy of a wonderful map of Rawmarsh Common produced originally in 1740 by William Fairbank and the other, a printed copy of the *Rawmarsh Enclosure Act and Award* with the accompanying map. Using these in conjunction with other supporting sources, such as the parish registers, it is possible to reconstruct a past landscape and discover more about the people living in that landscape. The impact of enclosure must have been very different for those who had encroached on the Common such as the Carr family, who were colliers in the local small coal pits, compared to Francis Ferrand Foljambe who was lord of two of the three manors in Rawmarsh parish. Similarly there must have been a difference in the way the Scorah family and the family of Joseph Clark(e) of Upper Haugh viewed the enclosure of the Common. Members of the Scorah family were involved in a long-lived pipe-making business and their house was built right on the boundary of the Common whereas Joseph Clark was already a substantial landowner before he received more than 24 acres of the Common in the *Enclosure Award.*

The use and comparison of maps is central to this particular local history study and serves to remind us of just how much information about the past can be collected from old maps if they exist. The information on a single map can sometimes quite easily be the equivalent of hundreds of pages of written material and is usually much more accessible than in written form. As with any source it should not be assumed that everything on maps is exactly accurate and correct, but used with care, and in conjunction with other sources if possible, they can be a real 'treasure chest' of local historical information. Any study of old maps should also not be divorced from what exists today on the ground, so to fully understand old maps it is necessary to walk over the area shown and relate it to what existed in the past. It is quite often surprising to discover just how much of what we see today on the ground can be linked directly with aspects of the past, sometimes hundreds or thousands of years ago.

To set the scene for a study of Rawmarsh Common it is necessary briefly to consider the whole of the parish of Rawmarsh and particularly its boundaries. Boundaries can often represent some of the oldest aspects of an area and this certainly seems true of Rawmarsh, where much of its north-western boundary is delineated by the earthwork feature known locally and confusingly as Roman Ridge. This can be clearly seen in Figure 1, a map of the parish of Rawmarsh with key

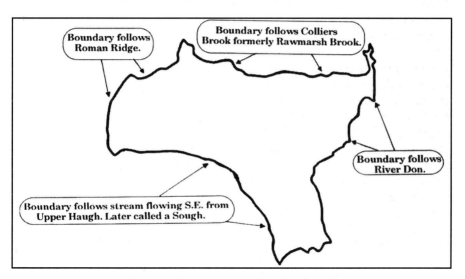

Figure 1. Rawmarsh parish with key features of its boundary labelled.

features of its boundary labelled. Roman Ridge, still clearly visible in the present-day landscape as a bank and ditch (e.g. directly east of Hoober House), separated Rawmarsh parish from Brampton Bierlow and Wath parishes. Its origins are essentially unknown although it may represent a boundary between tribes or peoples from the Dark Ages. In all it stretches for about ten miles from Sheffield to Mexborough and in some parts, including near Rawmarsh, there are in fact two dykes less than a mile apart. Figure 2 shows clearly the bank and ditch

Figure 2.   Roman Ridge, east of Hoober House on the western boundary of Rawmarsh parish. The bank and ditch are still visible today despite the antiquity of this feature. *The Author*

feature of Roman Ridge, and Fairbank describes one part of it erroneously on his Rawmarsh Common map as *Via Vicinalis Romana Antiqua*. At that time there tended to be an assumption that anything old in the landscape had to be linked to the Romans. Much of the rest of the northern boundary was defined by Rawmarsh Brook (as named by Fairbank but in more recent times called Colliers Brook). In the east the River Don was probably the original boundary but quite early on, Hunter believed in the 1160s, the south-eastern part of the parish known as Aldwarke was split from Rawmarsh to become a detached part of the parish of Ecclesfield. This estate at Aldwarke was associated in the Middle Ages with some noted families such as the Clarells and the Fitzwilliams, to be followed by the Foljambes who held it into the nineteenth century. The south-western boundary was again based on a water course, in this case a stream flowing south-eastwards from Upper Haugh and much changed by coal mining activity in the past 200 years.

Land such as Rawmarsh Common played a vital role in the economic system that had evolved in much of Lowland Britain in medieval times. Most crop growing was concentrated in the open fields but many villagers would have had rights to graze animals on the common lands. Particularly low-lying land close to rivers provided meadow pasture and was known locally as an *ing*. Much of the land around the village of Rawmarsh was taken up by the common fields with names such as Nether Field, School Field and Bank Field, the position of these being probably determined by the fertility of the soil and how easy it was to work. The lowest land in the parish was in the southern area and was called The Ings. It was fringed to the north by a small common. The main common, mapped by Fairbank, covered much of the northern third of the parish. As will be seen later there is considerable evidence of encroachment on to this common land, perhaps over a period of several hundred years, but it still constituted about 800 acres in the eighteenth century. Looking at Figure 3, the height of the Common was generally from 100 to 350 feet, not greatly different from the area of common fields but much of the land was on

Figure 3.   Variations in the height of land in Rawmarsh parish and the position of Rawmarsh Common.

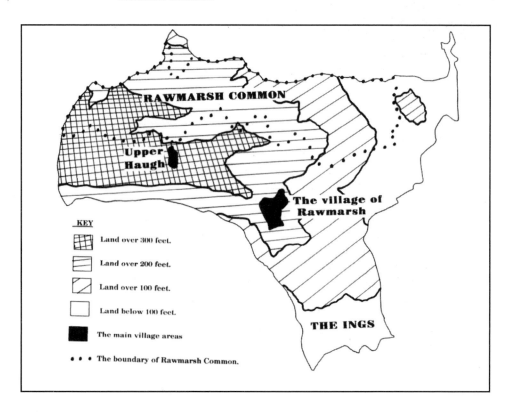

north-facing slopes and perhaps therefore not such an advantageous location for growing crops with regard to aspect (the position of the sun). The neighbouring parish of Wath-upon-Dearne had a very similar pattern of land use and land height except that the area furthest from the meadow land in that case was a wooded common (Wath Wood).

A common was owned by the lord of the manor, or in the case of Rawmarsh – lords of the manors, but some tenants had rights to graze animals on the common. One form of common rights was known as common appendant which entitled freehold tenants to pasture their beasts of the plough (horses or oxen) and animals which manure the land (cows and sheep). The number of animals that could be turned out onto the common was limited, or stinted, to the number the tenant could look after on his own land in winter when the grass on the common was not growing. The other form of common rights was common appurtenant which applied to occupiers of specific houses who had been given a grant, or could prove long use beforehand. Swine, goats, donkeys and geese were not commonable creatures but occasionally the right to graze these might be a common appurtenant.

There was more to rights of common than just pasture as is shown in Figure 4. They could involve the right to collect turf, peat, fish, stone and sand from the common as well as forage for pigs such as beech mast and acorns. Perhaps most important they included estovers which involved the right to take dead wood and underwood from the common. Estovers could be broken down into wood for burning,

Figure 4.   Rights of Common.

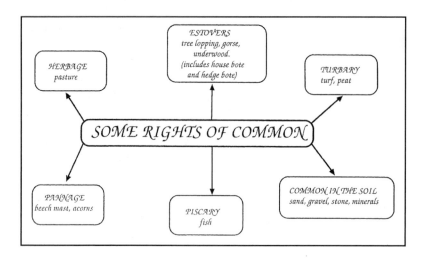

wood for housebote (i.e. used to build or repair houses) and wood for hedgebote (i.e. used to build or repair fences and hedges) and so on. As Melvyn Jones points out in his book *Rotherham's Woodland Heritage* these rights were important in Rawmarsh at an early date with a deed dated 1241 between William de Lichefield, parson of the church of Rawmarsh (written *de Rubio Marisco*) and Sibill de Sancta Maria concerning common of pasture and reasonable estovers. Similarly in a marriage settlement of 1557 between Lancelot Mountforthe of Kilnhurst and Margaret Wentworth of Wentworth Woodhouse the estate described includes:

access to the common and woods in Rawmarsh for pasturing animals and for wood to their fires, hedges and houses.

These rights did not usually include timber, which still belonged to the lord of the manor.

One other aspect of the commons generally that would have been relevant to Rawmarsh was the custom which prevailed that if a man went on to the common and could manage to erect, during the course of one night, some sort of dwelling which had a roof and which had a fire burning in the hearth by morning, then he was entitled to stay and call the primitive building his home. He did not need to seek the permission of the legitimate landowner i.e. the lord of the manor. This was likely to have been a source of friction as surely local people would have complained about squatters taking pieces of their common and depriving them of grazing but there was little they could do about it. Certainly the houses and crofts of W. Padley, Jn. Rodes, J. Carr and G. Pearson shown on Fairbank's map of Rawmarsh Common may have originated in just such a squatter's 'night exercise'! (See Figures 6a and 6b).

One really intriguing episode relating to Rawmarsh Common and Sir Francis Foljambe occurred in 1630–1631. At this time Sir Francis Foljambe was lord of two manors in Rawmarsh and owned the estate at Aldwarke. This became the main base for the family once he sold his estate at Walton near Chesterfield in 1633. Aldwarke Hall is shown in Figure 5. J. T. Cliffe in his book *The Yorkshire Gentry* tells us that Sir Francis inherited property worth £3,000 a year and at that time he was

a man of no estate or fortune, and of small understanding by reason of his education to manage so great an estate . . . and the rather because the Estate was so much troubled and incumbered with statutes and

Figure 5.   Aldwarke Hall in the 1890s. This was the home of the Foljambe family locally, back to the seventeenth century. *Rotherham Central Library, Archives and Local Studies Section*

divers other charges which did occasion many and great suites.

In 1630 Sir William Ellis of Kilnhurst, an important man in his own right, wrote of Sir Francis to Edward Marris, Sir Thomas Wentworth's steward:

> *My auld enemy – Sir Fran. Fulliambye hath taken in our principal beste pte of our common to the quantity of some three-quarters by estimation, wich my poure honest neighbours hath injoined hundreths of years as both by custom and antiente deds is aparante.*

Ellis continued:

> *Our selves are so affrighted by him and his men with threats of beggarye and undowinge by suttes, saying hee will pave it with silver before he will lose it.*

Sir Francis:

> *should in joy it so long to pin me up at my dore as he intends . . . even this day debarrs me wood of the comon wch I recovered by lawe.*

Ellis obviously wanted Sir Thomas Wentworth, a much 'bigger fish'
even than Sir Francis, to exert his influence over Foljambe and added
a poignant postscript:

many harts is enclosed in my petition whose hands dare not move.

Edward Marris passed on the information in his own letter to
Wentworth starting:

*Sir Francis Folliambay hath inclosed all or a great pt of the common
under Rawmarsh towards Kilnhiste wch must troble the inhabitants.*

He concludes:

*I have sent this petition whereunto yor Honor will be pleased to give
some answere, for indeed the manor of the inclosing, and keeping of it
enclosed, makes a great show of strength.*[1]

It would appear that later in the year the Council at York ruled against
Foljambe but that did not seem to resolve the problem. Even in the
family history Sir Francis is described as 'a man of profuse temper
and excessive hospitality' and perhaps the neighbours of Ellis
consoled themselves that he eventually found himself in severe financial trouble as the result, Cliffe tells us, of a mixture of bad fortune,
mismanagement and extravagance. At his death in 1640 he left property worth only £1000 a year. The Foljambes were to play an
important part in the final division of Rawmarsh Common in the
1780s but apparently with more co-operation locally than was the case
with their seventeenth century ancestor.

The 1740 map of Rawmarsh Common was originally produced by
William Fairbank but all that apparently remains is a copy of it held
in Rotherham Central Library, Archives and Local Studies Section.
It is because of the Fairbank family over several generations that
Sheffield is probably the best mapped city in England in the eighteenth and early nineteenth centuries. The first William
(*c.*1688–1759) was a schoolteacher and a Quaker who undertook
surveying and legal work. As T. Walter Hall writes in his book about
the Fairbanks:

*William, at the head of the pedigree, his sons, grandsons and great
grandson surveyed the whole of Sheffield and many miles round.*

Many parts of the Rotherham area were mapped by the family and the maps, fieldbooks (notebooks containing rough details of the maps completed on site) and letters are held in the Fairbank Collection in Sheffield Archives. Hall describes the Fairbanks' work as:

> *much . . . history . . . written not in words but in maps; and this form of local history brings into prominence many topographical facts and interesting events which are not to be found elsewhere.*

This is certainly the case for Rawmarsh Common because, as Figures 6a, 6b and 6c reveal, much that was unknown about the area is clearly exhibited on this map. Place names unrecorded elsewhere appear here along with locations of early industrial activity (such as coal pits and clay pits), the sites of houses and crofts that had encroached on the Common and, perhaps most remarkable of all, a record of a complex

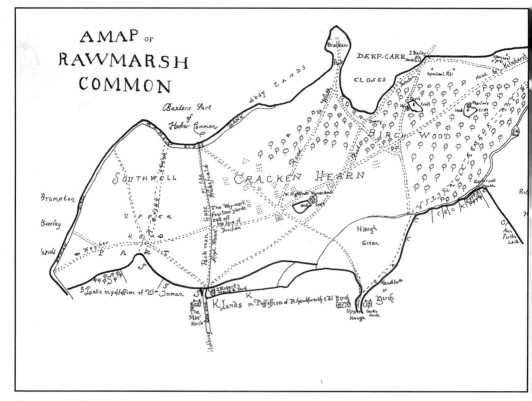

Figure 6a. The western half of Fairbank's 1740 map of Rawmarsh Common. *Redrawn from a copy of the original map in Rotherham Central Library, Archives and Local Studies Section*

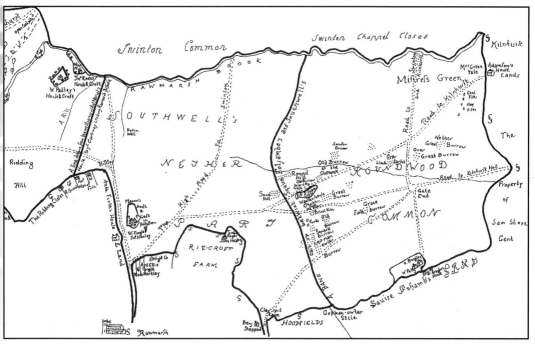

Figure 6b. The eastern half of Fairbank's 1740 map of Rawmarsh Common. *Redrawn from a copy of the original map in Rotherham Central Library, Archives and Local Studies Section*

Figure 6c. The Key for Fairbank's 1740 map of Rawmarsh Common. *From a copy of the original map in Rotherham Central Library, Archives and Local Studies Section*

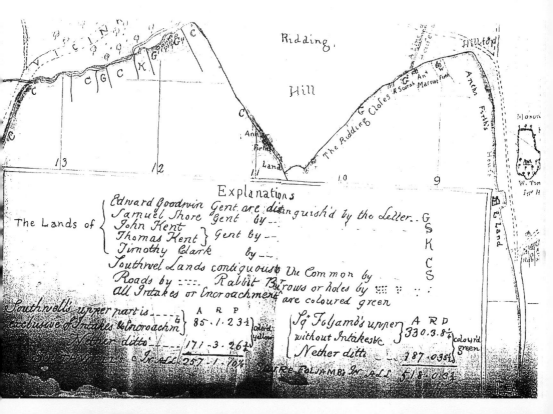

of rabbit burrows owned by the Foljambes and certainly unique locally for the detail provided about them. The pattern of pre-enclosure roads is clearly shown and for decorative effect each house is shown as a tiny drawing along with a drawing of the parish church (see Figure 7) right at the edge of the map. Land ownership on the southern boundary of the Common is shown with a key and the area of land on the Common held by Southwell Manor and by 'Squire' Foljambe is calculated. The Common is divided into four blocks, two owned by the Southwell Manor and two by the Foljambe manors.

Figure 7.
An enlarged copy of a drawing of St. Mary's Parish Church, Rawmarsh from Fairbank's 1740 map of Rawmarsh Common. *Redrawn from a copy of the original map in Rotherham Central Library, Archives and Local Studies Section*

Essentially the Southwell Manor held 257 acres of the Common compared to Foljambe's 518 acres (which related to the Foljambes being lords of two of the three manors in Rawmarsh). The remarkably accurate division of the Common into thirds suggests an arrangement going right back into the mists of time in the early Middle Ages and perhaps even links up with the information in Hunter's *South Yorkshire* where it is recorded that an early lord of the whole manor of Rawmarsh, Paganus de Sancta Maria, split the manor into three between his daughters, Lucy, Sibilla and Isolda. Adding to the confusion is the existence of a manor at Wheatcroft to the east of the village that may have been a separate manor in its own right (Hunter said it was given to Nicholas, a bastard son of Paganus) but it is generally tied in with the most eastern of the three manors of Rawmarsh.

The existence of quite a large wood, Birch Wood, is revealed in the central part of the Common and this had disappeared by the time the Ordnance Survey mapping started in the nineteenth century. The name lingered on and is shown on the 1854/5 Ordnance Survey Six Inch map along with the Birch Wood works (chemicals) which later became known as Chemical Cottages. Within this wood are marked the houses and crofts of J. Carr, Pearson, W. Padley and John Rodes who is named as living at the New Mill. This New Mill is marked on what is today Colliers Brook and just west of Warren Vale. At present there is no evidence that it operated as a mill but it is interesting to note that just upstream from this site are found two fish ponds. Fish was an important source of fresh food in the past and perhaps it was here that villagers could claim their rights of piscary. No Rodes are listed as millers in the eighteenth century parish registers. The earliest reference is to a Robert Rhodes dying in 1700 and to a William Rhodes married in 1709 to Mary Elam, a widow. William was a farmer who had four children baptised at St Mary's Parish Church. A little later Stephen Rhodes, a collier and Quaker, appears in registers followed by John, a potter, who married Susan Morton in 1752. The R(h)odes name continued to feature in the parish registers down to 1800. William Padley came originally from Tankersley and married Mary Shaw of Rawmarsh in 1707. He was a collier who had six children baptised in Rawmarsh, three of them dying before the age of six. His wife died in 1743 and, as so often seemed to happen then, William followed her within two months. His son George, although not married in Rawmarsh, had two children baptised in 1740 and 1742 but neither lived beyond the age of two. He was also a collier but the family disappears from the registers after 1743 apparently having moved away. George Pearson is listed as a collier and as father of Mary in 1727; his wife Margaret died in 1741. Twenty years later a Nicholas Pearson appears married in 1761 to Elizabeth Ramsden and is variously described thereafter as either a labourer or a collier. John Carr was also a collier married in 1723 to Elizabeth Megson and fathered nine children between 1726 and 1744. He may be the same John Carr born in 1698 and son of Richard, a woollen weaver and clothmaker. The Carrs remained one of the most numerous Rawmarsh families throughout the eighteenth century, the men mainly involved in coalmining and labouring. John Bailey, living right on the northern edge of the Common close to the other families, was also a collier but seems to have left the parish after 1750. The small coal pits named close to these families' houses surely represent their places of work for at least part of the century.

The shape of the Common as shown on Fairbank's map includes a number of characteristic features. Oliver Rackham in his *The History of the Countryside* points out that commons often have a straggling concave outline bordered by houses. They funnel into the roads which cross the common and join up with another common in the next parish. This certainly provides a good description of Rawmarsh Common and especially if we concentrate on the part shown in Figure 8. Here the funnelling of the Common from what is called Haugh Green into Upper Haugh is clearly seen with two houses, one being T. Clark's, set right on the boundary line. To the east the straggling concave outline is probably due to quite a large scale encroachment on the Common perhaps centuries earlier than 1740. The field sizes, shapes and positions are characteristic of a process called assarting, by which past inhabitants of Rawmarsh working individually or in a small group, cut down the woodland on the Common and enclosed it within their land. The map in Figure 8 includes information from the Fairbank map and the Enclosure Award Map of 1781. It shows the ownership of the land and the names of the fields as given in 1781.

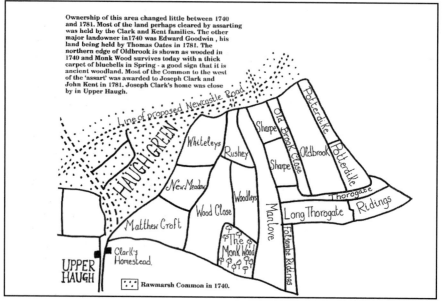

Figure 8. Part of the southern boundary area of Rawmarsh Common based on Fairbank's 1740 map of Rawmarsh Common and the Enclosure Award Map of 1781. It shows several characteristic features of a common and possibly evidence of 'assarting' in the past. Note the field names from the 1781 map; some of these suggest that much of this area was wooded.

Note the number of references to its previous wooded nature – field names such as Wood Close, Woodleys and Whiteleys (ley is a place name element that generally refers to land being cleared for pasture) as well as the Monk Wood that almost miraculously seems to have survived in part right up to the present day. A photograph of this remnant can be seen in Figure 9. The Riddings just to the east represents another obvious place name reference to woodland clearance and the houses of R. Scorah, Anthony Marriot and W. Firth are in the classic edge-of-common location. The Scorahs are a particularly interesting local family being represented in the parish registers in the seventeenth century – when Jonathan Scorer married Elizabeth Rodes in 1686 – and throughout the eighteenth century. The family was

Figure 9. The Monk Wood. A 'miraculous' survivor of the once extensive woodland in Rawmarsh parish and now totally surrounded by housing. *The Author*

involved throughout that time in making clay pipes from Richard Scorer described as a pipemaker in 1718 to Matthias Scorah, a pipemaker, in 1800. Where they lived was described as Pipe House on Ordnance Survey maps into the 1950s and Pipe House Lane survives today.

Other large scale encroachments on the Common would appear to have occurred when Rie-Croft Farm was created (this was on land owned by the Southwell Manor) and reference is also made in the south-eastern area of the map to Hoodfields (also on Southwell lands). One of the Rawmarsh manors had passed into the hands of the Chapter of Southwell Minster by a deed of 1408. The lands of this manor included eighteen dwelling houses, six furnaces or kilns (which G. Washington Rolls in his book *The Vicars Choral of Southwell Minster and Their Lands at Rawmarsh 1408 – 1850* has suggested might represent either metal smelting furnaces, brick kilns or pottery kilns), 20 agricultural holdings of two acres each, 200 acres of ploughland and 100 acres of pasture land – totalling about 350 to 400 acres. The 'Huddefelde' is mentioned in a lease of 1501 to Robert Dyson for 99 years 'without waste'. He was to pay ten shillings annually, half on St Martin's feast in winter and half at Pentecost at the 'Two Great Courts' of the Vicars Choral of Southwell Minster at Rawmarsh. These lands can be traced through a number of transactions from 1501 into the twentieth century when from 1950 onwards the Roundwood Estate was developed there; once again a quite startling example of continuity in the landscape.

The existence of extensive areas of rabbit burrows on two parts of Rawmarsh Common is perhaps the most remarkable aspect of Fairbank's map. These areas, known as warrens, were both watched over by warreners living in Warren Houses and the name survives in one case and was obviously considered when Warren Vale was named. Rabbits are so numerous today that we tend to take them for granted but there is no evidence of rabbits in Britain before the twelfth century. They were introduced from the Mediterranean region and protected in warrens for their meat, fur and for the sport of rabbit coursing. Many warrens probably failed in the past due to a lack of food in winter, bad weather and losses caused by poachers and natural predators. We hear little of the raising of 'coneys' (this was their name in the past, rabbits just being their young) because early agricultural writers considered warrens, like much else that went on upon the commons, as a negative use of land. John Sheail, an expert in this field, tells us that Aldbourne Warren in Wiltshire was let for as much as £40 per annum in medieval times and that

here and in other regions, the creation and sustenance of a warren repre-
sented a conscious and positive act of estate management.

Estate owners devoted as much attention to rabbits as to sheep and
other livestock. A warren lodge or house was often built to overlook
the warren and here the warrener and perhaps his family or men lived,
especially during the killing season. Certainly in the case of Rawmarsh
Common in 1740 Fairbank shows William Nightscales living at the
Warren House and Croft at Cracken Hearn on the western part of the
Common (see Figure 6a), while Richard and John Jubb were living at
the Warren House and Croft on Roundwood Common to the east.
Earlier in the century the western Warren House was probably occupied by Thomas Glover for he was described as a warrener in the burial
register in 1722. His widow, Sarah, died in 1728 and her maiden name
was Nightscales. William Nightscales first appears in the parish
register as a warrener in 1724 so it seems likely that he possibly
replaced his father-in-law. He died in 1753 and was apparently
replaced by Thomas, his son, aged 29, who was described as a
warrener at the baptism of two children in 1757 and 1758, but then
his family disappear from the registers until Mary, daughter of
Thomas Nightscales, weaver, was buried in 1779. If this Thomas is
the same (and the registers do suggest this) then his 'warrening' days
seem to have ended in the 1758 to 1779 period. Richard Jubb was
certainly the warrener on the eastern warren in 1714 and his son John
was described as a tailor when he married Sarah Ramsden in 1725.
By 1732 John was listed as a warrener contemporary with his father;
his last listing as a warrener was in 1736 and Richard's last was in
1739. At Richard's death in 1759 he was described as a tailor as was
John at his death in 1766.

The disappearance of references to these warrens in the second half
of the eighteenth century was perhaps linked to enclosure although in
the *Enclosure Act of 1774* Francis Ferrand Foljambe, Esquire, is
described as 'owner of two warrens for conies upon the said commons
or waste grounds'. The wording of the Act equating commons with
waste ground is clear evidence of the pressure that existed, especially
from large landowners, to get rid of the commons; the squatters and
poorer villagers perhaps had different views.

Figure 10 includes a map locating the main warren areas in the
parish together with a close up of some of the eastern rabbit warren.
It shows the burrows arranged in groups and often named, for
example Grace Firth Burrow and Square Burrow. These burrows were
almost certainly man-made. Typical earthworks often consisted of a

long straight, or slightly curved, bank possibly with ditches to aid drainage. The sloping land of both Rawmarsh Common warrens would have helped drainage. Surprisingly no outer walls or fences are marked around the warrens on the map although in the east the common land of Squire Foljambe was separated from that of Southwell Manor by a bank on Fairbank's map and this may have had a dual purpose. Open warrens, Sheail tells us, did exist in the eighteenth century and especially on the commons. The warren house would probably have had racks for drying rabbit skins and space would have been provided to store traps, nets and lanterns for night work. Ferrets were often kept to help capture the rabbits before the main 'harvest' in late autumn or early winter. Opposition locally to the coney warrens may have been considerable – there are certainly numerous references nationally to the damage caused by 'absconding' rabbits. In Henry VIII's reign farmers at Kingsthorpe in Northamptonshire complained that 'Their corn growing in the fields is yearly eaten, spoiled and destroyed'. At Settrington in East Yorkshire some time before 1537 Sir Francis Bygod had moved his coney warren from the low commons because he found his coneys were being destroyed (could this reflect local opposition?). The new warren near the Manor house saw their numbers multiply and

spread throughout the lordship that they are not only a great impoverishment to her majesty's poor tenants there but they do also great hurt in her majesty's woods by destroying the young springs (shoots). The tenants could be contented amongst them to pay the rent to her majesty to have the coneys destroyed.

E.P. Thompson in his book *Customs in Common* uncovered the lines of a 'Charnwood Opera' dated about 1753 and performed in North Leicestershire. Copious warrens had been planted on the commons by Lord Stamford, among others, and one part of the opera ran:

The turf is short bitten by Rabbits, And now
No milk can be stroaked from ye Old Woman's Cow.

In short, warrens were not favoured by many in the countryside but in Rawmarsh's case the closure of the warrens coincided roughly with the Common's enclosure so there was little time for local people to benefit. One mysterious reference on the Rawmarsh Common map to 'Holes for Poor' in the eastern warren suggests something quite philanthropic but that may be interpreting more than is really there.

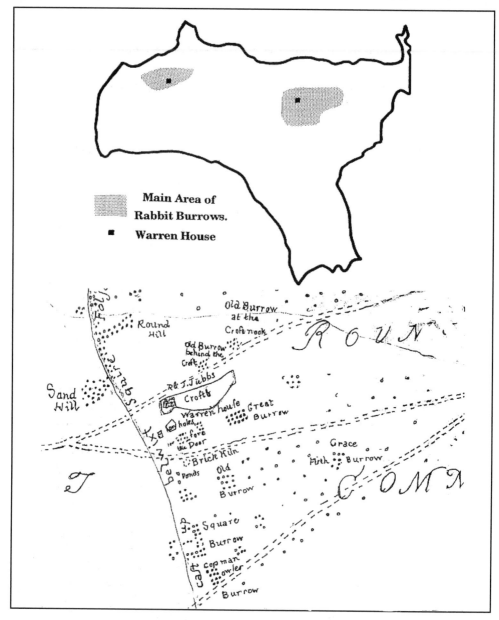

Figure 10. Location of the two main warrens in Rawmarsh parish with a detail from Fairbank's 1740 map of Rawmarsh Common showing most of the eastern warren. *Redrawn from a copy of the original map in Rotherham Central Library, Archives and Local Studies Section*

Towards the south-west corner of the Fairbank map, reference is made to 'The Manor House' where Stubbing Lane End becomes Packman Gate. Today this would be in the area known as Low and Higher Stubbin. The Manor House is set on land of Southwell Manor in the possession of William Inman. No other reference to a manor house on this site can be found. The site is certainly a commanding one with views down and across much of the south-western part of the parish. Within the records originally held by the Vicars Choral of Southwell Minster, Washington Rolls discovered a lease of land at 'Bellow Stubbyng and the Ickles', now the locality of Low Stubbin. The lease was between the Vicars Choral and Marjory, wife of William Dyson of Rawmarsh and dated 28 September, 1474. The lease involved a yearly rent of £35 and 'flitches of bacon' (beautifully described in Latin as *armis porcuibus!*). Within the lease reference is made to coals or metals being carried away by 'digger and bronze spade' but most interestingly it also includes an undertaking that Majory:

> *shall build upon the said estate four houses, namely one insethouse of ten posts and between two posts in length there shall be sixteen feet and between two posts in breadth there shall be forty-two feet , with one outhouse, one granary of ten crucks, one sheepfold of eight crucks and stabling of eight crucks.*

In all this represents about 7,000 square feet of floor space (if all one storey) and a building so large may well have had manorial signifi-cance. No link between Fairbank's Manor House and this building can be proved but it is tempting to speculate.

As Rawmarsh was divided quite early into three manors it seems likely that at one time there may have been three manor houses and if this Low Stubbin/Ickles reference is one, the second was certainly within the village itself on High Street, the last 'version' of which was demolished in 1965. The division of the parish would suggest that a third manor house should be located in the eastern part of the area but evidence for it is hard to come by. In the first edition of the Ordnance Survey map published in 1841 a Moat Wood is marked to the east of the village, perhaps suggesting a previous site of some distinction (a moat was sometimes constructed around a house in the Middle Ages as a status symbol), but the key reference is to another Fairbank map of 1758 held in Sheffield Archives. As can be seen in Figure 11 this map of the manor of Wheatcroft shows clearly an almost square enclosure named 'Site of the Old Manor House' and beside it a field named Moat Pasture. Here surely we have a link with Hunter's reference to John, son and heir of William de Haplesthorp, described in 1323 as lord of Whetecroft. Fairbank's map was drawn for John Moor of Hull as part of the arrangements following the death of Francis Foljambe. Figure 11 also includes an inset map of the whole

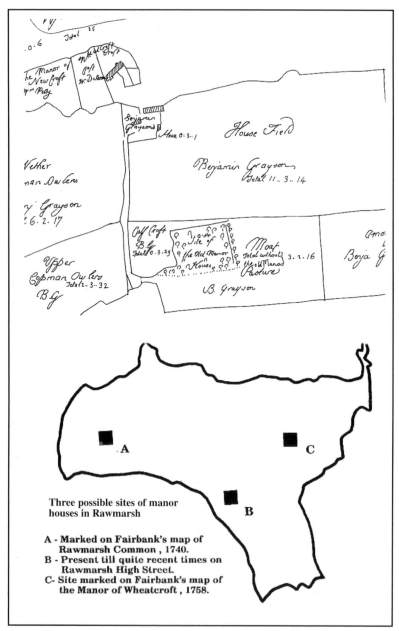

Figure 11. Part of Fairbank's 1758 map of the Manor of Wheatcroft. *Redrawn from a copy of the original map in Sheffield City Archives*

parish locating these three possible manor houses and it is striking to note their logical positioning if the parish had been split in the past into three parts. The balanced division of the Common into thirds (originally perhaps in one ninth units when the figures on Fairbank's 1740 map are studied) also suggests this same geographical symmetry.

The story of Rawmarsh Common is in many ways brought to a conclusion by the *Rawmarsh Enclosure Act of 1774* and the *Enclosure Award* of 1781. After the 1781 Award, Rawmarsh Common ceased to exist as an area where some local people had rights of common; instead it was divided up into big and small parcels of privately owned land. As W.E. Tate has pointed out, parliamentary enclosure was concentrated between about 1720 and 1860 but in particular in the six decades of the reign of King George III. It is interesting to consider the reasons why Fairbank was asked to draw up a map of Rawmarsh Common in 1740. Quite often common lands were enclosed separately from the common fields and it may have been that the map was seen as a prelude to the enclosure of the Common but that a dispute arose, perhaps between Francis Foljambe (see Figure 12) and the owners of Southwell Manor, and as a result the plans were shelved for several decades. Certainly Fairbank took great care to mark on the exact boundaries between the four 'blocks' of Common with reference to precise detail such as 'fourteen yards east of the line of division'. It seems likely that enclosure after 1774 did not proceed smoothly as seven years is a long time to complete the process, although one of the three Commissioners, Henson Kirkby of Worksop, did die in 1776. This no doubt created problems until his replacement by John Parker of Upper Haugh.

Before studying parliamentary enclosure at Rawmarsh in detail the point must be made, as J.C. Harvey stresses in his article on enclosure in the Lower Dearne Valley, that substantial evidence exists to confirm that by 1700 few South Yorkshire parishes had been unaffected by enclosure of common field land. Reference has already been made to Rie-Croft Farm and Hoodfields, north-east of Rawmarsh village, and to possible assarting activity to the north-west. By looking closely at the southern boundary of Fairbank's

Figure 12. The memorial to Francis Foljambe in Ecclesfield Church. *The Author*

1740 map it is possible to see that most of the land contiguous with the Common was already in private hands, such as the Goodwins, Kents and Clarks, and certainly not by that date part of the common fields. This enclosure on a private basis is often undocumented yet, as Harvey explains, must have been at least as important, in terms of the area affected, as parliamentary enclosure in the coal measures region of South Yorkshire.

As the first page of Rawmarsh's Enclosure Act emphasises (see Figure 13) the enclosure involved particularly common fields, common ings and commons or waste ground (the significance of equating commons with waste has already been mentioned). Some of the common arable areas are named such as Nether Field and School Field and can be located lying around the main village area. In all about 1250 acres of land were to be enclosed of which about two-thirds lay on Rawmarsh Common. Individuals named in the Act as pressing for enclosure include Francis Ferrand Foljambe, the Chapter of the Collegiate Church of Southwell, Samuel Shore Junior, Edward Oates, John Kent, John Hall, William Rhodes and the Rector of the parish, Reverend Rowland Hodgson. Just like the Fairbank map of 1740, the Foljambes, Kents and Shores figure prominently and Edward Oates seems to have acquired the Goodwin lands (note that William Oates of Wakefield married Mrs Gertrude Goodwin of Rawmarsh in June 1707). It is interesting that Joseph Clark of Haugh is not named despite being a substantial landowner. The date for enclosure seems to coincide with a plan to construct a 'Newcastle Road' (i.e. an early railway with wagons pulled by horses) across Rawmarsh Common to allow coal mined in the west of the parish at Low Stubbin to be transported to the River Don at Kilnhurst. This 'Cut or Coal Road' was to be made by William Cartwright and John Kent who leased mines in the area from the Southwell Chapter. At this time Lord John

A N

A   C   T

F O R

Dividing and Inclofing the Common Fields, Common Ings, Mefne Inclofures, Commons, or Wafte Grounds within the Parifh of *Rawmarfh*, in the Weft Riding of the County of *York*.

WHEREAS, there are within the Parifh of *Raw-* Preamble. *marfh*, in the Weft Riding of the County of *York*, feveral open common Fields, common Ings, and mefne Inclofures called or known by the Names of the *Nether Field*, *School Field*, *Long Orgreaves*, *Long Peafehill*, *Bankfield*, *Kirklands*, *Great Intake*, *Little Intake*, *Bear Trees*, *Short Orgreaves*, and *Crofs Orgreaves*, containing together by Eftimation Four hundred and Fifty Acres or thereabouts; and alfo feveral large Commons or Tracts
A   of

Figure 13. The first page of the Rawmarsh Enclosure Act of 1774 listing the main areas to be enclosed. *Rotherham Central Library, Archives and Local Studies Section*

Murray of Banner Cross (with a long and distinguished career in the British Army despite his half brother's involvement at Culloden as Commander in Chief of the Scots under Bonnie Prince Charlie) was leasing Southwell Manor from the Chapter of the Collegiate Church. Plans also existed for Foljambe and other freeholders of Rawmarsh to make use of this Coal Road. The possibility certainly exists that part of the pressure to enclose involved a desire on the part of some of the parish's main landowners to more effectively exploit the mineral riches of the area. The route of the Newcastle Road can be seen on the Enclosure Award map (see Figure 14) and was certainly completed eventually up to the line of the present day Warren Vale, but whether it ever reached Low Stubbin is in doubt as by 1850 the collieries in that area were connected to the canal at Parkgate by the Low Stubbin Incline.[2]

Rights relating to wood on the Common were obviously still of great importance and were referred to in detail in the Act. On page 18 of the Act we read:

> *And whereas the several persons intitled to Right of Common upon the said Commons or waste Grounds claim a Right to a Proportion of the*

Figure 14. The Enclosure Award Map of Rawmarsh (copy), 1781 with the line of the Newcastle or Coal Road highlighted. *Rotherham Central Library, Archives and Local Studies Section*

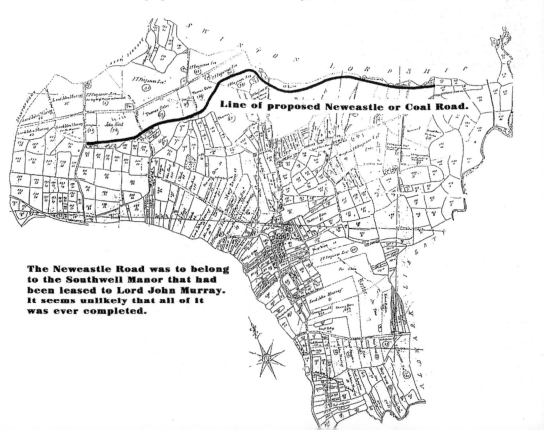

Trees or Underwoods . . . upon the Commons, and the Lords of the Said Manors object to such claim.

The Act empowered the Commissioners to enquire into any claim and they could allow the claimants or their servants or workmen:

within Three Calendar Months next after the passing of the Act, to fell, cut down, grub or stock up the same, and with Horse and Carriages to take and carry away the same for their own Use and Benefit.

This definitely sounds like 'one in the eye' for the lords of the manor!

The actual Enclosure Award was eventually made in 1781 and, with the accompanying map, includes a huge amount of fascinating detail about Rawmarsh. Each field is named, each homestead located and the ownership of every scrap of land in the whole parish definitively declared. Roads, carriageways and footways are defined and arrangements included for their construction if necessary. One fascinating detail in the Award should be highlighted. On page 20 it states:

Whereas some disputes and differences having arisen concerning the boundaries of the said respective Manors of Rawmarsh and Southwell upon the Commons or Waste Grounds within the said Parish of Rawmarsh and hereby inclosed NOW WE the said Christopher Alderson, William Fillingham and John Parker [the Commissioners] having heard the proofs and evidence considering the same and fully considered thereof do Award and Determine that the said Manor of Rawmarsh is bounded on the West by the West side of a Lane called Packman Road . . . and that the said Manor of Southwell is bounded on the East by the said Lane and that the said Manor of Rawmarsh is bounded on the East by the West side of a Road called Swinton Drove Way and that the said Manor of Southwell is bounded on the West by the West side of the said last mentioned Road.

This sounds very much like some very 'cheesed off' Commissioners finally putting their collective 'foot down' to end a long running dispute about ownership of the Common that surely has links with Fairbank's 1740 map!

The sub-division of Rawmarsh Common in the *Enclosure Award* is clearly shown on the accompanying map (Figure 14). It is obvious that seven major landowners got the lion's share of the land with the rest divided amongst 26 much smaller landowners. Figures 15 and 16 show by map and table the way in which the lands of the Common

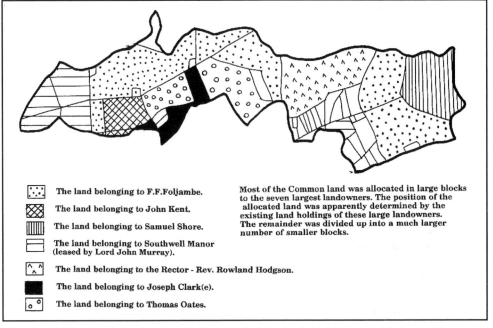

The land belonging to F.F.Foljambe.

The land belonging to John Kent.

The land belonging to Samuel Shore.

The land belonging to Southwell Manor (leased by Lord John Murray).

The land belonging to the Rector - Rev. Rowland Hodgson.

The land belonging to Joseph Clark(e).

The land belonging to Thomas Oates.

Most of the Common land was allocated in large blocks to the seven largest landowners. The position of the allocated land was apparently determined by the existing land holdings of these large landowners. The remainder was divided up into a much larger number of smaller blocks.

Figure 15. An extract from the Rawmarsh Enclosure Award Map showing awards of land on Rawmarsh Common to the seven main landowners.

were allocated. The position of the common land allocated to the largest landowners certainly does not appear to be random but related quite clearly to their existing landholdings. The large blocks of land acquired by the biggest landowners were not kept as such but often broken down into smaller blocks. Indeed maps exist in the Fairbank Collection from as early as 1776 showing the break up of Common land allotted to Thomas Oates and the Reverend Rowland Hodgson amongst smaller landowners such as Robert Amory and George Wright, and this fully five years before the Award!

The eighteenth century parish registers show us that some Rawmarsh families such as the Oxleys, Halls, Heatons and Blacksmiths were increasing their landholdings by carefully selected marriage 'unions' and this land and capital accumulation may have been vital in establishing the pre-conditions for the 'take-off' of the Industrial Revolution locally. Other families, such as the Scorahs (pipe-making) and the Ellises (pot-making), both with representatives on Fairbank's 1740 map, were from at least early in the eighteenth century exploiting their Common-side locations to develop local industries. E.P.Thompson was convinced that these individuals living

The Division of Rawmarsh Common in the Enclosure Award of 1781 (in size order)

NAME	Acres	Roots	Perches	NAME	Acres	Roots	Perches
Francis Foljambe Esq.	189	2	26	Francis Marriott	3	1	34
Rowland Hodgson Rector	86	2	1	Churchwardens	3	0	39
Lord John Murray (Southwell Manor)	83	0	6	George Marriott	3	0	14
Thomas Oates	80	2	34	Grace Marriott	2	2	13
Samuel Shore	56	2	12	Thomas Inman	2	1	2
John Kent	33	0	12	Richard Adron	2	0	2
Joseph Clark (Haugh)	24	1	31	John Lee	2	0	0
Mary Brunt	10	1	15	George Handley	2	0	0
William Rhodes	9	1	3	Susanna Bisby	1	3	31
Christopher Stephenson	9	0	6	Anthony Wright	1	2	7
Sarah & Jonathon Firth	8	2	1	Joseph Clark(Rawmarsh)	1	1	38
Robert Hallam	6	2	20	Ann Wright	1	1	32
John Awty	4	1	24	John Petty	1	1	27
School of Rawmarsh	3	0	32	Anthony Ellis (by house)	1	1	25
James Roberts	3	2	35	Thomas Steel	1	0	27
Joseph Parkin	3	2	34	John Hall	1	0	23

Figure 16. Post-enclosure landowners on Rawmarsh Common showing the area of their holdings. *The Enclosure Award of 1781*

on the common edge and switching from agriculture to industry were vital in the early stages of the Industrial Revolution. He also found evidence from around the country of the resistance of poor people to enclosure and the loss of Common rights (quoted extensively in his book *Customs in Common*), but this evidence is absent locally. It would be interesting to know how the labourers living round Rawmarsh Common in the eighteenth century such as the Sheppards, Pettys and Tingles felt about enclosure. It is hard to imagine them losing the right to exploit some of the resources of the Common without a word. Certainly by the early nineteenth century Rawmarsh could no longer be considered a predominantly agricultural community. The early censuses show clearly (see Figure 17) that Rawmarsh was by then already a mainly manufacturing settlement. This switch from farming was undoubtedly happening from early in the 1700s if the parish

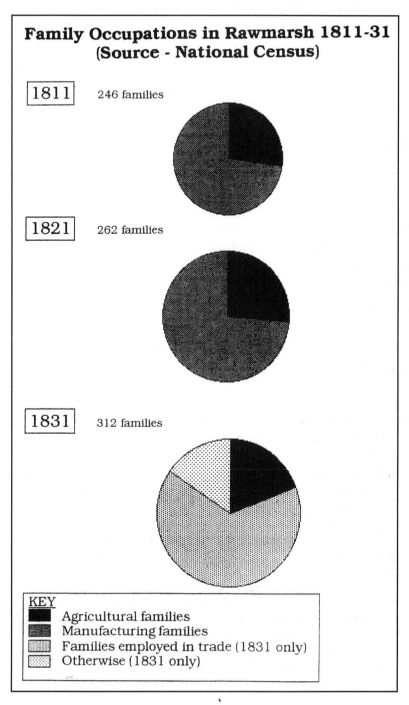

Family Occupations in Rawmarsh 1811-31 (Source - National Census)

1811   246 families

1821   262 families

1831   312 families

KEY
Agricultural families
Manufacturing families
Families employed in trade (1831 only)
Otherwise (1831 only)

Figure 17. The main occupations of Rawmarsh families 1811–1831. *Censuses of 1811, 1821 and 1831*

register information is to be believed but it seems likely that enclosure speeded the change.

So by focusing on one map of Rawmarsh Common produced in 1740 it has been possible to uncover some of the history of that area back into the early Middle Ages and forward into the nineteenth century. By comparing it with other maps and with the parish registers it has been possible to reach back in time to touch the lives of people long dead and to understand more clearly what we can see today in the landscape in and around Rawmarsh. Figure 18 is an aerial photograph of Rawmarsh west of Warren Vale. Compare the outline of the housing area arrowed with the possible area of assarting in Figure 8; could continuity in the landscape be clearer? As always research into a local area has raised as many questions as it has answered (e.g. Was it Wheatcroft Common that Francis Foljambe enclosed in 1630? What did happen to Birch Wood? When did coal mining start in the parish? and so on) but thank goodness that leaves plenty more to be discovered!

Figure 18. Housing in the northern part of the parish of Rawmarsh. *Rotherham Central Library, Archives and Local Studies Section*

References

1.The letters quoted here are part of the Strafford Letters collection held in the Sheffield Archives. I would like to thank Professor David Hey for sending me a full transcription of the letters quoted here as well as other helpful advice.
2. I would like to thank Judy Smith for the information relating to Low Stubbin Incline.

Map Sources

Fairbank's Map of Rawmarsh Common, 1740 (copy). 32/Z1/1. Rotherham Central Library, Archives and Local Studies Section.
Fairbank's Map of the Manor of Wheatcroft, 1758. Row 5L. Fairbank's Collection, Sheffield City Archives.
Rawmarsh Enclosure Award and Map, 1781. 63/B/33. Rotherham Central Library, Archives and Local Studies Section.

Bibliography

Cliffe, J.T., *The Yorkshire Gentry from the Reformation to the Civil War*, London, 1969.
Hall, T. Walter, *The Fairbanks of Sheffield 1688–1848*, 1932.
Harvey, J.C., 'Common Fields and Enclosure in the Lower Dearne Valley', *Yorkshire Archaeological Journal*, Vol 46, 1974, pp. 110–127.
Hunter, Joseph, *South Yorkshire*, London, 1828–1831.
Jones, Melvyn, *Rotherham's Woodland Heritage*, Rotherwood Press, 1995.
King, H. and Harris, A., 'A Survey of the Manor of Settrington', *Yorkshire Archaeological Society*, Record Series, 126, 1962.
Mountford, Frances, *A Commoner's Cottage*, Alan Sutton, 1992.
Preston, F.L., 'A Field Survey of the "Roman Rig" Dyke in SW Yorkshire', *Transactions of the Hunter Archaeological Society*, VI, pt 5, 1949, pp. 197–220 and VI pt 6, 1950, pp. 285–309.
Rackham, Oliver, *The History of the Countryside*, Dent, 1986.
Sheail, John, *Rabbits and their History*, David & Charles, 1971.
Sheail, John, 'Rabbits and Agriculture in post-medieval England', *Journal of Historical Geography*, Vol 14, Part 4, 1978, pp. 343–355.
Tate, W.E., *The English Village Community and the Enclosure Movements*, Gollancz Ltd, 1967.
Thompson, E.P., *Customs in Common*, The Merlin Press, 1991.
Turner, Michael, *English Parliamentary Enclosure*, Dawson-Archon Books, 1980.
Washington Rolls, G., *The Vicars Choral of Southwell Minster and their Lands in Rawmarsh 1408–1850*.

Acknowledgements

Once again I am indebted to Mel and Joan Jones for their encouragement and advice. I would also like to thank particularly the staff in the Local Studies and Archives Section of Rotherham Central Library who have dealt so expertly and patiently with all my requests. I am also grateful to the staff of Sheffield Archives for the assistance they provided. The Rector of St. Mary's Church Rawmarsh, the Rev. Roger Bellamy, kindly lent me some bound copies of the parish registers which proved very useful. Thanks also to Rose Hoppitt for providing some references and to Cynthia Hobson for the presentation of Figures 4, 16 and 17. Finally thanks again to Jane, my wife, for all the hard work of checking and word processing and to Helen for putting up with discussions about Rawmarsh Common even at the breakfast table.

12. EARLY LENDING LIBRARIES IN ROTHERHAM

by Freda Casson

THE ART OF READING AND WRITING began a process which caused people to be dependent on letters to such an extent that the capacity to take part in a society's culture was governed by the literacy level of an individual. Initially reading and writing were restricted to religious, legal and political affairs, but with the development of printing the art of reading began to spread slowly through all classes of society. Social change became inseparable from the development of a literate society as reading became essential to the advancement of science and learning. Thus a relationship began to develop between the rise of literacy and the development of libraries and each age developed its own pattern of library service whose character reflected the social stratification and intellectual habits of its time.

In Rotherham a library, founded in 1728, was held at the Parish Church of All Saints. This came into being at the instigation of Mrs Frances Mansel. She was the daughter of George Westby, of Guilthwaite, and married Henry Saxton, of Harworth. After his death she married a second time and became the wife of the Rev. Edward Mansel, Vicar of Ecclesfield. He died in 1704, and in her second widowhood Mrs Mansel 'gave a library, chiefly of theological works to the value of £100 for the use of the clergy and parishioners for ever.'

A wooden shield bearing details of the origin of the library still survives, as does a volume containing a catalogue of its books, together with rules and issue details. Volumes could be borrowed for a period of two months with the exception of two works (*Collyer's Universal Dictionary* and a *Commentary*) which were for consultation only in the Church.

The first recorded loan of a book was in March, 1730 when the Rev. Mr Ferrand (Vicar of Rotherham, 1704–1733) borrowed the first volume of Backwell's *Sermons*, closely followed by the Rev. Mr Hemingway who chose five volumes.

Persons borrowing books had their names, together with very brief details of the books, entered into the loan book and these details were crossed out when the book was returned (Figure 1). Not everyone observed the rules. In April, 1744, is a note that Mr Thomas Westby had the 14th volume of Rapin's *History*, 'which volume he has had in his possession for upwards of three years'. As this entry has been

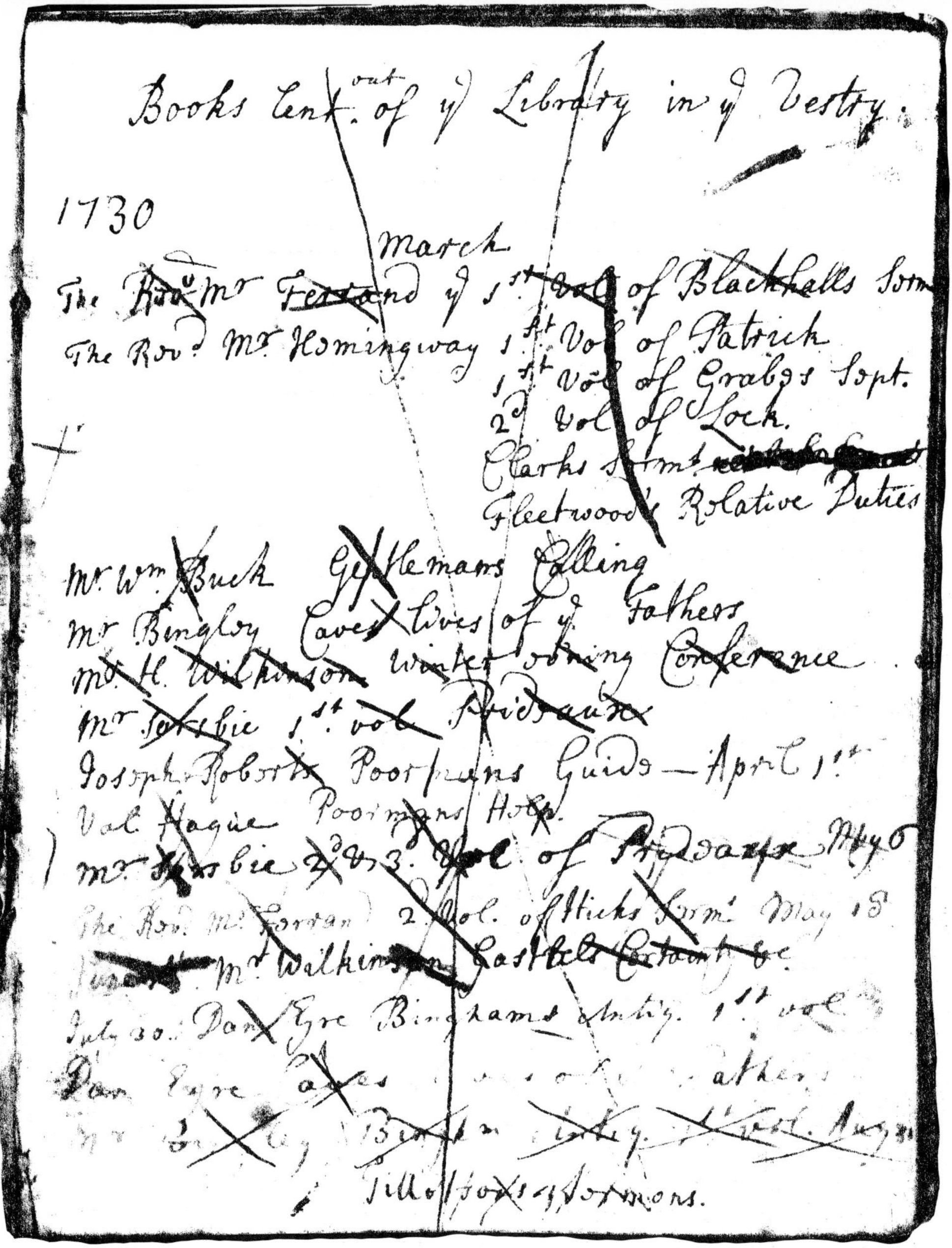

Figure 1. Mansel Library Loan Book: the opening page for 1730.

crossed out it would appear that Mr Westby did return the book at
some point. As other volumes of the *History* were frequently borrowed
Mr Westby must have caused annoyance to other users of this set, but
as a kinsman of the founder of the library perhaps he thought himself
above the rules. Another user of the library, Mr Tunnicliffe, also

merited a special note that he had borrowed books and lent them to
Mr Stanley '*qua authoritate*'.

There is a list of books held by the library in 1782. The Vicar and
his curate were the principal librarians, but they were allowed to
deputise a librarian who was not allowed to be a 'salaried mercenary
officer' as such a person would be 'an encumbrance and dead weight
and a perpetual burden'. It was also hoped that gentlemen of public
spirit would donate money to repair books and improve the collection.
There is a list of books given by Mrs Westby in 1758 and 1759, and
on the evidence of bookplates both the Earl of Effingham and the
Honorable Thomas Wentworth each gave a book to the library.

The number of books borrowed declined over a period of years, the
last record of a loan being in March 1868 when Mr Verey borrowed
Epistles of the Father. The books remained in the Parish Church until
1893 when they were handed over to the Free Public Library, and
housed in a specially built bookcase. The Public Library in Main
Street was destroyed by fire in 1925 but the books from the Parish
Church Library were rescued.

A Subscription Library had been founded in Rotherham in 1775.
A volume of 'Rules, subscribers' names and catalogue of books'
survives for the year 1826. At that date there were sixty subscribers
paying a three guinea entry fee and a subsequent annual subscription
of one guinea. All the subscribers are listed by name, and, in cases
where they lived out of town, a word to indicate their address. Four
women are listed – Mrs Dennis (Brecks), Miss Oxley (Moorgate),
Miss Walker (Masbrough) and Mrs Wigfield. According to the rules
they were excused from attendance at the monthly meetings at the
Library (which male members were expected to attend), but they were
allowed to propose books to be bought either by proxy or by letter.
Many of the names of the male members can be connected to local
industry, trade or the professions. Seven clergymen are also included
in this list.

The Treasurer of the Library was Mr Heseltine. He was Edward
Heseltine, Manager of the Walker, Stanley and Eyre Bank in High
Street (later the Sheffield and Rotherham Joint Stock Bank). About
this time it is written that he was often to be seen 'sunning himself
daily . . . with his blue coat and gilt buttons, a chevalier of the old
school.' As Treasurer he had to produce accounts each June, pay the
Librarian's salary, and pay other bills as they were received.
Subscriptions were due in June, and he had to report to the
Committee the names of subscribers who had not paid their dues by
August.

The Librarian in 1826 was John Clarke. He was elected to the position at the Annual General Meeting. He had to 'attend to the Library each day (Sunday excepted) from nine in the morning till eight at night', and keep an accurate record of all books borrowed. When books were returned he had to examine them and inform the Committee of any damage in order that a fine could be imposed. If a book already on loan was asked for then he had to tell the person making the request the date of its expected return together with the name of the person who had the book on loan.

Open access to library books was far in the future and in the Subscription Library they were arranged by size, and then allocated a call number, which had to be cited by the person wishing to borrow a book. Examples of books available range from Bruce's *Travels to Discover the Sources of the Nile* in five volumes, and Howett's *Christian Researches in Syria and the Holy Land* to such lighter sounding volumes such as *Lights and Shadows of a Scottish life*, by the author of *The Trials of Margaret Lindsay*, and Cunningham's *Velvet Cushion*. Periodicals such as the *Edinburgh Review* and the *Literary Gazette* were also available, together with back runs on file.

By 1858 the number of subscribers had risen to eighty-four, together with three honorary members. At this date only three clergymen are subscribers – the Rev. Richard Moseley, Vicar of Rotherham, the Rev. John Foster, Vicar of Wickersley and the Rev. P. L. Sandberg, Vicar of Kimberworth. The Earl of Effingham and Earl Fitzwilliam were also subscribers, and the number of women members had risen. One of these women was Mrs Hinchliffe, High Street. She was possibly Ann Hinchliffe and would have been involved in the printing of the Library's Catalogue at the premises of Hinchliffe and Epworth and also being the publisher of the *Rotherham and Masbrough Advertiser* which had started publication in January, 1858.

The Treasurer of the Library in 1858 was J. Haywood and the Librarian was Miss M. Newton. She had to be present during opening hours which were 10.00 a.m. to 1.00 p.m. Monday to Saturday, with a half day closure each Thursday. The books were still shelved by a call number and a subscriber, or their messenger, had to cite this, together with the title of the book in order to borrow it. To prevent 'disarrangement of books' subscribers were requested not to help themselves to books but 'to apply to the Librarian to take down and replace any work into which they may wish to look.'

The range of periodicals available had been extended and now included such practical titles as *The Farmer's Magazine* and *The Mechanic's Magazine*. Also available in the Library were books now

---

CATALOGUE.

A.

Abernethy, Dr., Memoirs of, by George Macilwain. 1 vol. 1856.

Accum, Frederick, Treatise on the Use of Chemical Tests. 1 vol., 1818.

Achilli, Dr., Dealings with the Inquisition. 1 vol., 1851.

Adair, James, History of the American Indians. 1 vol., 1775.

Adams, George, Essays on the Microscope. 1 vol., 1787.

Addison, G. G., Knights Templars. 1 vol., 1842.

Addison, Joseph, Life of. 2 vols., 1843.

,,   ,,   Remarks on several Parts of Italy. 1 vol., 1767.

,,   ,,   Works in Prose and Verse. 3 vols., 1766.

Aguilar, Grace, The Days of Bruce. 1 vol.

,,   ,,   Home Influence. 1 vol.

,,   ,,   The Mother's Recompense. 1 vol., 1866.

,,   ,,   The Vale of Cedars. 1 vol.

,,   ,,   The Women of Israel. 2 vols., 1865.

Figure 2. Beginning of the Catalogue of Rotherham Subscription Library, 1868.

regarded as classics, but were then recently published books written by authors such as Charles Dickens.

Ten years later these and other popular authors of the time were well represented on the shelves of the Library. Possibly the women-folk of the male subscribers were having an effect on the titles purchased. Some titles are intriguing (Figure 2). What, for example, was *Aunt Maud's Trouble*, or *The Mother's Recompense*? At that time (1868) the members of the Library are listed as either a Proprietor or a Subscriber, there being eighty-six of the former and twelve of the latter, together with two honorary members. Miss Newton was still Librarian, but at some point between 1876 and 1881 she was succeeded by Miss Eliza Raybould. The Library continued in existence until 1886, at which time it amalgamated with the Literary and Scientific Society.

Earlier in the century there appears to have been a small circulation library operating from a High Street shop. In 1890 Mr W. Naylor wrote to the *Rotherham Advertiser* saying that in the 1830s and 1840s:

Naylor's, top of High Street, had a circulating library of over one thousand volumes, mostly novels and romances. One set of three or four volumes was called A bride and no wife. *It was always out and they could have done with another set. Another set was Rev. Isaac Watts'* Work *in seven volumes. During the Thirties and Forties they were not out once.*

The two libraries founded in the eighteenth century appear to have been used by the upper and middle classes of the town. By the nineteenth century working class people began to have greater access to books as local churches and chapels began to organise and operate small libraries and reading rooms.

In a letter to his parishioners written in 1862 the Vicar of Masbrough, the Rev. H. Master White, who at that time was holding services in a temporary church prior to St. John the Evangelist being built, wrote

For a Parochial Lending Library I have received a grant of books from the Society for Promoting Christian Knowledge. Applications for the books should be made to me, at my house, where the books are available for lending.

In 1863 the Rebecca Hussey Book Charity, administered from Westminster, provided ten pounds to buy more books. A letter written to the Rev. H. Master White said that the books could be purchased at a reduced price which meant that thirteen pounds worth of books would be provided, but that the order must not include bibles, prayer books, tracts or chap books. The list of books chosen included *Tom Brown's Schooldays*, *The Heir of Radcliffe* and Lamb's *Tales from Shakespeare* for recreational reading, whilst those readers in search of more serious reading could choose from such titles as *Introduction to Gothic Architecture* and *Health for the Household*. As could be expected a number of books on religious topics were chosen including *Scripture Topography* and Bishop Trower's books on the Epistles and the Gospels.

At Kimberworth a Reading Room was provided at the Church Institute 'for the benefit of the working classes', a similar establishment also being available at Greasbrough. A number of non-conformist churches provided similar facilities, specific examples being Talbot Lane Chapel, Masbrough Independent Chapel and the Baptist Chapel in Westgate.

The Temperance Society was inaugurated in 1838, starting with

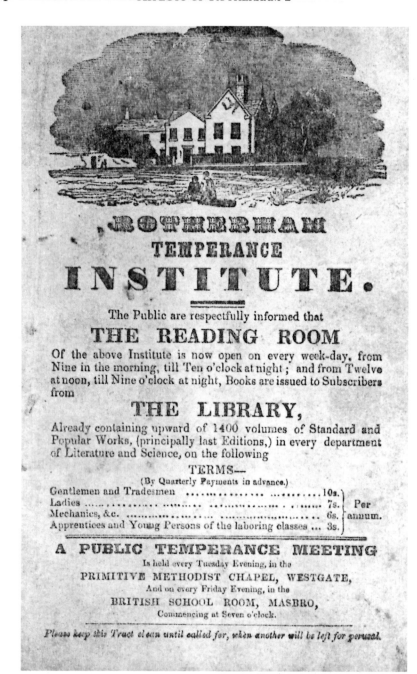

Figure 3. Handbill for the Temperance Institute Reading Room and Library.

meetings in both the open air and in hired halls. The Committee, anticipating a need to provide recreational and educational facilities for its younger members, bought the old vicarage in the corner of the Churchyard in order to use it as a Temperance Institute. Following a visit to London by some members, 1,500 books were bought, a Librarian appointed and the Institute's library opened in 1843 (Figure 3). The books provided were 'standard and popular works in every department of literature and science.' The cost of equipping the library and classrooms, and the provision of books cost between £350 and £400.

Unfortunately after its initial success the Institute failed to attract sufficient members to finance its running costs. In 1849 a meeting was held at the Court House at which a resolution was passed 'that the Temperance Institute be changed . . . into a Mechanics' Institute.' Following negotiations the library and other effects of the Institute were transferred to the new organisation for the sum of £220 10s.

In the same year a decision was made to build new premises, taking two years to negotiate a site. This was to be on land leased from the Earl of Effingham. The original cost of the lease was to have been £12 10s per year, but the Earl agreed that this cost could be lowered to £5 in consideration of the public good likely to be derived from the Institute. The Rotherham and Masbrough Literary and Mechanics' Institute was formally opened in 1853 (Figure 4). Immediately an

Figure 4. The Rotherham and Masbrough Literary and Mechanics' Institute.

ambitious programme began with classes in elementary and advanced reading, writing, arithmetic, vocal music, French, German and phonography (shorthand).

The Library was an attractive part of the Institute and more books were bought to complement the teaching. It was found that there was a demand for general literature and fiction so the Committee decided to buy more books that were 'attractive and popular'. Between 1858 and 1860 the lady members of the Institute were responsible for supplying funds for book purchases and by the end of this period they had the sum of only 7$\frac{1}{2}$d in hand!

By 1858 the Institute had 318 members, made up from seven honorary members, seven gentlemen and thirteen ladies, the rest being tradesmen, artisans, females and juveniles. Each category of member paid a different subscription level. The classes were well attended and between 50 and 60 books were borrowed each week from the Library. The number of books held grew from 1,500 in 1861 to 3,000 in 1868. Over the next three years, possibly as books were discarded, this number fell to 1,800, but by 1881 the number of books reached the 1868 level again.

The period of loan for books was either seven or 14 days, depending on the size of the volume – quarto or octavo. In 1875 the Reading Room was open between 9.00 a.m. and 10.00 p.m. daily. It contained eight daily newspapers, 17 weekly papers, together with monthly and quarterly periodicals (Figure 5). A Librarian (George Cusworth in 1861, Miss Wright in 1868 and William Cusworth in 1871) was on duty between 7.00 p.m. and 9.00 p.m. to issue books. Only one could be borrowed at a time unless the work comprised several volumes, then the set was issued for the same period as a single book. Many books were donated to the Library, including such titles as *Female Piety, The Curse of Britain – Intemperance* and *A treatise on the Teeth of Wheels*.

After 1878 no more new books were purchased as the question of the opening of a Free Public Library was being discussed by the Borough and it was expected that the Institute's Library would be bought to form the nucleus of the new library. This did not happen, but the opening of the Free Public Library led to a slow reduction in the number of members of the Institute, as they gradually used the new source of books. The Institute did survive until 1891, at which time the Borough Council purchased the property in order to incorporate it into the new Town Hall being built at that time.

The Rotherham Ivanhoe Club was founded in 1871, the year Rotherham was incorporated as a Borough. Initially it held weekly

THE ROTHERHAM AND MASBROUGH
Literary and Mechanics' Institute

Offers to its Members the following advantages, viz.:

.1. A NEWSROOM. A comfortable, well-lighted, and well-ventilated READING ROOM, open from Nine o'Clock in the Morning till Ten at Night, and supplied with the following London and Provincial Newspapers, Periodicals, and Magazines :—

DAILY.		MONTHLY.
The Times	Punch'	Blackwood's Magazine
The Daily News	Saturday Review	Macmillan's ,,
The Daily Telegraph	Spectator	Cornhill ,,
The Standard	Society of Arts' Journal	All the Year Round
Sheffield Daily Tele-	Doncaster Gazette	Chambers' Journal
graph	Midland Counties'	Leisure Hour
Sheffield & Rotherham	Herald	Animal World
Independent	Newcastle Chronicle	
Leeds Mercury	Judy	
Manchester Daily Exa-	Derbyshire Times	
miner and Times	Belfast Northern Whig	QUARTERLY.
	English Mechanic	
WEEKLY.	Iron	Edinburgh Review
The Illustrated London	Builder	Quarterly Review
News	Stamford Mercury	London Quarterly Re-
The Graphic	Rotherham and Mas-	view
	brough Advertiser	

2. A LIBRARY. The Library contains about 1750 volumes of well-selected works on Science, History, and Popular Literature, for circulation and reference, to which additions will be made from time to time.

3. LECTURES. During the Winter Session there are numerous Lectures on Scientific and Popular Subjects. Members are admitted *Free*.

4. CLASSES. Every facility is afforded in the formation of Classes for the instruction of members in the elementary branches of Education, Science, and Drawing.

Figure 5. Details of the Reading Room, Library, Lectures and Classes at the Literary and Mechanics' Institute 1875.

meetings which took the form of a paper being read on a topic prepared by a member, followed by a discussion on the subject. Members of the Club were men over the age of 21, who were admitted to the Club by ballot. One of its objects was to acquire knowledge by mutual consideration and discussion on any subject other than one of a disloyal nature. The Club was suspended in 1968 due to lack of members and was formally wound up in 1971.

During its first year, two of the subjects discussed were the introduction of compulsory education and the reduction of income tax from sixpence to fivepence in the pound. A library was soon initiated, its first books being donated by members. By 1874 a halfpenny from each member's subscription was being allocated to the purpose of purchasing books. The first to be acquired by this means were a selection bought for £4 7s 6d, and included *Self-help* by Samuel Smiles, *Facts and Hints of Everyday Life* and ten volumes of *Chambers' Miscellany*.

The library, small as it was, developed into a circulating library and rules for borrowing were drawn up. A Librarian and his assistant had to be members of the Club and attend to issue books between 8.00 p.m. and 9.00 p.m. Books were issued for 14 days and a fine of a halfpenny a week was levied on overdue books. This sum could be paid either in cash or in postage stamps.

Books continued to be given by members, an appropriate gift being Sir Walter Scott's *Ivanhoe*. In 1879 the members decided to buy a copy of the newly published *Historic Notices of Rotherham* by John Guest, which is hardly a book to be read in 14 days. A member was severely reprimanded in 1882 for borrowing the book without permission and not returning it within the loan period. Possibly as a result of this a Club resolution was passed in the following year:

> *That any member wishing to take out John Guest's* History of Rotherham *can only have the same by a two-third majority of the members present, and the Librarian shall carefully examine the book when returned to see if there are any finger marks upon it.*

As membership of the club fluctuated so did the number of books borrowed, but the Club did produce a small printed catalogue of its books which was sold for a halfpenny. The opening of the Free Public Library had a detrimental effect on both borrowing and purchasing of books and no more were bought after 1900.

Rotherham was incorporated as a Borough in 1871 and so gained power to establish a Free Library under the Public Libraries Act,

1850. This Act allowed any borough with a population of over 10,000 to establish such a library. The decision to do so had to be taken at a meeting of local government electors and could involve no more than an expenditure of a halfpenny rate on building, furnishing and operating a library (this sum was raised to one penny in 1885).

In 1873 Rotherham Council elected a committee to consider the best way to establish a library, but this body never made a report to Council. A new Committee was set up in 1875, resulting in a public meeting being held in February 1876. It was reported that 'There was not a large attendance, the audience numbering something like one hundred.' Those present passed a resolution that the Public Libraries be adopted for the town.

Later that month a Free Library Committee was set up by the Council which would work for several years before a library was opened. One of the issues discussed by this Committee was whether workmen, on their way home wearing dirty clothes, should be allowed to use the library. A decision was made that, providing he had clean hands, a workman could change books, but not sit in the Reading Room in working clothes. Much effort was expended on trying to find premises for the library, and in 1879 it was agreed that rooms in the old Gas Offices in Frederick Street should be used, the rent being £10 per year. Early in 1880 tenders were accepted for the provision of furniture and fittings, a sub-committee was formed to select books, and a penny rate levied.

An advertisement for the appointment of a Librarian appeared in the *Rotherham Advertiser* on 12 June, 1880.

The Free Library will at their meeting to be held on Thursday, the 24th inst. consider Applications for the Office of LIBRARIAN. Applications, in the handwriting of the candidate, stating age, present occupation and salary required and accompanied by Testimonials of recent date, should be sent to my office marked "Librarian".

The Town Clerk received 25 replies to this and three names were selected to be put forward to the Council meeting to be held in July. The names, together with the salaries asked were William Hall (£52 10s), Thomas Machin (£60) and Thomas Woodger (£50). The *Advertiser* reported that voting took place by 'scratching' and that eventually William Hall was appointed to the post. His first task was to become involved with buying books, spending £350 during the next two months.

When the Library was deemed ready for the public the Mayor (Ald.

MINUTES OF THE COMMITTEES

To be Presented to the MONTHLY COUNCIL MEETING to be
holden on WEDNESDAY, the 6th day of OCTOBER, 1880

FREE LIBRARY COMMITTEE, 23rd September, 1880.

1 The Sub-Committee submitted the following Periodicals, and the Committee recommend
that they be purchased for the use of the Free Library :—

QUARTERLY REVIEWS.

Edinburgh Review.	The British Quarterly Review.
The Quarterly Review.	The Westminster Review.

MONTHLY REVIEWS.

The Art Journal.	Chambers' Journal.
Nineteenth Century.	Contemporary Review.
Macmillan.	Cornhill Magazine.
Blackwood.	Frazer's Magazine.
All The Year Round.	Leisure Hour.
Band of Hope Review.	Scribner's Mercury.
British Workman.	Science Gossip.

WEEKLY PERIODICALS

Builder.	Land and Water.
English Mechanic.	Notes and Queries.
Engineer.	Punch.
Gardener's Chronicle.	Scientific American.
Graphic.	Cassell's Magazine.
Illustrated London News.	

Figure 6. Periodicals provided in the Reading Room at Rotherham Free Library, 1880.

R. Marsh) performed the opening ceremony in October 1880. Suitable speeches were made after which 'those present sat down in the Reading Room to partake of a light lunch'. The Library then began to serve the people of the town and was such a success that two months later Mr Hall was urging the Library Committee 'on the desirability of providing more books as the present stock is quite inadequate to the demands made on it.'

More books were bought and periodicals provided in the Reading Room (Figure 6), opening up a source of reading material to many of the town's inhabitants previously without ready access to material for learning and leisure, and gradually the former privately run libraries, clubs and other organisations were closed.

Sources

A brief history of the Parish Church of St John the Evangelist, Masbrough (1964).

Casson, Freda, 'The Mansel Library', *The Ivanhoe Review*, No 8, Summer, 1995, pp. 44–46.

The Mansel Collection. Held at the Archives and Local Studies Section of Rotherham Central Library.

Rotherham and Masbrough Literary and Mechanics' Institute. *Annual Reports.*

Rotherham Library. Rules, subscribers and catalogue of books. 1826, 1858, 1868.

Rotherham and Masbrough Advertiser.

Steeple, T. W., 'A history of adult and further education in nineteenth century Rotherham', Unpublished thesis, 1977.

13. THE HORSE OYLE MILL

by Tony Munford

TRAVELLERS MAKING THEIR WAY SOUTH out of Rotherham along Westgate may pause to wonder about the origin of the name of one of the streets that lead off to the left. Oil Mill Fold leads steeply up the hill from Westgate, continuing up steps into Downs Row and into Moorgate Street. It is now the only street in the town to retain its stone setts. Today it provides access only to a funeral director and a second-hand car dealer. In the nineteenth century the land between Oil Mill Fold and Wilfred Street was occupied by houses. In the eighteenth century, however, Oil Mill Fold was the site of the horse-powered oil mill which gave the street its name.

Some of the history of the site can be deduced from the records of Rotherham's Unitarian congregation. Probably the oldest nonconformist congregation in the town, the Unitarians initially met in a building in Allenby's Yard, Church Street, but in 1704 a new chapel was erected in Downs Row with the aid of a trust established by Thomas Hollis.[1] The chapel was supported by a considerable trust estate, part of which was the site of the oil mill. The early history of the site can be traced in the deeds to the site which form part of the chapel archives.[2]

The earliest deed dates from 1753 but recites earlier deeds. In 1734 Robert Haslabie of Rotherham, gent, had sold a parcel of land in a croft off Westgate, known as Royds Croft, measuring 45 yards by 25 yards, to Thomas Buck of Sheffield, grocer. Buck subsequently erected a 'horse oyle mill' on the land. Four years later Haslabie leased to Buck a kiln and malthouse which he had erected on Royds Croft with the right to use a pump in Royds Croft to water the horses at the oil mill and a right of way for carriages and top loads to the mill, for a term of 5,000 years at a rent of 7s [35p] a year. In 1739 Buck took a lease from the Hon. John Finch of Thrybergh and Dame Elizabeth his wife of a newly erected house at Ickles with an adjacent ancient water-powered corn mill (lately converted into an oil mill), standing on the River Don, and various fields (including Castle Garth and Temple Brough) totalling 40 acres, known as Ickles Low Farm. The term was 21 years and the annual rent £55-15s-9d [£55.78½]. In February 1753 Thomas Buck sold the oil mill in Westgate to Thomas Atkinson of Tinsley, oil drawer, for £1,000. The transaction also included the assignment to Atkinson of the right to use the pump and the right of way, with the remainder of the lease at Ickles and all the lead vats, vessels and utensils about the two oil mills.

Atkinson obtained a new lease, from the now widowed Elizabeth Finch, of Ickles Mill and Ickles Low Farm together with Ickles High Farm (45 acres) for 21 years at £94-11s [£94.55] a year. He did not enjoy the property for long and was dead by May 1755. In that month Atkinson's widow Elizabeth and his father, Joseph Atkinson of Rawcliffe, merchant, sold the Royds Croft property and assigned the Ickles leasehold to John Walton and John Hall of Thurlstone, oil drawers. The price was £530-5s-6d [£530.27$\frac{1}{2}$]. The Hall/Walton partnership was to continue for almost 30 years but eventually failed. In 1781 John Hall and Isaac Walton of Eccles [sic], describing themselves as oil drawers, dealers, chapmen and partners, had been declared bankrupt by a commission consisting of John Parker of Woodthorpe, in the parish of Handsworth, Samuel Tooker of Moorgate, Josiah Beckwith of Masbrough, James Wheat of Sheffield and John Foljambe of Rotherham. The horse oil mill etc on Royds Croft was assigned to James Walton of Thurlstone and Thomas Bloom of Trumfleet, gents, in recompense for £1,552-2s-6d [£1,552.12$\frac{1}{2}$] which Hall and Walton owed to James Walton. In August 1784 Walton and Bloom sold the parcel of land in Royds Croft with the horse oil mill and other buildings and the use of the pump etc to John Rimington of Sheffield, attorney, for £200.

In the days before society learned to exploit mineral oils, oil for lubrication, medicinal or culinary uses had to be obtained from animal sources (tallow or whale oil) or from vegetable sources. In England, with no olives or other oily fruit available, oil was produced by crushing seeds, the commonest being linseed and rape seeds. Rape seeds produced colza oil which was used in oil lamps. The oil extracted from linseed or flax has the property of drying on exposure to the air and is therefore used in paints, varnishes and printing inks. The seed is first crushed and then ground to a fine meal before being pressed to extract the oil. The percentage of oil extracted could be increased by heating the meal before pressing. In the eighteenth century the Dutch or stamper press was in wide use. A wooden (later cast iron) box was filled with bags of oil meal which were placed under pressure between perforated iron plates by driving in wedges. The oil was then driven out by heavy iron stampers. This type of press was generally superseded in the nineteenth century by the hydraulic press which had been invented by Joseph Bramah in 1795.

The oil could be refined by exposing it to light in shallow trays under glass and could also be boiled to improve its drying properties.

The surviving documents give no technical information about the mill in Rotherham. On a site where water power was not available and in a period when the steam engine was used only to drive pumps, horse power was the only means available to power such a mill. The seeds would have been crushed and ground in an edge running mill in which a millstone was driven around a circular trough. The stone could have been driven by shafts and gears from a horse gin or, more simply, by a shaft pivoted in the centre of the trough with the horse harnessed to the other end. Horses could also be used to power the screw presses that were used before the stamper press came into use. We also have no information about the source of the seeds used in the mill. There was certainly a linen industry in late eighteenth century Rotherham. Today different strains of flax (linum) are grown, optimised for linen production and for oil seed production. In the eighteenth century it is likely that the same strain

Figure 1. The Oil Mill Fold area, redrawn from 'A plan of the town of Rotherham', drawn for the Rt Hon Earl of Effingham by Bartholomew Rotheram (master of the Feoffees School). *Rotherham Central Library, Archives and Local Studies Section*

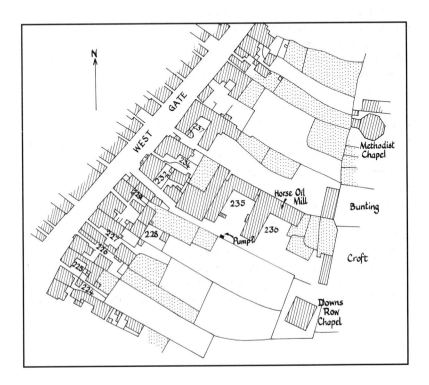

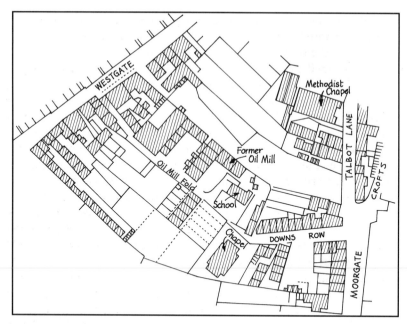

Figure 2. The Oil Mill Fold area redrawn from 'A map of the township of Rotherham' by Charles Rawson. *Rotherham Central Library, Archives and Local Studies Section*

was used for both purposes. It is also likely that the crop was grown locally although Arthur Young made no mention of it being grown in the Rotherham area.[3]

Rimington kept the property for four years before selling it at a profit (for £300) to Sheffield banker William Shore. By the time of this sale in October 1788 the mill had ceased to work and the property was described as 'a parcel of land, part of Royds Croft, with several dwelling houses etc thereon, formerly a horse oil mill'. Shore was not operating for himself but on behalf of the trustees of Downs Row Chapel. The site was acquired specifically to allow the erection of a new building for the Hollis School, founded in 1702, which had been held in the chapel since 1704. A total of £399-6s [£399.30] was raised from subscribers (including Timothy Hollis of London) towards the cost of the site and building which cost £481-10-7d [£481.53].[4]

Unfortunately the original deed was never registered at the West Riding Registry of Deeds at Wakefield and no declaration had ever been made of the trusts affecting the property. This was rectified in 1791 when, as part of another transaction, it was declared that the

£300 purchase money had been the property of the chapel trustees and that Shore had been operating on their behalf. Shore released his interest in the property to Samuel Shore of Clapham (Surrey), John Shore of Sheffield, banker, Jonathan Mellor of Ickles, book keeper, John Hollis of High Wycombe (Buckinghamshire), Isaac Solly of London, Samuel Shore jnr of Norton (Derbyshire), Joseph Turner of Rotherham and William Favell of Rotherham. The trusts affecting the property were declared as the application of the rents and profits from the property to maintain and augment the salary of the minister of the chapel and 'towards the support of a school lately erected by private subscription on part of the said piece of ground'.

The new Hollis School stood near the bottom of the steps leading up to Downs Row Chapel and the 1791 deed therefore enables the position of the horse oil mill to be located. It can be identified on the earliest surviving map of the town, dating from 1774 when the mill was still in operation (Figure 1).[5] Unfortunately the book of reference that accompanied the map is lost but it is certain that the mill was the L–shaped building numbered 236 and lying north of Oil Mill Fold. The site of this building with the yard and the gardens above it approximate very closely with the dimensions of the plot in the deed of 1734. The plan shows a small, square structure half way up Oil Mill Fold. This may perhaps be the pump. The 1788 deed indicated that the mill building had been converted into dwellings. The 1843 rating map of Rotherham township shows the Hollis School numbered 789 and the mill building divided into eight cottages (Figure 2). It is not possible to speculate how much of the structure of the mill survived in these cottages as no photographs of them have survived. The building below the mill (no 235 on the 1774 map – possibly the kiln and malthouse referred to in the 1753 deed) had also been divided into cottages. These survived long enough to be photographed in 1933.[6]

Today the site of the mill looks unsuitable for a mill of any type, sloping steeply towards Westgate. A nineteenth century engraving of Downs Row Chapel before its rebuilding in 1841, shows the upper part of the site as relatively level with Oil Mill Fold rising up to the steps between retaining walls (Figure 3). The upper part of the site

Figure 3. The original Downs Row Chapel and the top of Oil Mill Fold, early nineteenth century. *Rotherham Central Library, Archives and Local Studies Section*

had been terraced to provide a level site for the new school and its playground. The rest of the site must always have sloped much as it does today. The eight cottages that succeeded the mill were demolished in 1901 when the Hollis Trustees erected a terrace of six houses fronting onto Wilfred Street. These survived until the 1970s.

The new school was originally single storey. A second storey, with a staircase tower was added in 1860 so that boys and girls could be accommodated on different floors (Figure 4). The Hollis School was leased to the Rotherham School Board in 1893 and used as a temporary board school until 1896 when the new Alma Road Schools were opened. The Hollis School was then converted into three cottages which continued to provide a rental income to the trustees until they too were demolished in the 1970s.[7]

Figure 4. The Hollis School as it was after the additions of 1860. *Rotherham Central Library, Archives and Local Studies Section*

Figure 5 shows Oil Mill Fold in 1936. Now only a tarmac car park, stretching between Oil Mill Fold and Wilfred Street, marks the site of the 'horse oil mill'. The venerable stone wall at the top of the site supports the terrace on which the Hollis School stood. Of the pump where the horses were watered after their exertions in the oil mill, there is now no sign.

References

1.   The site of Allenby's Yard is now occupied by Phillip Howard Books on Church Street. Thomas Hollis (1634–1718) was the son of Thomas Hollis of Rotherham, whitesmith, and was apprenticed to his uncle, a Sheffield cutler. In 1654 his uncle sent him to manage a cutlery business in London and four years later he married Anne Thorner whose brother was an early benefactor of Harvard College. Hollis contributed towards the building of Sheffield's first nonconformist chapel on Snig Hill and its successor, the Upper Chapel on Norfolk Street. He was also responsible for providing a site for the new chapel in Downs Row in 1704, having two years earlier endowed a school for the education of poor children. His son, Thomas Hollis

junior, was a trustee of the Rotherham chapel and endowed two professorships and several scholarships at Harvard. For the history of the congregation and the chapel, see Rev William Blazeby, *Rotherham: the old meeting-house and its ministers*, Rotherham 1906.

2. The chapel archives are deposited with the Archives and Local Studies Section of Rotherham Central Library.

3. Arthur Young, *A six month tour through the North of England*, 3 vols, Dublin 1770.

4. Accounts quoted by Rev. William Blazeby, op cit, pp. 146–8.

5. The original map is also lost. It was borrowed from Winder's, the Earl of Effingham's agents in Sheffield, in the 1930s and copied by the Borough Engineer's Dept. The original was returned to Winder's and when enquiries were made about it after the War, it could not be found. Several of the copies are now held by the Archives and Local Studies Section, Rotherham Central Library.

6. See the photograph reproduced on p.295 of *Aspects of Rotherham 1*, ed. Melvyn Jones, Wharncliffe Publishing, 1995.

7. The school building bore a stone recording its foundation and rebuilding. This was moved to the chapel when the school closed and has misled some people into thinking that the inscription referred to the chapel building. The stone currently to be seen on the chapel wall is a reproduction, erected when the chapel surrounds were refurbished in recent years.

Figure 5. Oil Mill Fold in 1936 after the demolition of Alma Place and Jubbs Yard which stood below the chapel, which can just be seen at the top right. The houses on the left occupy the site of the horse oil mill, with the former Hollis School standing above them. *Rotherham Central Library, Archives and Local Studies Section, ref 8744*

14. THE RUDDLE MINES AT MICKLEBRING AND THE RUDDLE MILL AT BRAITHWELL

by John Goodchild, M. Univ.

THE VARIOUS USES OF RADDLE OR REDDLE or ruddle, as the word was variously spelt, were conveniently described in the 1895 edition of *Chambers' Encyclopaedia*, at a time when this mineral substance was still in common use from English sources:

> *an impure peroxide of iron . . . It varies greatly too in hardness... In colour it passes from a pale brick-red to a tint occasionally nearly as bright as vermilion. It is found in many places abroad, and in England in Somersetshire, the Forest of Dean, at Wastwater in Cumberland, and, of a quality valuable for polishing optical glasses, near Rotherham in Yorkshire. Some kinds of it are used for marking sheep, others for carpenters' and masons' pencils, and the finer qualities for artists' crayons. Red ochre is one of the varieties.*

Over a long period, although always on a small scale so far as employment was concerned, this red or reddish mineral was mined at Micklebring, and later also processed at a mill in Braithwell, which are adjoining villages some six miles to the east of Rotherham (see Figure 1).

It is the historian's pleasure to initially find and then bring together in a story, references in manuscripts, books, maps and human memory to the subject which is being studied, and in the case of the history of ruddle mining – as here we will henceforth describe it – the sources of references to the industry are widely scattered. Numbers of such references were used by Dr Ivor Brown and F. W. Cowdell in essays published in the *Bulletin of the Peak District Mines Historical Society* in 1967 and 1970, and to these the present writer has been able to add more, although there is little doubt but that, as is usually the case with historical research, further references will ultimately come to light – and of these, the present writer would much like to hear. The present study is then one reflecting the present state of knowledge on this fascinating subject.

A reference occurs in the parish register of Stainton – a parish adjoining to that of Braithwell – in 1622NS to the burial of 'a poore Radleman' there, of the unusual and possibly significant name of

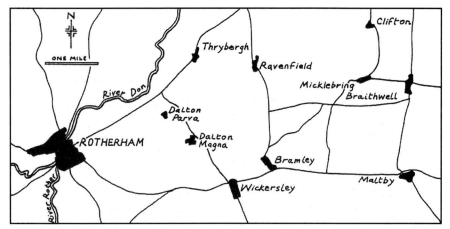

Figure 1. Location of Micklebring and Braithwell. Settlement sizes and shapes and the main road routes are as they would have been in *c*.1840.

James Meridolla. Ralph Thoresby, FRS, the Leeds historian and diarist, refers in about 1712 to a specimen of ruddle in his own museum, which came from Edlington, the estate of his friend Robert Molesworth; the more recent (1973) detailed study of Edlington Wood makes no reference to such mines there. It is possible that no organised, capitalistic form of ruddle mining and processing occurred until the eighteenth century, and documents indeed suggest that such may be the case. In 1750 an agreement was entered into whereby the common land of the lord of the manor of Braithwell (the Duke of Leeds) was to be explored for ruddle:

> *it was apprehended that there was a Vein of Rudd or Raddle in some parts of the Wast ground belonging to the Towne of Braithwell and Micklebring*

and one George Brooke

> *was desirous to try where there was any such Vein of Rudd . . .* [and was granted permission] *to sink Pitts or otherwise to try to get and Carry away to his own use the same in any part of the Highways or Waste Ground belonging to the said Duke as Lord.*

Brooke was to pay £20 as rent for every 100 lbs of ruddle produced, and an account was to be produced each year. Who this George Brooke was, is difficult to tell, as several of that name were baptised at Braithwell at the end of the seventeenth and the beginning of the eighteenth centuries, but Brooke created a partnership to exploit his grant, taking as equal partners George Staniforth of Braithwell, farmer (almost certainly born in 1725 and married in 1751), Thomas Townrow of Conisbrough and Jonathan Smith of Ravenfield, both described as millwrights. The partners negotiated ruddle-working leases from the Duke and from a Mr Wilford, and in 1766 they agreed to deliver up all – but to whom is not stated or inferred – in return for a modest £46. 10s. 0d; George Brooke signed as 'Miner'.

When Thomas Jefferys surveyed Yorkshire in 1767–70 he found 'Reddle Pitts' immediately to the south of Micklebring village, but it is not obvious if there was continuing working of these pits.

What was certainly if not a revival at least a new beginning, and the beginning of a very active period of working at Micklebring, occurred under a lease of 1792. A water-powered mill to grind and process the mineral was built at Braithwell, and a company was formed for the purpose: the mines and mill are referred to in Miller's *History of Doncaster and its Vicinity*, published in 1804: Micklebring, he says, was

> *remarkable for a curious mineral called raddle, which it is said, is to be found only in this and one other place in England. Large quantities of this mineral are raised here both for home consumption and for exportation . . . at this place Messrs. Gleadhill and Shepherd have mills for grinding it.*

The Proprietors of the Union Colour Mill or Ruddle Mill, described as a water-powered colour and oil mill and used by 'The Union Colour Co', had ceased to operate as such by 1815, although the mill continued to be used for similar purposes.

The interest in the mines and mill of the Gleadall family continued until 1840: they were farmers locally, and sold interests in the mill in 1840, which was then in the tenancy of William Thompson. The 1838 trade directory had referred to the 'excellent stratum of reddle' at Micklebring, and to John Gleadall, 'reddle pit owner'. The Union Colour Mill was ultimately converted to corn grinding – this had occured by 1850/51, and then Francis Turner occupied the mill and farm.

The 'Colour Mill and Manufactory' were advertised to let in the *Doncaster, Nottingham and Lincoln Advertiser* in November 1812: newly built, with ample water and 'a plentiful supply' of ruddle, found near the mill at one of the only two locations in England: it was occupied by Messrs Gleadall & Co, of Micklebring. At the end of 1837, a quarter share in the Ruddle Mill was advertised for sale in the *Doncaster Gazette*, with a farm, all in the tenancy of William Thompson, the land including 'a thick vein of RED Ochre' only a few yards below the surface which had for many years past supplied the mill, with another field containing brown ochre, never yet worked, all the property of John Gleadall of Micklebring. Figure 2, which is from the First Edition 25-Inch Ordnance Survey Map, shows the Mill and the Mill Dam in 1891. The mill buildings still stand (Figure 3).

It is useful to remember both that coal in workable thickness (some 17 inches) was got at Micklebring, and that the Don Navigation lay only a few miles to the north of the area.

The process of ruddle mining was described by George Walker in his *Costume of Yorkshire*, first published in 1814:

> *The mineral called Ruddle, or Raddle, is obtained near Micklebring, a hamlet in the parish of Braithwell, near Doncaster. A shaft is sunk of about twenty-three feet in depth, and five in diameter, which passes through strata of limestone and gritstone, and immediately under this last the ruddle is embedded universally in clay, which is three feet thick above and below the vein. It lies nearly horizontal, and is generally*

Figure 2. The Ruddle Mill and Mill Dam in 1891. *O.S. 25-Inch Sheet 290.7, First Edition, surveyed in 1891, published 1892*

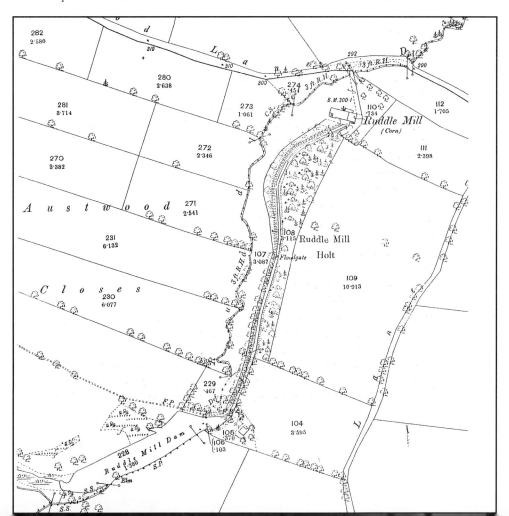

about nine inches in thickness. The miner in working sits down and uses a short sharp axe, similar to that of the lead miner. He excavates to the distance of about four yards from the centre of the shaft; but, as the clay cannot be easily supported, as soon as he has reached this distance, a new shaft is sunk near to the other. The ruddle is carried to a mill, where it is ground to a powder; then mixed with water and ground afresh, and afterwards let off into a reservoir, where the raddle subsides, and the water is evaporated. It is afterwards cut into small squares, packed up in casks and sent to Hull and London, whence it is exported. The price is about £5 per ton. We understand ruddle is also found near Bristol, very near the surface, which injures the more expensive preparation of it here. This substance is used for the coarser purposes of painting, such as carts and waggons, and also by carpenters for marking their timber, &c.

The accompanying illustration (Figure 4) shows a man working a horizontal hand winch (a jack roll in West Riding mining parlance) and a boy landing a wooden basket from the rope at the shaft top; a ladder provides access to the workings.

In fact there are three seams or beds of ruddle, the topmost of five inches, then two feet of clay, a four inches bed of ruddle, then another two feet of clay and finally a nine inch bed of ruddle.

It seems probable that there was no regular working of ruddle from about 1840. The mill was converted to corn grinding, and had ceased to be used when sold by auction in 1877: the accompanying plan and particulars also locate fields in which ruddle pits had been worked. But a new exploitation of the mineral began at the end of the nine-teenth century, after a number of decades when the mineral and its working are not referred to in the trade directories. Mines were opened

Figure 3. The Ruddle Mill in 1996. *Joan Jones*

by R. E. Horrox of Dore House, Handsworth, who is described in the official lists of mines as working coal and ironstone in 1901: ruddle is a form of decomposed haematite. He had then two underground and two surface workers, and there were two underground workers in 1905, although the mine had no workers in 1911. Horrox had ceased to work at Micklebring by 1918. In sale particulars of 1908, it is mentioned that some plots were believed to contain 'a valuable bed of Ruddle', which the 1877 sale plan and particulars had identified the location – immediately south of Micklebring village – of fields known as Ruddle Leys and Ruddle Pit Shutt (two such). Horrox is not mentioned in the trade directory of 1897 under either Sheffield or Handsworth; was his perhaps the timber business which became Horrox & Co. Ltd, of 53, Norfolk Street in Sheffield?

Figure 4. Ruddle Mining in the early nineteenth century. *George Walker, Costume of Yorkshire*

References

This essay is based upon the essays by Dr I. J. Brown and Mr F. W. Cowdell which are cited in the text and full details of which are provided below, and upon manuscripts in The John Goodchild Collection at Wakefield (Lime MSS and M.141). Employment figures are from the annual Lists of Mines, copies of some of which are in The John Goodchild Collection.

Brown, I. H. and Cowdell, F. W., 'The Mining of Ruddle in the Rotherham area', *Bulletin of the Peak District Mines Historical Society*, Vol. 3, Pt 3, May 1967, 133–142.

Brown, I. H., 'Supplementary Notes on the Working of Ruddle at Micklebring, Rotherham', *Bulletin of the Peak District Mines Historical Society*, Vol.4, Pt.3, May 1970, 244–48.

15. CHRONICLES OF A TITAN: TEMPLEBOROUGH STEELWORKS, 1916-1993

by Trevor Lodge

If thou didst ever hold me in thy heart, absent thee from felicity awhile
and in this harsh world draw thy breath in pain to tell my story.
William Shakespeare, *Hamlet,* Act V, Sc II.

Introduction

WHEN ROTHERHAM STEELMAKERS Steel, Peech & Tozer Ltd (SPT) commissioned a modest 15 ton capacity openhearth steel-making furnace in1892/93, no one at the company's Phoenix Bessemer Steelworks could have realised just how important the process would become for SPT's future well-being. They had, after all, no real reason to think otherwise. SPT made steels essentially for rail-ways, in the form of rails, tyres, wheels, axles and springs.[1] And since the railway companies exclusively specified steels made by the acid Bessemer process for these products, SPT's decision to produce steel by any other method could have been regarded as somewhat fool-hardy.

Yet thirty years later – following a major national shift in metallur-gical thinking – the bulk of the company's steel was being produced from 21 openhearth furnaces in two melting shops. One of these, Templeborough Melting Shop (TMS), born of the First World War's insatiable appetite for shell steel, was the largest of its type in Europe. Templeborough quickly became an icon to progress in the world of steelmaking, ever ready to adopt and develop new technology in the quest to improve steel quality, operating efficiency and productivity. This enthusiasm for embracing new technology served Templeborough well, twice coming to the very salvation of the works. Templeborough pioneered the UK production of bulk carbon steels by electric arc melting in the 1960s, giving up obsolete openhearth melting in the process, and twenty years later became the stage for British Steel's first plant to produce engineering steels by the contin-uous casting process.

Despite this progressiveness, however, Templeborough today lies cold and still, a victim of the 'unlevel playing field' within the European steel industry which has allowed foreign governments to give subsidies to their steel industries, and in doing so to distort the true economics of manufacturing costs. Its productive life now over, Templeborough at least deserves an obituary – a chronology of the events which shaped its destiny and at times even influenced the fortunes of the very nation.

Concept and Construction

If it starts anywhere, Templeborough's story can be said to start in France. The outbreak of hostilities in August 1914, especially the adoption of trench warfare on the Western Front, was to have a profound effect on the UK's steel industry. Artillery was perceived to be the solution for breaking the trench stalemate, but Britain was ill-equipped to respond to this initial challenge. Quite simply, the UK's manufacturing industries could not get enough steel of the right sort from which to make artillery shells.

Not until June 1915 was the Ministry of Munitions (MoM) formed to address the problem and oversee all aspects of production of war materials. One month later, James ('Jim') Peech, a director of SPT and son of William Peech (one of the original company partners), was appointed to the Iron and Steel Department of the MoM. His specific duties were quite straightforward but somewhat onerous: he was given the task of ensuring the supply of shell steel throughout the nation met demands. Peech's most pressing job was to overcome the War Office specification strait-jacket which required shell steel to be made by the acid process. After many months of negotiations between the MoM and the War Office some relaxations were allowed on shell steel composition, and in 1916 trials were carried out on shells made with basic openhearth, basic Bessemer and acid Bessemer steels.[2] Throughout this period, the shortfall of steel deemed suitable by the War Office was made good by importing billets from the USA.

David Lloyd George, Minister of Munitions during this period, and shortly to be appointed Secretary of State for War, became personally involved in the shell steel problem. Jim Peech suggested to him that the adoption of basic steel was the only practical solution to the dilemma. Peech had knowledge of basic openhearth steel production from SPT's Rotherham Melting Shop (RMS) at the Ickles, and this must have influenced matters, for the story goes that Lloyd George personally gave Peech the go-ahead. Whatever the truth of the matter, it is fact that early in 1916, with Government assistance, SPT was committed to the installation of a large melting shop at

Figure 1. Construction of Templeborough Melting Shop, *c.* 1917. A rail-borne vertical boiler steam crane is being used to position roof supports.

Templeborough capable of producing basic shell steels (Figure 1). Apart from initial munition demands, it was felt that the shop would perform a useful post-war function by putting SPT in a strong position to supply UK re-rollers and forgers with billets which in the pre-war period had been imported from Continental sources.

Peech's success in persuading Lloyd George to allow basic steels for shell production had far-reaching implications. In addition to initiating the Government programme to install new steelmaking capacity (at Templeborough and elsewhere) it also meant that the existing basic openhearth plants in this country were finally able to make a significant contribution to the war effort.

Bill Kitching, one-time Chief Engineer at SPT, personally witnessed the result of Jim Peech's influence on Lloyd George. His wife's cousin, Colonel Hanson of the 49th Division (Sheffield Gunners) confirmed the acute shortage of shells which existed in the initial months of the First World War. According to Hanson, his 18lb guns were effectively rationed to one shell per day in the 1914–16 period! The watershed occurred at the Somme. Bill Kitching joined the 49th RE in time to witness the second battle of the Somme on 16 September, 1916, by which time Jim Peech's basic shell steel programme was well under way. In Bill's own words:

Zero hour was 12.30 mid-day. I had prepared with others the way for tanks. You could not hear yourself speak for (British) shells going over. I saw the result of Jim Peech's work at Thiepval – I was there.

Construction of the new works at Templeborough took place on what was essentially a greenfield site but the choice created some controversy for the area was known to have been occupied by the Roman Fort of Templeborough. In the event, some archaeological excavations were possible before SPT's strip and bar mills were built over the site, and a number of Roman artifacts from Templeborough are deposited in Rotherham's Clifton Park Museum. Initial Government plans called for an eleven furnace openhearth shop, and this seems to have been carried out in two phases – schemes A and C. Scheme B was for associated plant, including a 36-inch cogging mill, a 21-inch continuous billet mill and parallel slab mill, in which the cast steel ingots from the melting shop, after reheating, were rolled down to semi-finished products.*

Work began on site in April 1916 and the first cast (ex 'B' furnace) was tapped on 12 July, 1917. All eleven of the planned 60 tons capacity furnaces were melting steel before hostilities ceased in November 1918, and in the event the shop was extended to house three more identical furnaces. Metallurgically, the melting shop was of the 'cold charged' type, its principal raw material feedstock consisting of scrap and pig iron (Figure 2).

The order for the cogging mill was placed with Davy Brothers Ltd. of Sheffield in March 1917, and one month later the 18-inch and 21-inch billet mills, to the designs of the American Morgan Construction Company, were ordered from the Brightside Foundry Co. Ltd., also of Sheffield. Davy's contract, costing £63,000, included the roller table and manipulator and bloom and slab shears. Templeborough

---

*Readers with little or no understanding of the workings of a steelworks should consult the glossary at the end, which gives brief descriptions of the fundamental plant employed at Templeborough, and its purpose.

Figure 2.   Interior of Templeborough Melting Shop in the 1930s, showing a train of moulds being assembled (right) by overhead crane and an assembled train (left) awaiting a cast of steel. The man visible (centre right) is standing on the furnace stage, which extends the full length of the shop.

Cogging Mill (TCM) and its associated continuous billet mill completely revolutionised the rolling of steel in this country. For the first time it was possible to roll the re-heated 3 ton ingots down to $1^{1}/_{2}$ inch square billets in one operation: in older mills such rolling was a two stage process where it was necessary to also reheat the product of the cogging mill – steel blooms – before they could proceed to the final rolling sequence through the billet mill stands. The works conformed to the highest standards of practice in the world, and with the exception of the shearing machine every unit was electrically driven.

It is not known when the cogging and billet mills were first operational, but they were certainly rolling by December 1919, at which time the slab mill was 'at present under construction'.[4] These primary rolling operations would soon be supplemented by re-rolling facilities in the shape of an adjacent semi-continuous bar mill (Templeborough Bar Mill) and a strip mill, both of Morgan design (see Figures 3 and

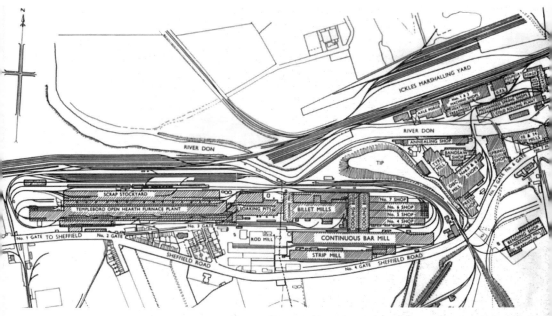

Figure 3.   Layout of SPT's Templeborough complex about 1950. The neat efficient layout makes for an interesting comparison with the older, poorly arranged Ickles Works (top right).

4). The original scheme had also included plans to establish an adjacent continuous rod mill in conjunction with two wire rope manufacturers, who would take the product of the mill as feedstock for their own wire drawing operations. This partnership created what subsequently became Templeborough Rolling Mills Ltd., and the rod mill was reported as 'now complete' by the end of March 1919.

Figure 4.   Coiling narrow strip, Morgan Strip Mill.

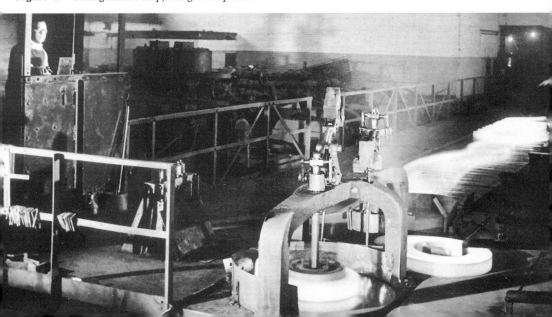

The Early Years

Harry Steel and his colleagues on the Board of SPT were fully aware of the problems associated with operating a large cold charged open-hearth shop in terms of material supplies and running costs. Tentative plans were drawn up for an iron-smelting plant to cut costs by supplying TMS with liquid iron (so-called 'hot metal'). A drawing dated 13 October, 1917, shows a line of no fewer than six blast furnaces which would have been located south of Sheffield Road on the present Slag Reduction Company's site, i.e., on the Sheffield side of Ickles Way. Such a scheme had several attractions – so much so that it was again considered in the late 1920s – but for one reason or another was never adopted. Instead, SPT chose to pursue an alternative solution – that of acquiring (in conjunction with steelmakers Samuel Fox & Co. Ltd. of Stocksbridge) other companies with a view to stabilising its sources of raw materials and fuel. A simple enough statement in itself, but one which resulted in the formation of the United Steel Companies Ltd., a combine which in its heyday was the largest steel producer in the British Empire.[5]

United Steel was the brain-child of Harry Steel (son of the founder of SPT), and there was never any doubt of SPT's senior position within the group in its formative years. The original capital for the acquisition of the Frodingham Iron & Steel Co. Ltd. in 1917, for example, came from SPT and Fox's in the ratio of 3:1. It was said that Steel was keen to gain control of Frodingham not only to provide SPT and Fox's with a cheap source of basic Lincolnshire pig iron, but to prevent Frodingham becoming a potential competitor in the field of billet and bar production – a feature of particular importance to Templeborough's future well-being.

To facilitate the merger of further acquisitions into the new SPT/Fox/Frodingham group an entirely new company – the United Steel Companies Ltd. – was formed on 25 March, 1918, with the objective of acquiring the share capitals of all the businesses involved. Notable early acquisitions by USC included the Rothervale Collieries Ltd. and the Workington Iron & Steel Co. Ltd.

The unexpected death of Steel, USC's first Chairman, in 1920 could easily have proved a serious body blow to the company,

Figure 5.
Harry Steel, the man who masterminded the creation of the United Steel Companies Ltd.

which was still struggling to find its way in the depressed commercial world following the end of the First World War (Figure 5). Fortunately, the Board of USC was of sufficient calibre to take the loss of such a central figure in its stride. A number of modernisation projects previously mooted were sanctioned, in spite of severe misgivings due to the economic climate then prevailing. Such misgivings can be understood when one realises, for example, that Templeborough Melting Shop (TMS) and its associated ingot cogging and billet rolling mills were idle for virtually the whole of 1922 due to lack of orders. Indeed, trading conditions were so bad that by 1922 USC was just about breaking even, and from 1924 to 1927 generated a deficit of nearly £1 million.

The new strip and bar mills at Templeborough were completed and began producing in 1922, under the management of United Strip & Bar Mills Ltd., a wholly owned subsidiary of USC for which finance had been obtained by a public issue of 8 per cent preference shares on the Stock Exchange. To allow SPT and S. Fox & Co. Ltd. to develop better access to UK billet re-rolling and forging markets, USC developed links with Sheffield forgemasters Daniel Doncaster & Sons Ltd.; also Birmingham merchants Martino Steel and Metal Co. Ltd.

USC's expressed intention in its formative years was that the various branches would 'continue as individual producers, maintaining their own identity', but outside influences soon changed this view. There was much false optimism about in the early 1920s, and the long-awaited upturn in business seemed to be forever just around the corner. In reality, the country lurched from one economic crisis to the next. The whole situation was aggravated by iron and steel imports which flooded in from 1921 onwards. These grew at such a rate that by 1924 they exceeded the pre-war level of imports – some $2^{1}/_{4}$ million tonnes per annum. In 1927 some $4^{1}/_{2}$ million tonnes were imported, over half coming from Belgium and Luxembourg. Much of these imports competed directly with steel melted and rolled at Templeborough.

USC experienced a particularly shaky period in 1926, when the General Strike practically brought to a standstill all its works, collieries, coke ovens and ore mines. The effects of the General Strike and of the later 1926 coal strike were disastrous for Britain's heavy industries generally, since the underlying problems were also largely responsible for the loss of confidence by former overseas customers in Britain's ability to fulfil commitments efficiently. Realising that grave difficulties still existed after the unhappy events of 1926, USC eventually called on the services of a widely respected firm of American consulting engineers, H. A. Brassert & Company, with a view to obtaining a blueprint for future operations policy based on best American practice.

Towards A New Role

A notable move which set the pattern for USC's survival technique through the 1930s was the appointment of an engineer, Captain Robert S. Hilton, as Managing Director in 1928. Hilton, previously Managing Director of the Metropolitan Vickers Electrical Co. Ltd. of Manchester, was brought in at the insistence of USC's bank, being a condition for the large overdraft which the company had run up through the 1920s. Hilton soon centralised the management of USC, making it independent of influence or bias from any of the various branches, and also exercised tight control over spending on new capital development. Together, these were major factors in stabilising USC's precarious position. Another of Hilton's far reaching decisions was the creation of a centralised research function for USC. Though this department was based at Stocksbridge, the research personnel soon found TMS particularly receptive to innovation in steelmaking techniques, and as a result SPT went on to pioneer many metallurgical developments within USC.

Hilton and the USC board of directors were quick to act on many of the recommendations made by Brassert & Company following the latter's survey of USC's properties. Produced in 1929, Brassert's report[6] recognised that at the time of the General Strike, SPT's Templeborough complex was still the only comprehensive plant installed in the UK for the production of large tonnages of small sections with minimum expenditure of power, fuel and labour in conversion from the ingot. Likewise, the strip and bar mills at Templeborough were the most modern in the country. Obviously, Templeborough was to play a key role in the reorganisation plans, which resulted in sweeping changes, both at Rotherham and Stocksbridge. Despite all this, the consultant's recommendations for Templeborough itself – to cut the operating costs of TMS by making it part of a fully integrated iron and steelmaking plant – were never acted upon. The coke oven battery, two 400 tons/day blast furnaces and 600 ton capacity metal mixer proposed for Templeborough were all destined to remain on paper only.

At SPT's older Ickles Works the outlook was less favourable. The

'Old' Siemens melting shop was considered obsolete, as were the cogging and rail mills. Indeed, by the time of the report these were essentially no longer in use, and SPT's nearby Rotherham Melting Shop was also (temporarily) out of use. Similarly, the 'Old' tyre mill, though still used, was described as being in poor condition, and lacking modern handling devices. On the brighter side, a future could be seen for the axle forge, the 14-inch bar mill, the 'New' tyre mill, the Disc mill and the Spring Department.

Under Brassert's plan, SPT ceased rail production in 1928/29 and began to concentrate on steel semis (essentially billets for re-rolling), bar and strip products and railway materials (wheels, tyres and axles). Rail orders formerly dealt with by SPT and Samuel Fox & Co. Ltd. were all transferred to USC's works at Workington, which specialised in the production of low phosphorus acid Bessemer steels.

Improving the Adolescent

The Thirties were to be notable throughout the UK iron and steel industry as years of rationalisation and consolidation. Under Hilton, USC, including SPT, fared better than many companies. To his credit, Hilton introduced the concept of joint consultation, which made USC a pioneer in the creation of Works Councils. He also fostered policies which improved the social lot of his workers, including contributory pension schemes for all USC employees in 1935 – one of the first such schemes in the UK. This progressive attitude of USC in personnel-related matters was widely recognised as a model within British industry but unfortunately cannot be dealt with in more detail here.

Economic recovery proceeded steadily through the early 1930s, initially as a result of the government's policy aimed at protecting home industry. Despite all its problems, during these difficult years, USC continued to invest in new schemes designed to improve competitiveness and operating efficiencies, and established an ethos in the company which recognised that ongoing modernisation was crucial in helping to guarantee the long-term future of the business.

At SPT, it had become painfully obvious that the high capacity cogging mill at Templeborough was tied almost exclusively to a billet mill which rolled only small square sections, a product which had not found a ready sale in the depressed 1920s, largely due to the dumping of continental steel. In 1930, sanction was given for a new 30-inch roughing mill fed by the Templeborough cogging mill and costing £71,000, with the specific intention of improving flexibility by allowing the works to produce rounds, gothics sections and bigger slabs. In an attempt to secure a further 'captive' outlet for Templeborough billets, in 1933–34 USC invested some £25,000 in Tinsley Wire Industries Ltd., an associate company of one of its partners in Templeborough Rolling Mills Ltd.

Large quantities of by-product coke oven gas were produced at USC's Rothervale Collieries. To utilise this valuable fuel within the group, a gas main costing £16,000 was laid in 1933 between Orgreave and SPT, a distance of three miles. This gas was used in place of producer gas to reheat ingots prior to rolling through TCM, thereby relieving rail traffic congestion in the stockyards by reducing the amount of coal needed to feed the producer gas plants. (The latter were, however, still necessary for providing gas to the openhearth furnaces at both Templeborough and Rotherham Melting Shops).

Several important metallurgical advances were also made in the 1930s. One of the most far-reaching was the development of low carbon-free machining steels, following their ready sale in the UK from continental suppliers. The first (experimental) casts were made in 1931. Ultimately, SPT progressed so well in developing low carbon-free cutting steel of consistent quality that, by early 1933, it introduced Phoenix Rapid-Machining Steel, one of the fore-runners of British Steel's present range of free cutting steels. Such developments were aided by a growth in the understanding of production metallurgy in its widest sense, this in turn coming as feedback from a team of quality controllers – or mill observers, as they were initially known.

Generally, SPT was recognised as being to the fore in the introduction of quality control, and was regarded within USC as the branch with the most scientific approach and willingness to experiment. This was especially true in the field of refractories, materials which could withstand high temperatures and the corrosive action of liquid steel and slag and were therefore indispensable for the lining of furnaces. Much pioneering work on improving existing refractories, and developing new ones, was carried out at TMS by Dr J. H. Chesters of USC's Central Research Department. Jack Chesters' work soon established him as a leading authority on refractories and his monumental treatise, *Steelplant Refractories*, became the standard work on the subject.[7]

The driving force behind all this pre-occupation with refractories was the desire for faster working and reliability of the openhearth furnace. Templeborough's K furnace was rebuilt to an improved Maerz design in 1937/38 to compare with the standard type. The Maerz furnace had modified air/gas ports, which minimised flame impingement to exit ports and allowed for greater access to the flues for repairs. Trials showed K furnace to be fully 40 minutes faster, on average, than a standard furnace, which had an average charge to melt time of $9^{1}/_{2}$ hours. A later development, the semi-Venturi ports fitted about 1942 to S furnace, showed an even better gain.

A particularly important advance made at TMS in the 1930s was the introduction of pyrometers, which meant that for the first time accurate temperature monitoring became possible for both the vulnerable linings of the openhearth furnace and also its liquid steel content (the bath). Pyrometers liberated the melter from the agonising dilemma he faced every working shift, when he was torn between driving his furnace harder for increased productivity, but at the risk of bringing his furnace roof down if he overheated it. Despite these advantages, however, pyrometers were initially regarded by melters with suspicion as a management tool and referred to scornfully as 'spy'-rometers.[8] These initial misgivings were soon swept away as their benefits became apparent.

By the late 1930s, with trade improving, an efficient working pattern had been established within TMS. The shop usually ran 10 to 12 furnaces simultaneously, with one or two off for repair, and one

Figure 6.   Taking a steel sample on the furnace stage at Templeborough. Two of the charging doors (left) were deliberately left partially opened to provide illumination for the photograph. Liquid steel from a sampling spoon is poured into a small cast iron pot (centre) and the solidified piece then sent for analysis.

Figure 7. Tapping B furnace at Templeborough. Operatives on the furnace stage (right) are busy throwing additives into the ladle (centre). The vessel in the lower centre of the picture is a slag pot which will shortly receive the ladle overflow (liquid slag). The openhearth furnace is marked by the group of girder uprights – eight in all – and cross members.

Figure 8. A train of recently cast ingots, with moulds removed, ready to be taken to Templeborough Cogging Mill.

undergoing a complete rebuild. Weekly output was between 10,000 and 12,000 ingot tons, with approximately 75 per cent going through TCM for rolling to billet. Figures 6, 7 and 8 illustrate aspects of production.

Going to War

As a result of the government's policy of re-armament from about 1937, Britain's industry was better prepared for the Second World War than it had been for the First World War. The country's steel-makers, in particular, played a vital role in supplying the country with essential war materials, and nowhere was this more true than at SPT. Templeborough, with its high capacity continuous production capa-bility, now came into a league of its own. Between them, TMS and RMS produced almost 4 million tons of ingots during the war years. The output of steel 'semis' (billets and slabs) at Templeborough amounted to nearly 3 million tons, half of which were then re-rolled in the company's adjacent Morgan bar and strip mills. Over a quarter of a million tons of billets were despatched to shell forging concerns, and almost half of the output from TBM (i.e., a further quarter of a million tons) consisted of shell steel bars. TBM also supplied a consid-erable tonnage of concrete reinforcing bars for incorporation in the pre-fabricated 'Mulberry' harbours so vital to the success of the D-day landings.

At the company's Ickles Works, the forging departments were largely turned over to ordnance manufacture, where total deliveries reached a peak in 1942/43, and drew complimentary comments from both the Minister of Supply and the Director-General of Weapons Production. SPT became the largest producer of barrels and breech parts for the six-pounder anti-tank gun, introduced in 1941, and the following year actually delivered more components for guns of all type than any other single UK forging firm. The Drop Stamping Department at Ickles contributed nearly 2 million hammered rings (many used in aircraft engines) and 124,000 bomb forgings for infantry mortars. Finally, the output of the Ickles 10-inch and 14-inch mills included bars used in the fabrication of 9,400 barrels for the Hispano-Suiza Cannon and $1\frac{1}{4}$ million shoulder rifle barrels.

As a precaution against enemy actions a fairly sophisticated Air Raid Precaution (ARP) system was introduced. A central control room, situated at the Ickles, received all official communications of Air Raid Warnings, and notified the works areas accordingly. The more serious warnings, 'purple alerts', which necessitated personnel going into air raid shelters, were of particular concern in the melting shops. These were almost impossible to black-out fully, and partially or fully charged furnaces suffered very severe damage if they were held on stand-by conditions for all but the shortest of such interruptions. Fortunately, further research done by Chesters (*op cit*) improved the furnace hearth refractories to such an extent that breakouts – the escape of liquid steel – were virtually eliminated.

Despite Lord Haw Haw's propaganda claims that the distinctive line of Templeborough's chimneys had been flattened by the Luftwaffe, SPT escaped remarkably unscathed. On the Sunday night of the Sheffield Blitz (15 December, 1940), a land mine was dropped near TMS and blew off a quantity of the shop's corrugated roof sheeting. The Shift Superintendent, 'Tubby' England, wanted to restart the furnaces before repairs could be carried out to the shop roof but was prevented from doing so by the threat of imprisonment from the local Air Raid Warden, who happened to be one of his employees![9]

Two particularly important plant modifications at SPT had been sanctioned in the early months of the war, namely the reconstruction of TCM and a further chance to evaluate the Maerz design of open-hearth furnace, when the rebuilding of 'L' furnace in RMS was sanctioned.

It is no exaggeration to state that the improvements carried out to openhearth furnace linings and operating practice, following Jack Chesters' work, brought the Templeborough furnaces up to levels of productivity and availability that were previously undreamed of for cold charged practice. As a result, Templeborough was able to hold its own on liquid steel costs well into the 1950s, by which time new steel-making methods were threatening the viability of all openhearth methods.

For more efficient handling of materials at the works, improvements to railway sidings at Templeborough were sanctioned in 1941 at an estimated cost of £30,000, and helped considerably by removing a former traffic constraint. These improvements could not have been more opportune, for in the six war years (1939–1945) SPT's rail transport department hauled nearly 25 million tons of material, with road transport accounting for much less ($1^{1}/_{2}$ million tons).

Despite its potential for high outputs – in the region of 12,000 tons per week – the condition of Templeborough Cogging Mill had been giving cause for concern at the beginning of the war. It was felt that a real risk of serious breakdown existed at a time when maintaining shell

Figure 9.(right)   Aerial view of the Templeborough complex looking down the Don Valley in the 1950s, with the openhearth chimneys prominent. The site is tightly bounded by the main Sheffield Road (right) and the River Don (left).

steel billet output was vital. Consequently, approval was given for the full reconstruction of the Cogging Mill. Though it was actually ready for delivery from the manufacturers in 1943, installation of the mill was deferred until the Summer of 1944, with work arranged to minimise disruption to production. The new mill had a designed capacity to roll 14,000 tons of ingots per week, but within a few years of commissioning was actually dealing with 18,000 tons per week.

Post War Recovery

The war left SPT tired. Desirable maintenance had been deferred on TMS, RMS and TBM, and much capital expenditure was required to bring these departments back to pre-war efficiency. In addition, complete reconstruction was necessary for much of the Ickles Works. Figure 9 shows the Templeborough complex in the 1950s.

The culmination of Chesters' work on openhearth refractories came in 1948 when Templeborough's B furnace became the first in the UK to be fitted with a successful basic roof constructed from British-made chrome-magnesite bricks. By 1953 a second furnace was similarly converted and this was soon giving steel outputs 10 per cent better than the shop average.[10]

The works was essentially unaffected by the 'stillborn' steel nationalisation of 1950/51, though the Government did offer USC the option of acquiring the Park Gate Iron & Steel Co. Ltd., with its possibility of supplying TMS with liquid iron from the Park Gate blast furnaces. USC declined, and it would be another 20 years before integration of SPT and Park Gate production facilities was begun in earnest.

Figure 10. The last harvest is gathered from the field which was soon to be transformed into the site for Brinsworth Strip Mill. The Fourteen Sisters of TMS make for an interesting skyline. *R. Dyal*

Figure 11. Furnace hands at TMS. Note the length of the handle on the fettling shovel, specially made for the job.

Efforts to improve steel output continued throughout the 1950s, with all TMS furnaces being uprated from 80 ton to 100 ton capacity. Oil firing was also extensively employed, resulting in major gains. The 1930 output of 423,000 ingot tons (for TMS plus RMS) rose to 599,000 in 1940, and 785,000 tons in 1950. The corresponding figure for 1960 was 1.1 million tons, and something of a swansong for openhearth steelmaking at SPT, as we shall see. New strip rolling capacity in the shape of Brinsworth Hot Strip Mill (Figure 10), costing £6.5 millions, was commissioned in 1957, with cold rolled facilities following four years later. The original Morgan Strip Mill remained in production, however, not closing down until 1969.

On a lighter note, Templeborough played host in the 1950s and 1960s to several show business personalities, who were always suitably impressed by the scale of operations and the whole aura of steelmaking (Figures 11 and 12). TMS was even chosen to epitomise northern heavy industry in the film *Tread Softly Stranger*, starring Diana Dors, George Baker and Patrick Allen. A crime melodrama, the film was shot in 1957 in the imaginary northern town of Rawborough, in reality a hybrid of the Rawmarsh and Masbrough districts of Rotherham. The steelworks scenes include a sequence shot on the openhearth stage of TMS, with actor Patrick Allen, who later became well known as a voice-over man for TV commercials, seen as a member of a real openhearth furnace crew. Needless to say, his fettling action readily identifies him as the odd man out!

Figure 12. Actor Kenneth More tries his hand at fettling.

Project SPEAR

By the late 1950s the openhearth facilities at SPT were beginning to
show their age, despite all the efforts made to improve their
efficiency and productivity. Several options were considered as
means of retaining a steelmaking capacity at SPT, and though it
seemed an extremely bold move at the time, the decision was made
to replace all 21 of the firm's openhearth furnaces with electric arc
steelmaking.

USC announced the £10 millions scheme in December 1959.
Project SPEAR – it stood for Steel Peech Electric Arc Reorganisation
– would increase the plant's annual ingot capacity from 1.2 million to
1.35 million tons. The six arc furnaces that were the centrepiece of the
scheme would be housed in TMS in a development that would,
amongst other things, sweep away the 'Fourteen Sisters' that had been

Figure 13. Project SPEAR well under way, 1962. At the same time that substantial civil engineering was carried out for the new shop, openhearth melting continued in those areas of the site (right) not yet affected.

Figure 14. The first of Templeborough's arc furnaces (upper left) is tapped for the first time in front of an audience of operatives and managers. The ladle receiving the steel is located in a pit (lower centre) and suspended from an overhead crane.

such a dominant feature of the Templeborough skyline for half a century. Incredibly, the new melting shop (TEMS) was actually built piecemeal over the existing one, starting at the Sheffield end (Figure 13). This was done in such a way that steel production from individual openhearth furnaces was maintained until such time that they had to be taken out of service pending demolition as the 'new look' gradually advanced through the shop (Figure 14). SPT's last openhearth – M furnace – tapped its last cast of steel on 23 December, 1964.

USC's Technical Adviser on Steelmaking, Albert Jackson, switched on the last of the six arc furnaces on 1 February, 1965, to signify the completion of the SPEAR Project. He told those present that

> *United Steel Companies' steelmaking is now in the forefront of world best practice . . .* [This new plant] *enables SPT to expand into wider markets because it now has the ability to make the highest quality electric steels as well as to continue making traditional openhearth qualities.*

Ironically, the whole scheme had only been made possible because of improvements made by Jackson in openhearth steelmaking elsewhere within USC! His 'Ajax' (Albert Jackson) process developed at the Appleby Frodingham Works boosted productivity of that plant's existing openhearth capacity by using oxygen injection coupled to a 100 per cent liquid iron feedstock from the adjacent blast furnaces. The steel scrap arising during ingot rolling at Appleby Frodingham, previously melted in the plant's own openhearth furnaces, was now all available as feedstock for SPT's arc furnaces and thereby justified the viability of SPEAR.

The statistics behind SPEAR were impressive to say the least. Once the shop was fully commissioned – ahead of schedule – SPT became responsible for producing almost 25 per cent of the UK's electrically melted steel. Indeed, TEMS proved to be the world's largest electric steelplant. The electricity consumed by TEMS during full production amounted to 750 million units – over one third of the existing industrial load in the Sheffield area. Put another way, Templeborough consumed as much electricity as the whole of a medium-sized town such as Rochdale!

Nationalisation and Rationalisation

No sooner had SPT got over the major technological changes of the SPEAR Project, which had meant redeployment and early retirement for some 900 personnel, than it was faced with a further major upheaval. The UK's steel industry was nationalised in 1967 and as a result SPT was brought together with a long standing local commercial rival – the Park Gate Iron & Steel Co. Ltd. The two operations collectively became British Steel's Rotherham Works, and it was soon apparent that there was scope for rationalisation. Thanks to SPEAR, TEMS could now produce more ingots than TCM was capable of rolling, while at the former Park Gate Aldwarke complex, the modern primary (cogging) mill was under-utilised.

As an interim measure cold ingots from TEMS were sent to Aldwarke for rolling, but the obvious longer-term solution was to transfer some of the Templeborough electric arc furnaces to Aldwarke steelplant, where the two Kaldo steelmaking vessels were proving expensive to operate. Two arcs were moved in 1974, after which time the output of TEMS, with four furnaces remaining, was better balanced with the needs of TCM. However, there were new problems to face, partially due to the knock-on effect of British Steel's modernisation plans, and partially because of a change in steel markets. In particular, there had been a rapid contraction in demand for railway materials, and the oxygen (BOS) steelmaking process being introduced elsewhere by British Steel was soon found to be a cost effective alternative for producing several of Templeborough's steel grades.

In 1973 BSC's development plans to modernise the UK public steel sector were published in a parliamentary white paper.[11] Under 'Implications of the Strategy' it cast doubt on the longer term future of some existing steelworks with a sombre statement that 'Steelmaking and associated activities at Consett, Cleveland arc plant, Normanby Park and Templeborough are expected to continue until the latter part of the decade.' It then offered something of a life line with a rather indeterminate 'sweetener', saying 'one or more of these four works might well have a longer-term future as a supplementary source of steelmaking for billet production.' In the event, there would only be one such works. Templeborough put in a world-class performance to ensure it was the chosen one.

For a week in the autumn of 1977 Templeborough's 'E' furnace was driven at such a rate that it averaged 74.2 tonnes liquid steel output per hour – better than Japanese, German or other world competitors in electric steelmaking. This display of the plant's potential – achieved by management/union co-operation – even earned recognition from Prime Minister Jim Callaghan, who sent the workers (and the furnace!) a suitably endorsed Christmas Card. More importantly, it provided vital currency for a survival plan, but at another cost. A £22 million investment in continuous casting equipment for Templeborough was approved by BSC's board in a scheme that would spell the end of TCM's billet rolling line and result in the loss of some 500 jobs.

Through the mid-1970s, BSC's losses had been running in excess of £200 millions annually, and a cut-back to profitable 'core' manu-facturing units was seen as vital if the industry was to have any future, and able to compete effectively in an increasingly aggressive world marketplace. Naturally unhappy about the social consequences of such a move, the main steel unions called a national 13 week strike in the winter of 1979–80, but to no real avail.

Later in 1980 British Steel's Chairman, Ian MacGregor, announced details of the plan to save British Steel from incurring further massive trading losses. As part of the plans, Templeborough was to run on reduced capacity with just a single furnace, and all liquid steel going through the billet caster. Complete closure of all TCM and related activities, including the 30-inch Mill slab line, took place in February 1981. Thereafter, the Brinsworth Strip Mill was sourced from other slab producers, notably Scunthorpe.

Phoenix Project

The scheme to install a world-class continuous caster at Templeborough was appropriately named the Phoenix Project. The name was a reminder of the very roots of the steel industry hereabouts, and signified re-birth for the industry, albeit on a reduced scale. Supplied by Distington Engineering, plant was commissioned in February 1981. Its prime function was to produce high quality billets for re-rolling into bars and rods. A six strand machine incorporating a curved mould system, it was the first in the UK to incorporate features essential for ensuring the high levels of surface and internal quality of the product required by engineering steels users (Figure 15). The machine was sourced with liquid steel from E furnace – by this time uprated, much modernised and fitted with continuous charging facilities, and capable of producing half a million tonnes of liquid steel annually.

In 1986 as part of a Government initiative to encourage greater participation between the private and public sectors in steel, BSC and GKN merged their engineering steels interest to form United Engineering Steels Ltd., Europe's largest manufacurer of such steels. Templeborough became part of Rotherham Engineering Steels, one

Figure 15. Templeborough's billet caster in action for the first time, with six hot strands of solidified steel emerging from the continuous casting machine, which is off the top of the picture.

of the businesses within UES.[12] That same year, a ladle furnace was commissioned at Templeborough which would allow for even closer control of steelmaking and further enhance quality of the product, and in 1992 the size range of billets cast was extended to 180mm.

Finale

The last cast of steel was produced on 25 November, 1993, with the furnace tapping being witnessed by many employees, past and present, who effectively were paying their respects to an old friend. Templeborough Steelplant Manager, Brian Short, in a voice obviously charged with emotion, told the gathering (many of them former 'Steel- oes' men) that

> *Anyone who has ever worked at Templeborough cannot fail to have been touched by today's event in some way. When I came here in 1961 I joined what was effectively a large family, and the pride of being part of that family I'll always remember.*
>
> *This closure has been brought about by the desperate situation in which we are caught, with high raw material and power costs, coupled with poor selling margins brought about by a market surplus of steel made worse by unlawful government subsidies in certain European countries.*

March 1995 marked the start of a new chapter for Rotherham steel, when British Steel plc, by this time denationalised, acquired full control of UES Steels. Sadly, Templeborough was no longer a direct part of the story, but former 'Steel-oes' employees can take heart from the fact that the Templeborough spirit for innovation, together with some of the plant's expertise in special steelmaking and bar rolling, have been inherited by the modern British Steel Engineering Steel's complex at Aldwarke.

And if Rotherham Metropolitan Borough Council's ambitious Magna plans to establish a major adventure museum at Templeborough come to fruition, then the melting shop, currently a mausoleum to steel's past, will be transformed into a national centre celebrating man's metal-working technologies down the ages. Who knows? This is certainly a story worth telling, and the success of Magna might yet result in our tragedy ending on a somewhat happier note than Hamlet's.

GLOSSARY

Furnace Types
Openhearth furnace A typical 60 ton (nominal) openhearth furnace consisted of a large shallow oblong hearth, approximately 40ft long by 13ft wide, lined with dolomite. This was enclosed in a steel frame which incorporated refractory brick walls and a roof. Raw materials for melting (scrap,

pig iron and lime) were charged through several doors in the front of the furnace. The contents were heated by burning producer gas (made from coal) with air at special combustion ports on the ends of the furnace. The gas and air passed into the furnace after being preheated in regenerative chambers located beneath the furnace and charging stage. Developed by Charles Siemens, the regenerative process was crucial to the success of the openhearth process, for without it the high temperatures needed to melt the steel could not be sustained. After the contents were melted and refined (9 to 12 hours total time) the furnace was tapped, and the liquid contents drained through a taphole opened out for the purpose at the back of the furnace. The steel ran down a special channel – a launder – and was collected in a refractory-lined vessel called a ladle, where alloys were added. The slag – the lime plus impurities – was allowed to overflow into sumps in the melting shop floor, from which it was extracted after cooling. Before a further charge could be loaded into the furnace, any damage to the hearth lining had to be made good by 'fettling' – manually shovelling dolomite through the charging doors to patch over the affected areas. If the furnace had a particularly bad 'bottom' this fettling process could take several hours.

Electric arc furnace A large (150 ton nominal capacity) electric arc furnace consists of a circular steel vessel about 8 metres (24 ft) in diameter lined with refractories, and fitted with a removable roof and a tilting mechanism. To start the melting cycle, the roof is swung to one side and scrap charged in through the top of the open furnace. The roof is swung back into place and three graphite electrodes are then gradually lowered through holes in the roof until they are just above the scrap. A powerful electric arc is now struck, and heat from this melts the scrap. Lime and other refining agents and/or alloys can be charged through a door at the front (stage side) of the furnace. Liquid slag is removed by tilting the furnace towards the stage side, when it runs out of this door into a waiting slag pot. The furnace is tapped by tilting it away from the stage side, whereupon the liquid steel flows down the launder into a waiting ladle.

Melting and refining by electric arc was a much faster process than in the openhearth. Originally the Templeborough arc furnaces were each tapped every three hours on average, and this performance was much improved by the introduction of more powerful electrical transformers and oxygen injection. Modern electric arc furnaces incorporate water cooled panels in place of some of the refractory linings, and may also be charged continuously be means of a conveyor system.

Rolling Mill types

Cogging Mill This is a reversing mill in which the reheated steel ingot is passed to and fro between two rolls and is progressively reduced in section as the rolls are moved closer together by the mill operator. Slots of different sizes in the rolls (pass holes) enabled the operator in the original Templeborough Cogging Mill to roll a 3 ton ingot down to a 150mm (6-inch) square intermediate product known as a bloom.

Continuous Mill This consists of a series of stands in a line, each containing a pair of rolls in a fixed configuration, which run in one direction only. The hot steel passes through the rolls in each stand in turn and receives a fixed rolling reduction at each stand.

Semi-continuous Mill The initial stands in such a mill are of the reversing type, and the part-rolled stock then passes on to a series of continuous stands for further rolling.

Steel conversion (liquid to solid)

Ingot teeming In this traditional means of producing solid steel, the liquid steel was poured from the ladle in a controlled fashion – a process called teeming – into groups of waiting moulds, where the steel was allowed to solidify. At TMS the moulds were set on flat topped railway bogies, to allow transfer of the ingots to other parts of the works, as necessary. A fresh train of empty moulds was then brought in to await the next cast. Meanwhile the solid ingots, now out of the moulds were sent to the cogging mill, where they were reheated prior to rolling.

Continuous Casting In this modern method for producing solid steel shapes, the liquid steel in the ladle is poured in a controlled manner into one or more water-cooled copper moulds. The solidifying steel strand, which is still liquid in the centre, is withdrawn from the bottom of the mould(s) where it is further cooled by water spraying, and after solidifying completely is cut to the required length. The Templeborough Continuous Caster produced square billets of various cross-section (100mm, 115mm, 140mm, 180mm) and its introduction meant that the more costly traditional steel conversion route (liquid steel to ingot; followed by the ingot being rolled through the cogging mill and billet mill) could be eliminated.

Abbreviations

To avoid needless repetition in full of some company, government department and works titles which appear frequently in the text these have been abbreviated as shown below:

BSC	British Steel Corporation
GKN	GKN plc (originally Guest, Keen & Nettlefold Ltd.)
MoM	Ministry of Munitions
RMS	Rotherham Melting Shop
SPT	Steel, Peech & Tozer Ltd
TBM	Templeborough Bar Mill
TCM	Templeborough Cogging Mill
TEMS	Templeborough Electric Melting Shop
TMS	Templeborough Melting Shop
TRM	Templeborough Rolling Mills Ltd
UES	United Engineering Steels Ltd. (later traded as UES Steels Ltd.)
USC	United Steel Companies Ltd

Notes and references

1. For a summary of the inception of SPT, and some details of the production of railway materials at the company's Ickles Works, see my article 'Rotherham's Railway Trades: An Early Chapter in Heavy Engineering' in *Aspects of Rotherham, Volume 1*, edited by M. Jones, Wharncliffe Publishing Ltd, 1995.
2. The terms acid and basic refer to the type of refractory material lining the furnace. The substances involved were silica (acid) and dolomite (basic).
3. W. Kitching, personal communication.
4. *Iron & Coal Trades Review*, 12 December, 1919.
5. A much fuller account of the United Steel Companies Ltd. can be found in *Capital Development in Steel*, by P.W. S. Andrews and E. Brunner, published by Blackwell (Oxford) in 1951. Regrettably, there is no comprehensive history of the final 25 years of the United Steel Companies – a period which many would argue to be its most fruitful period.
6. *Report on the Properties and Operations of the United Steel Companies Limited*, by H.A. Brassert & Co., printed in 1929 for private circulation.
7. *Steelplant Refractories* by Dr J. H. Chesters, published by United Steel Companies Ltd. The book first appeared in 1945, and ran to two editions and several reprints.
8. Dr J. H. Chesters, personal communication. Initial trials were carried out in conjunction with the National Physical Laboratory, and are believed to be another steel industry 'first'.
9. R. Dyal, personal communication.
10. The furnace bricklayers had a particularly thankless task. They had to produce work of a very high class – better than 'civvy street' brickwork – yet within five months of building an open-hearth furnace roof in silica bricks they were obliged to wreck it and build a new one! Similarly, the general brickwork in the furnace structure needed replacing about every 36 weeks. The introduction of superior refractories (especially basic bricks for the roof) significantly lengthened these times.
11. *Steel. British Steel Corporation: Ten Year Development Strategy* by the Department of Trade and Industry, HMSO, February 1973.
12. Shortly after this, British Steel disposed of its remaining assets at the former SPT Ickles Works to Firth Rixson plc. Much of the information in the article is drawn from the author's archive of manuscript material relevant to the USC businesses, assembled over the last thirty years. This information has been verified and/or amplified as necessary by reference to Company Minute Books, USC Annual General Meeting statements and other official records in the archives of British Steel plc, together with information in the public domain (USC press releases, publicity brochures, etc).

Acknowledgements

In addition to those individuals cited under **Notes and References**, the author also wishes to thank Ron Dyal, former Press and Public Relations Officer for BCS's Sheffield Division, and Bill Dunn and Liz Green, former Manager and former Archivist repectively at BSC's Northern Region Record Centre, Teesside, for assistance. He is grateful to British Steel plc for permission to quote from the company's extensive archive holdings on SPT.

CONTRIBUTORS

1.   'IN THE NAME OF GOD AMEN'; WILL-MAKERS OF
TUDOR ROTHERHAM

Stephen Cooper was born in 1948 and was educated at the Holt Grammar School, Liverpool and Balliol College, Oxford, where he read Modern History. He qualified as a solicitor in 1972. He was in private practice in Sheffield for a number of years, but joined the Government Legal Service in 1989. Stephen married his wife Gaye in 1970 and they have two daughters, Elizabeth and Rosemary. The family has lived in Thorpe Hesley since 1979. Stephen's interest in local history was awakened in 1985 by the chance discovery of a document relating to a disputed will. This led to the publication of *A House Divided* in 1987, a story of madness and litigation in the late eighteenth century. Stephen's other publication is *Burglars and Sheepstealers* (1992), which concerns crime and transportation in the early nineteenth century. Apart from history and law Stephen's other hobbies include walking and running.

2.   LIONELL COPLEY: A SEVENTEENTH CENTURY
CAPITALIST

14. THE RUDDLE MINES AT MICKLEBRING AND THE
RUDDLE MILL AT BRAITHWELL

John Goodchild, M.Univ, is a native of Wakefield and was educated at the Grammar School there. He has been active in local historical research since about the age of thirteen, and he is the author of some 130 books and published essays on aspects of the history of the West Riding. He was the founder-Curator of Cusworth Hall Museum near Doncaster, and subsequently Archivist to Wakefield M D C; in his retirement, he runs a Local History Study Centre at Wakefield which houses his immense collections of manuscripts and research materials, and which is open to all to use, free of charge by appointment. Mr Goodchild holds an honorary Master's degree from the Open University, awarded for academic and scholarly distinction and for public services. Outside historical research, his interests lie in Freemasonry and in Unitarianism – and in his dog.

3. THOMAS SALKELD (1778–1844): ESTATE WORKER, WENTWORTH

Joan Jones (née Gregory) was brought up in Charlton Brook near Chapeltown and was educated at Ecclesfield Grammar School, Matlock College of Education and what is now Sheffield Hallam University. She has taught in primary schools in the West Riding, Nottingham and Sheffield, latterly as Deputy Head at Bankwood School. She is currently on secondment to Sheffield Hallam University where she is a Senior Lecturer in the School of Education. She is Honorary Secretary of the Chapeltown and High Green Archive which was founded in 1987. The Archive is noted for its wide range of publications and Joan has most recently co-edited *A Most Enterprising Thing* (a history of Newton Chambers at Thorncliffe) and *Ecclesfield Parish: People and Places*. Between 1983–86 Joan acted as adviser to the award-winning BBC TV's schools history series *Now and Then*. She is co-editor of *Chapeltown and High Green*, a new title in Chalford Publishing's Archive Photographs series.

4 THE PAYNE FAMILY OF NEWHILL; A QUAKER FAMILY IN THE EIGHTEENTH AND NINETEENTH CENTURIES

Alexander Fleming was born and educated in Liverpool. After obtaining graduate and post-graduate qualifications from London, Newcastle and Keele Universities he joined the staff of Wath Comprehensive School in 1972, where he is Head of History. As secretary of Wath History Group since its inception in 1979 he has given many illustrated talks at its quarterly meetings and organised several local history exhibitions at Wath library. His published contributions include a Wath town-trail, a photographic history of the town (jointly with Steve Hird) and commentaries on reprints of old Ordnance Survey maps of the area. A long-term project is the creation of an oral history archive for Wath. For many years a long-distance runner, Alex tries to spend as much time as possible walking, climbing and cross-country skiing with his wife Susan in Scotland and the Alps.

5   'A SAPPER'S DREAM' – SIR DONALD BAILEY
AND HIS BRIDGE
and
13.   THE HORSE OYLE MILL

Tony Munford was born and raised in Surrey but claims to be a semi-Yorkshireman as his mother was born in the county. Educated at Dorking County Grammar School and the University College of Wales, Aberystwyth, he began his working life at the Derbyshire County Record Office, later moving to the South Yorkshire County Record Office. Since 1986 he has been head of the Archives and Local Studies Section of Rotherham Central Library. His other published works include *Victorian Rotherham* (1989), *Rotherham: a pictorial history* (1994), *A walk round Rotherham: the town centre* (1994), and *Around Rotherham in Old Photographs* (1995). He also edits the *Ivanhoe Review,* the Archives and Local Studies Section's biannual local history journal.

6   'WAT TYLER WAS MY FRIEND': MIKE HAYWOOD,
WRITER 1934–1973

Ray Hearne is a poet/singer-songwriter from Parkgate, now living in Wath. He has worked across South Yorkshire for the Workers' Educational Association since 1981, teaching Literature and Writing. He contributed an essay on 'Ebenezer Elliott, Corn Law Rhymer' to *Aspects of Barnsley 1* and another on 'Roger Dataller of Rawmarsh' to *Aspects of Rotherham 1.*

7. 'LIFTING THE DARK VEIL OF EARTH': ROCHE ABBEY
EXCAVATIONS 1857–1935

Alice Rodgers was born and brought up in Burton-on-Trent on the borders of Derbyshire and Staffordshire. She came to South Yorkshire in the late sixties after qualifying as a teacher and, for ten years, lived and worked in Sheffield eventually marrying a local. In 1978 she and her family moved to Maltby where, in her spare time, she has been able to pursue her life-long interest in local history. In 1981, she co-founded Maltby Local History Society whose regular monthly meetings now draw people from the wider Rotherham area and beyond. Research into the history of the local 'miners' church led to her contribution, in 1990, of an article on the 'South Yorkshire Coalfield Church Extension Committee' to the South Yorkshire Industrial Mission publication *God's Coal*. This, in turn, sprang from her work on Maltby Colliery Disaster. She is now employed part-time as a lecturer and community outreach worker at Rother Valley College at Dinnington.

8. THE MEDIEVAL DEER PARK AT KIMBERWORTH

Melvyn Jones, who also edited *Aspects of Rotherham 1*, was born in Barnsley and educated at the Holgate Grammar School and the Universities of Nottingham and Leeds. He taught for seven years at Myers Grove, Sheffield's first comprehensive school, and then for nine years at Sheffield City College of Education before its amalgamation into Sheffield City Polytechnic in 1976. He is now Head of Academic Resources in the School of Leisure and Food Management at Sheffield Hallam University. He has written extensively on the economic and social history of South Yorkshire. Recent publications include *A Most Enterprising Thing* (an illustrated history of Newton Chambers) and a revised edition of the widely acclaimed *Sheffield's Woodland Heritage*. A new book on *Rotherham's Woodland Heritage* was published by Rotherham Libraries, Museum and Arts in 1995. He is a co-editor of *Chapeltown and High Green*, a new title in Chalford Publishing's Archive Photographic series.

9. ROTHERHAM'S ROLE AS A MARKET TOWN AND THE PROPOSED ROTHERHAM TO BAWTRY RAILWAY

Tom William Beastall was born in Doncaster and brought up in Tickhill. After attending Maltby Grammar School and Manchester and London Universities he made the study of the Lumley archives a major leisure time interest. He published *A North Country Estate: the Lumleys and Sandersons as landowners* in 1975 and *The Agricultural Revolution in Lincolnshire* in 1978. He contributed to the *Victorian Countryside*, volume 2 in 1981 and has edited publications on the history of Tickhill for the University of Sheffield. His latest book, *Tickhill: Portrait of an English Country Town* was published in September, 1995. A churchwarden at St Mary's Parish Church Tickhill, he was deputy headmaster of Maltby Comprehensive School after teaching history at Chichester High School for Boys, West Sussex.

10. SOME DOVECOTE SITES IN THE ROTHERHAM AREA

Brian Elliott was born in the Barnsley area, the son of a miner. He left Edward Sheerien Secondary Modern School at the age of fifteen and had several jobs until part-time study enabled entry to Matlock College of Education where he obtained a B. Ed. (Hons) degree. Whilst teaching at Royston Comprehensive School Brian tutored a series of local history courses for the WEA and University of Sheffield and published short histories of Royston parish. He continued his interest in local history, researching his home town for an M. Phil, completed at the University of Sheffield in 1990. His book, *The Making of Barnsley* (1988) was the first published history of the town since Victorian times. He initiated the *Aspects* series, edits the Barnsley volumes and forthcoming Doncaster volume, and advises Wharncliffe Publishing Ltd. on matters relating to local books. Since 1984 he has worked at Rother Valley College, Dinnington, where he is now Head of the School of General Education.

11. RAWMARSH COMMON: A STUDY IN LANDSCAPE HISTORY

Tony Dodsworth was born in Crystal Palace and grew up in South London. He attended St Joseph's College, Beulah Hill, before studying for a combined degree in Geography and History at Birmingham University. He began teaching in London but moved north in 1974 and has now taught for twenty years at Pope Pius X School, Wath upon Dearne, where he is Head of Humanities. It was under the influence of Professor Harry Thorpe at Birmingham University that he developed a keen interest in the historical geography of England and learned to recognise ridge and furrow at more than  twenty paces! This interest has continued to grow through membership of English Heritage and the National Trust and he is an enthusiastic visitor of churches, particularly as a member of the Church Monuments Society.

12. EARLY LENDING LIBRARIES IN ROTHERHAM

Freda Casson was born in Rotherham and received her education at the High School for Girls. An Associate of the Library Association, she has worked, both full-time and part-time, in most departments of Rotherham Library, culminating in the position of Local Studies Librarian. She has written (some under a former name) many pamphlets and articles on different aspects of the history of Rotherham. It has given her great pleasure to have been able to help many students and researchers and to have had her help acknowledged in books and theses written by them. She was both touched  and honoured to have had a recent book dedicated to her. Having recently retired she is hoping to be able to devote more time to her family and friends and to being able to continue to work on her own family history after many years helping other people to do theirs.

15.   CHRONICLES OF A TITAN: TEMPLEBOROUGH STEELWORKS, 1916–1993

Sheffield born and bred, **Trevor Lodge** was educated at Abbeydale  Grammar School, and Manchester and Sheffield Universities. An industrial chemist by training, he had an early career which comprised spells of teaching interspersed by a memorable (but all too brief!) period as research chemist with Newton, Chambers & Co Ltd at Chapeltown. He retrained as a metallurgist in the early 1970s, largely through development work carried out at British Steel's Templeborough Steelworks. He has been carrying out research since the mid 1960s into the UK's heavy industries (coal, steel and engineering) and the railways that served them. His most notable published works – the histories of the Park Gate Iron & Steel Co Ltd, the Steel, Peech & Tozer Co Ltd, and Samuel Fox & Co Ltd – appeared in serialised form in British Steel's *Steel News* and United Engineering Steel's Journal, *Stocksbridge Gazette* between 1981 and 1993.

INDEX

PEOPLE & PLACES

PLACES